SAT®
Math Workbook
Third Edition

D1288397

RELATED TITLES FOR COLLEGE-BOUND STUDENTS

SAT Comprehensive Program
SAT Premier Program
SAT 2400
SAT Critical Reading Workbook
SAT Writing Workbook
SAT Vocabulary Prep Level 1
SAT Vocabulary Prep Level 2
SAT in a Box
SAT Strategies for Super Busy Students
The Ring of McAllister: An SAT Score-Raising Mystery
Frankenstein: A Kaplan SAT Score-Raising Classic
The Tales of Edgar Allan Poe: A Kaplan SAT Score-Raising Classic
Dr. Jekyll and Mr. Hyde: A Kaplan SAT Score-Raising Classic
The War of the Worlds: A Kaplan SAT Score-Raising Classic
Wuthering Heights: A Kaplan SAT Score-Raising Classic
Domina El SAT: Preparate para Tomar el Examen para Ingresar a la Universidad

SAT Subject Test: Biology E/M
SAT Subject Test: Chemistry
SAT Subject Test: Literature
SAT Subject Test: Mathematics Level 1
SAT Subject Test: Mathematics Level 2
SAT Subject Test: Physics
SAT Subject Test: Spanish
SAT Subject Test: U.S. History
SAT Subject Test: World History

AP Biology
AP Calculus AB/BC
AP Chemistry
AP English Language & Composition
AP English Literature & Composition
AP Environmental Science
AP European History
AP Human Geography
AP Macroeconomics/Microeconomics
AP Physics B & C
AP Psychology
AP Statistics
AP U.S. Government & Politics
AP U.S. History
AP U.S. History in a Box
AP World History

SAT®

Math Workbook

Third Edition

By the Staff of Kaplan Test Prep and Admissions

PUBLISHING

New York

SAT® is a registered trademark of the College Entrance Examination Board, which neither sponsors nor endorses this product.

SAT® is a registered trademark of the College Entrance Examination Board, which neither sponsors nor endorses this product.

This publication is designed to provide accurate and authoritative information in regard to the subject matter covered. It is sold with the understanding that the publisher is not engaged in rendering legal, accounting, or other professional service. If legal advice or other expert assistance is required, the services of a competent professional should be sought.

© 2008 by Kaplan, Inc.

Published by Kaplan Publishing, a division of Kaplan, Inc.

1 Liberty Plaza, 24th Floor

New York, NY 10006

All rights reserved. The text of this publication, or any part thereof, may not be reproduced in any manner whatsoever without written permission from the publisher.

Printed in the United States of America

July 2008

08   09   10   10 9 8 7 6 5 4 3 2

ISBN-13: 978-1-4195-5213-7

Kaplan Publishing books are available at special quantity discounts to use for sales promotions, employee premiums, or educational purposes. Please email our Special Sales Department to order or for more information at kaplanpublishing@kaplan.com, or write to Kaplan Publishing, 1 Liberty Plaza, 24th Floor, New York, NY 10006.

Table of Contents

Section Three: Important Math Concepts for the SAT

Section Four: Practice Tests and Explanations

AVAILABLE ONLINE

FOR ANY TEST CHANGES OR LATE-BREAKING DEVELOPMENTS

kaptest.com/publishing

The material in this book is up-to-date at the time of publication. However, the College Board may have instituted changes in the test after this book was published. Be sure to carefully read the materials you receive when you register for the test. If there are any important late-breaking developments—or any changes or corrections to the Kaplan test preparation materials in this book—we will post that information online at **kaptest. com/publishing.**

FEEDBACK AND COMMENTS

kaplansurveys.com/books

We'd love to hear your comments and suggestions about this book. We invite you to fill out our online survey form at **kaplansurveys.com/books.** Your feedback is extremely helpful as we continue to develop high-quality resources to meet your needs.

How to Use this Book

This book will prepare you for the math you'll see on the SAT. Many of you are intimidated by math on the SAT. There is math up to Algebra II, with symbols, shapes, and formulas to learn and master. Never fear: We'll show you the Kaplan math strategies that will help you get your highest score.

We'll also make you practice, practice, practice. Well, "make" is a strong word. We ask you nicely to practice, practice, practice. Once you know the Math section as well as we do, you'll be ready, willing, and able to ace it.

Kaplan has helped students improve their scores on standardized tests for more than 60 years. Plus, we are a HUGE company. No other test prep company has our long history, and our expert resources. We know the SAT like the backs of our many hands.

This is how we *strongly suggest* you use this book:

Take a Practice Test

Take one of the practice tests *before* you work through the chapters. This will give you a bench-mark score, so you can see how much improvement you make after you complete this book. It doesn't take long to take a practice test—under an hour—and it's worth it.

Become Familiar with the SAT Math Section

Educate yourself about the Math section—what kinds of questions are on it, how it's scored, and how best to approach it. This will get your brain into SAT Math mode. You'll also want to master the strategies we offer for tackling Grid-ins—the question type that students most fear. Using Kaplan's techniques, you will learn how to maximize your time and strengths—even if you don't learn *one single thing* about linear algebra or multiple figure geometry. It's all in your approach.

Do the Practice Sets

Remember the part about forced practice? This is it. Each of the 18 Practice Sets is devoted to a common SAT Math concept. Each chapter begins with an introduction that will familiarize you with the broader topic, and includes a list of in-depth topics you can reference at the back of the book (see 100 Essential Math Concepts). The practice questions are followed by detailed answer explanations, to help you understand what you're doing wrong and what you're doing right. In order to simulate test conditions, we recommend that you time each practice set, use a calculator where appropriate, and have plenty of scrap paper on hand.

Test Again

It's time to put it all to use and take another practice exam. How much better did you do? 20 points? 30 points? More?

Evaluate Your Strengths and Weaknesses

Read through the answers and explanations for the questions you got wrong on *both* of your practice tests. Go back to the book and review any sections you feel shaky on. This is where 100 Essential Math Concepts comes in handy. It provides a comprehensive review of 100 of the most commonly tested SAT Math topics—and you can go back to it over and over again.

The Basics

Chapter One: **How to Prepare for the SAT**

Here is a breakdown of the entire SAT, from start to finish.

FORMAT AND TIME

The SAT is 3 hours and 45 minutes long.

The Math Section

There are two kinds of questions on the Math section: **Regular Math** questions, which are straightforward multiple-choice questions, with five answer choices; and **Grid-Ins**, which require you to write your response in a little grid. Grid-ins test the same math concepts as Regular Math questions—they're just a different kind of question.

Math questions will be arranged in order of difficulty. The first few questions in a set will be fairly easy, the middle few questions a little harder, and the last few the most difficult. Keep this in mind as you work.

The Critical Reading Section

The Critical Reading section contains three types of questions:

Sentence Completion questions test your ability to see how the parts of a sentence relate to each other. They are basic fill-in-the-blank questions. About half the time you'll have to fill in one blank, and half the time you'll have to fill in two. Both types test vocabulary and reasoning skills.

Sentence Completion questions will also be arranged in order of difficulty. The first few questions in a set will be fairly easy, the middle few questions a little harder, and the last few the most difficult. Keep this in mind as you work.

Short Reading Comprehension questions test your ability to understand a short piece of writing. You are given a short passage of around 100 words, and are asked a couple of questions about the text.

Long Reading Comprehension questions test your ability to understand a longer piece of writing. The passages here are a few paragraphs long,. You'll be asked about such things as the main idea, contextual references, and vocabulary. There will be several reading passages in total; of those, one will be a set of two related readings, which you'll be asked to compare and contrast.

Reading Comprehension questions are *not* arranged in order of difficulty. The passages are all time-consuming to read, so you need to keep moving at a good pace. If you find yourself spending too much time on a Reading Comp question, skip it and come back to it later. The next question may be a lot easier.

Most Reading Comprehension questions test how well you understand the passage, some make you draw conclusions, and some test your vocabulary.

The Writing Section

The Writing section is broken into two parts: an essay (that you compose) and multiple-choice questions. The essay tests your ability to organize and communicate ideas clearly in response to a given topic (a prompt). The multiple-choice questions test your grasp of grammar, usage, and vocabulary.

The essay assignment comes first. In fact, it is the very first section on the test. You'll have 25 minutes for that. As for the multiple-choice questions that come in later sections, those will test whether you can recognize—and in most cases fix—grammatical, diction, or structural errors in sentences and in paragraphs.

GENERAL SAT STRATEGIES

Now that you know some basics about how the test is set up, you can approach each section with a plan. Kaplan has a seven-step method for handling all SAT questions:

1. Think About the Question First
2. Pace Yourself
3. Know When a Question Is Supposed to Be Easy or Hard
4. Move Around Within a Section
5. Be a Good Guesser
6. Be a Good Gridder
7. Two-Minute Warning: Locate Quick Points

Note: These steps work for the multiple-choice questions in the Writing section. But there is a different approach we suggest you take with the essay.

1. Think about the Question First

Before you look at the answer choices, consider the question. The people who write the SAT put distractors among the answer choices. Distractors are answer choices that look right, but aren't. If you jump into the answer choices without thinking about what you're looking for, you're much more likely to fall in a test writer's trap. So always think for a second or two about the question—before you look at the answers.

2. Pace Yourself

The SAT gives you a lot of questions to answer in a short period of time. To get through a whole section, you can't spend too much time on any one question. Keep moving through the test at a good speed. If you run into a hard question, circle it in your test booklet, skip it, and come back to it later if you have time.

3. Know When a Question Is Supposed to Be Easy or Hard

Some sections will have their multiple-choice questions arranged in order of difficulty. In other words, the questions get harder as you move through the problem set. Here's a breakdown:

		Arranged Easiest to Hardest?
Math	Regular Math	Yes
	Grid-Ins	Yes
Critical Reading	Sentence Completions	Yes
	Short Reading Comprehension	No
	Long Reading Comprehension	No
Writing	Essay	N/A
	Usage	No
	Sentence Correction	No
	Paragraph Corrections	No

As you can see, all question sets in Math are arranged in order of difficulty, as are sentence completions in Verbal. As you work through a section that is organized this way, *be aware of where you are in a set*. When working on the easy questions, you can generally trust your first impulse—the obvious answer is likely to be right. As you get to the end of the set, you need to be more suspicious of "obvious" answers, because the answer should not come easily. If it does, look at the question again because the obvious answer is likely to be wrong. It may be one of those distractors—a wrong answer choice meant to trick you.

Hard SAT questions are usually tough for two reasons:

- Their answers are not immediately obvious.
- The questions do not ask for information in a straightforward way.

Here's an easy question:

What is the value of $x^2 - 2x$ when $x = -2$?

(A) -8
(B) -4
(C) 0
(D) 4
(E) 8

If you plug -2 into the equation, it ends up being $-2^2 - 2(-2) =$. This reduces to $4+4$, which equals 8. The correct answer, (E), probably jumped right out at you. This question would likely be at the beginning of a practice set. Easy questions are purposely designed with obvious answer choices.

Here is an example of a harder question:

A $7\frac{1}{2}$ liter mixture of water and molasses is 60 percent molasses. If 1 and $\frac{1}{2}$ liters of water are added, approximately what percent of the new mixture is molasses?

(A) 40%
(B) 50%
(C) 63%
(D) 64%
(E) 68%

Fist find the amount of molasses in the original mixture. There are 7.5 liters of the mixture, of which 60 percent is molasses, so there are $\frac{60}{100} \times 7.5 = 4.5$ liters of molasses. An additional 1.5 liters of water is added so now the mixture is $7.5 + 1.5 = 9$ liters, of which 4.5 liters is molasses. Percent=Part/Whole, so in this case, $\frac{4.5}{9} \times 100\% = 50\%$. So (B) is the correct answer. This question would appear at the end of a question set. For one thing, the answer choices are far more difficult. In addition, the question requires several steps to reach a solution.

4. Move Around Within a Section

On a test at school, you probably spend more time on the hard questions than you do on the easy ones, since hard questions are usually worth more points. *Do not do this on the SAT.*

Easy questions are worth as many points as the tough ones, so do the easy questions first. Don't rush through them just to get to the hard ones. All the questions are worth the same number of points, so you want to rack up points as much as you can. If you work too quickly through the easy questions, you might carelessly—and needlessly—make a mistake. When you run into a question that looks tough, circle it in your test booklet and skip it for the time being. (Make sure you skip them on your answer grid, too.)

Then, if you have time, go back to it AFTER you have answered the easier ones. Sometimes, after you have answered some easier questions, troublesome questions can get easier, too.

5. Be a Good Guesser

You may have heard there's a penalty for guessing on the SAT. That's not quite accurate. There's no penalty for guessing—there's a penalty for a *wrong answer*. That's not the same thing. Here's how it works:

If you get a multiple-choice question wrong, you lose a fraction of a point. If you get a Grid-in wrong, you lose nothing. The fractions you lose on multiple-choice questions are meant to offset the points you might get "accidentally" if you guess the correct answer.

So then, if you can eliminate one or more wrong answers, you turn the odds in your favor, and you'll actually come out ahead by guessing.

Take a look at this question:

> Herman's test scores in a certain class were 79, 84, 85, 90, and 92. What is the average (arithmetic mean) of Herman's test scores?
>
> (A) 15
> (B) 75
> (C) 86
> (D) 90
> (E) 110

Chances are, you recognized that choice (A), *15*, was wrong. You then looked at the next answer choice, and then the next one, and so on, eliminating wrong answers to find the correct answer. This process is usually the best way to work through multiple-choice questions. If you still don't know the right answer but can eliminate one or more wrong answers, you should *guess*.

6. Be a Good Gridder

Don't make mistakes filling out your answer grid. When time is short, it's easy to get confused skipping around a section, and going back and forth between test booklet and grid. If you mis-grid a *single* question, that will throw your entire grid off. Even if you discover the mistake, you'll waste valuable time fixing it. You can lose a ton of points this way, so make sure you keep track of your grid.

To avoid mistakes on the answer grid:

- In your test booklet, circle the answers you choose. By circling your answers, you'll have an easier time checking your grid against your book later.
- Grid five or more answers at once. Don't transfer your answers to the grid after every question. Transfer your answers after every five questions, or, in the reading comprehension questions, at the end of each passage. That way, you won't keep breaking your concentration to mark the grid. You'll save time and improve accuracy.

There is one *exception* to this rule: When time is running out at the end of a section, start gridding one by one so you don't get caught at the end with ungridded answers.

- Circle the questions you skip. Put a big circle in your test book around the number of any questions you skip, so they'll be easy to locate when you go back later. Also, if you realize later that you accidentally skipped a box on the grid, you can more easily check your grid against your book to see where you went wrong.

- Write in your booklet. Take notes, circle hard questions, underline things, etcetera. Proctors collect booklets at the end of each testing session, but the booklets are not examined or reused.

7. Two-Minute Warning: Locate Quick Points

When you start to run out of time, locate and answer any of the quick points that remain. For example, some Critical Reading questions will ask you what a specific word means within a passage. These can be done at the last minute, even if you haven't read the passage.

CHAPTER ONE SUMMARY

The SAT Writing section has two parts: a written essay and multiple-choice questions on usage, sentence corrections, and paragraph corrections. The Math section tests math up through Algebra II and has multiple-choice and grid-in questions. The Critical Reading section has three kinds of questions: sentence completions, reading comprehension, and critical reading.

There are general SAT strategies that work for all question types (except maybe the essay):

1. Think About the Question Before You Look at the Answers
2. Pace Yourself
3. Know When a Question Is Supposed to Be Easy or Hard
4. Move Around Within a Section
5. Be a Good Guesser
6. Be a Good Gridder
7. Two-Minute Warning: Locate Quick Points

Chapter Two: **Introduction to SAT Math**

The first thing you should know about SAT Math is how it's set up. If you can go in to the test knowing what to expect, it will give you a sure-fire leg up—if for nothing else, because there won't be any surprises. In fact, in a lot of ways, SAT Math can be kind of predictable, despite the recent changes to the test. Year after year, test-makers ask the same kinds of questions, and throw in the same kinds of traps, so it pays to be able to see them coming. As we've discussed before, there are three scored math sections, two 25-minute sections and one 20-minute section. These three sections are composed of Multiple Choice and Grid-In questions. There may also be an "experimental" math section that won't be scored, but you won't be able to pick it out, so treat every section as if it counts toward your score.

MULTIPLE-CHOICE QUESTIONS

This is the kind of question you are most likely familiar with. It is simply a question followed by five answer choices. The correct answer is right in front of you—you just have to pick it out. Just like on any other section of the SAT, the key to working quickly and efficiently through the Math section is to think about the question before you start looking for the answer. Kaplan has developed a five-step method for tackling all SAT Math questions:

1. Read the question.
2. Estimate the difficulty of the question.
3. Skip or do?
4. Look for the fastest approach.
5. Make an educated guess.

1. Read the question.

This is obvious. If you try to solve the question without knowing all the facts, not only will you be unable to assess the difficulty of the question, you'll also most likely come up with the wrong answer.

2. Estimate the question's difficulty.

Let's talk about the topic of difficulty level again. As was the case with the old SAT, all sets of math questions will start off with basic questions and then gradually increased in difficulty. When dealing with a hard question, you are more likely to encounter a trap. Also be aware that hard questions don't count for any more points than easy ones, so don't be afraid to skip around within a section and tackle all of the questions you're comfortable with. In other words, don't get hung up on a question you can't answer. Move on and spend the time on a question you can answer.

3. Skip or do?

If a question leaves you seriously scratching your head, circle it and move on. Spend your time on the questions you can do, and then at the end of the section, if you have more time, come back to the difficult ones. Remember, easy questions are worth as much as hard ones.

4. Look for the fastest approach.

All the information you will need to answer the question is right there in front of you. You never need outside knowledge to answer a question. Your job is to figure out the best way to use that information. There's more than one way to use given information. Look for shortcuts. Sometimes the most obvious way of finding a solution is also the longest way. Take the following question:

> At a certain diner, Joe orders 3 doughnuts and a cup of coffee and is charged $2.25. Stella orders 2 doughnuts and a cup of coffee and is charged $1.70. What is the price of 2 doughnuts?
>
> (A) $0.55
> (B) $0.60
> (C) $1.10
> (D) $1.30
> (E) $1.80

The cost of doughnuts and coffee could be translated into two distinct equations using the variables d and c. You could start by finding c in terms of d, then you could plug the values into the other equation.

If you stop for a minute, and look for a shortcut, you'll see that there's a faster way: The difference in price between three doughnuts and a cup of coffee and two doughnuts and a cup of coffee is the price of one doughnut. So the cost of one doughnut can be figured out by subtracting the two costs, $2.25 − $1.70 = $0.55. Notice that that's choice (A)? *Don't get caught in the trap!* This is one of those "distractor" answers we've been talking about. $0.55 is the price of one doughnut, but if you read the question carefully you'll see that it's asking for the price of two doughnuts, which is $1.10. Choice (C) is the correct answer.

There are also special Kaplan strategies you might use:

Picking Numbers

This strategy says that instead of always trying to wrap your head around abstract variables, pick numbers for them. This way you end up making your calculations with real numbers and you can really "see" the answer. For example:

If n Velcro tabs cost p dollars, then how many dollars would q Velcro tabs cost?

(A) $\dfrac{np}{q}$

(B) $\dfrac{nq}{p}$

(C) $\dfrac{pq}{n}$

(D) $\dfrac{n}{pq}$

(E) $\dfrac{p}{nq}$

[handwritten: $n=p$ $q=3$ $2=,4$ $\frac{2}{4}=\frac{3}{x}$ $x=6$ $\frac{12}{2}=\frac{2x}{2}$]

Plug in some numbers for those variables. Lets say $n = 2$, $p = 4$, and $q = 3$. Then the question becomes, "If two Velcro tabs cost $4.00, how many dollars would three Velcro tabs cost? That answer is simple—$6.00. So now that you have a "solution" to work with, plug the numbers into the solution and see which answer choice gives you 6. The answer is (C) by the way. It's the only answer that yields 6. In the event that more than one answer choice gave you 6, you would pick out another set of numbers. In general, we recommend that you avoid using one or zero, as these often yield a few "possibly correct" answers.

Here's another example where picking numbers is effective:

If s skirts cost d dollars, how much would $s - 1$ skirts cost?

(A) $d-1$

(B) $d-s$

(C) $\dfrac{d}{s-1}$

(D) $\dfrac{d(s-1)}{s}$

(E) $\dfrac{d(s-1)}{s}$

[handwritten: 4 skirts cost 8   3 skirts $\frac{4}{8}=\frac{3}{x}$ $4x=24$ $\frac{4x}{4}=\frac{24}{4}$ $x=6$]

First pick numbers for the variables s and d. Try to use numbers that will keep the question simple, in this case maybe 3 and 15. Now plug the numbers into the existing equation to find the values. If 3 skirts cost $15, then each individual skirt must cost $5, so 2 skirts would cost $10. Finally, plug 3 and 5 into the answer choices to see which one will give you 10. When you do that, you realize that (D) yields 10. (D) is $\frac{d(s-1)}{s}$ which in numbers is $\frac{15(3-1)}{3} = \frac{15 \times 2}{3} = \frac{30}{3} = 10$.

Backsolving

With some math questions, it's easier to work backward from the answer choices than to try and trudge through the question. Basically, with backsolving, you are plugging the answer choices back into the question until you find a solution. This method works best when the question is a complex word problem and the answer choices are numbers, or when your only other choice is to set up multiple algebraic equations.

> A music club draws 27 patrons. If there are 7 more hippies than punks in the club, how many patrons are hippies?
>
> (A) 8
> (B) 10
> (C) 14
> (D) 17
> (E) 20

Try each of the answers as a substitute for the number of hippies in the club. Plugging in choice (C) gives you 14 hippies in the club. Since there are 7 more hippies than punks, there are 7 punks in the club, but $14 + 7 < 27$, so 14 doesn't work. You know the solution has to be higher, so you can eliminate (A), (B), and (C). Already you've upped you're odds of getting to the right answer. Now, if you plug in (D) you see that it gives you 17 hippies and 10 punks. $17 + 10 = 27$. Eureka, that's the right answer. It's a good idea to start with letter (C), because it's the median choice. Since the answer choices are always listed in increasing or decreasing order, if choice (C) is too large, you'll know to move to smaller choices. If it's too small you'll move to the bigger ones. This will definitely save you time.

Here's one more example of backsolving, for good measure:

> Two packages have a combined wight of 120 pounds. If the weight of one package is $\frac{1}{4}$ the weight of the other package, how many pounds does the lighter package weigh?
>
> (A) 12
> (B) 16
> (C) 20
> (D) 24
> (E) 30

Plugging in (C), 20, gives you 80 pounds as the weight of the heavier package, for a total weight of 80 + 20, or 100 pounds. That total is too small. Now you know that the weight of the package must be greater than 20 pounds, so you can eliminate (A), (B), and (C) immediately. Plugging in (D) gives you 96 pounds as the weight of the heavier package and 24 as the weight of the smaller package, for a total of 120 pounds. (D) is the answer.

GRID-INS

Just to reassure you, Grid-ins test the same math concepts as Multiple-Choice questions. The only difference is that with Grid-ins, there are no answer choices. You have to fill in your own, in a special grid that looks like this:

Grid-ins can really help you gain points because there's no wrong-answer penalty. If you get an answer wrong you don't gain any points, but you don't lose points either. So we advise that you never leave a Grid-in blank, because you have nothing to lose.

You'll need to make sure to fill in the grids correctly. See how there are boxes across the top where you can write in the answer and then bubbles where you HAVE TO fill in your answer? So here's the deal: The computer reads only the bubbles. So why bother writing in the answer, you ask? Good question. Because writing in the answer can help ensure that you grid the right number or symbol in each column. In other words, it won't get you any extra points if you write the answer before you grid it, but you're likely to make fewer mistakes if you do—and accuracy means points!

Don't get nervous if there seems to be more than one right answer. For example, if the question asks for a two-digit integer that is a multiple of 2, 3, and 5, there's more than one right answer (30, 60, 90...). Don't panic if there's more than one answer. It doesn't mean your answer is wrong. The computer is programmed to accept multiple answers in a case like that.

Placement

You can start writing your answer in any of the boxes, but we recommend you always start your answer in the first (far left) box. It keeps confusion to a minimum, and it also ensures that your answer will always fit. You'll note that there's no oval for zero in the first column, so you'll have to start a zero answer in the second column.

Fractions

Gridding fractions can get a little tricky. If you look at the grid, you'll see the (/) sign, which separates the numerator from the denominator, in two of the four columns. This means you have limited options when gridding a fraction. Basically, you can express your answer as a fraction in any form that fits. In other words, you don't have to reduce a fraction to its simplest form, but a fraction like 32/64 won't fit in the grid. You can either reduce it to 1/2 or .5. If the fraction is too big to fit in the grid and can't be reduced, it doesn't necessarily mean your answer is wrong, it just means you can only express it in the form of a decimal.

Another potential problem is gridding a mixed number. If you try to grid 4 1/2, it will be read as 41/2, which in mixed numbers is actually 20 1/2. So when dealing with mixed numbers, you must either change it to a regular fraction (In the case of 4 1/2 it would be gridded as 9/2) or convert it to a decimal before gridding.

Decimals

Now let's concentrate on decimals for a minute. Try, for the sake of consistency, to start in the first box. If the number starts with a decimal point—no problem—there's a bubble for that in the first column. There's no need to put a zero before a decimal less than one. It's not a good idea for several reasons. First, there's no zero in the first column, so you'd have to start gridding in the second column. Second, you might end up running out of room. For example, when gridding .5, you don't need to grid 0.5. A simple .5 will suffice.

When gridding decimals, don't shorten or round up your decimals. If you get an answer that's a repeating decimal, such as .333333333… (you get the point), don't be tempted to grid .3 or .33. Write out the longest version of the answer that will fit in the grid. In this case it's .333.

How would you grid .45454545…?

Hopefully you gridded in .454.

If the answer is an infinite but nonrepeating decimal, like 1.4285736… do the same thing: Write out the longest version of the answer that will fit, which in this case would be 1.42. Remember, rounding up is not necessary.

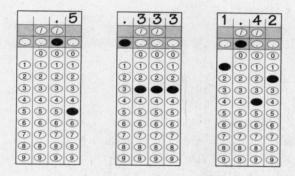

By the way, these are all good examples of why we recommend that you start gridding to the far left, in the first box.

CALCULATORS AND THE SAT

If you didn't know, you can breath a sigh of relief—yes, you're allowed to use your calculator on the SAT—but you don't ever *need* a calculator to solve an SAT Math question. Actually, statistically speaking, students who use a calculator score an average of 10–20 points higher than those who don't, but don't let that tempt you into blindly using your calculator every chance you get. Using your calculator will not always make problem solving easier. SAT Math questions test a lot more than your ability to do computations. The trick is learning when to use the calculator and when to leave it alone.

Choosing a Calculator

You might be thinking to yourself, "I wonder what kind of calculator I should bring to the SAT?" Well we say, "Good question," and fortunately we have the answer. These are the kinds of calculators that are allowed:

- Four-function calculator (one that simply adds, subtracts, multiplies, and divides)
- Scientific calculator (able to perform slightly more complex operations with radicals, exponents, etcetera)
- Graphing calculator (able to perform and display graphing functions)

Just to make sure that it's crystal clear, these are the kinds of calculators you should NOT bring:

- Calculators that print out your calculations
- Handheld mini-computers or laptop computers
- Any calculator with a typewriter keypad
- Calculators with an angled readout screen
- Calculators that require a wall outlet

So then, what kind of calculator does Kaplan recommend? We recommend you use one that you're comfortable with. If you don't have one already, buy one immediately and practice using it between now and the day of the test.

When to Use Your Calculator

Calculators are particularly helpful on the Grid-in questions. Since Grid-ins don't give you answer choices to choose from, it's especially important to be sure of your work. Calculators can help you check your work and avoid careless errors. They can also help you speed up arithmetic. The thing is, you have to be the one to decide which questions a calculator will speed up and which ones it will slow down.

You also have to remember that a calculator will never be able to tell you how to set up a question. In fact, trying to use a calculator when it's not appropriate can really mess things up. A good rule of thumb is to always think the question through and look for the fastest way to approach it before you just start punching numbers into the calculator. For example, the following question would be a disaster if you were to just immediately reach for your calculator:

> The sum of all integers between 1 and 44, inclusive, is subtracted from the sum of all the integers between 7 and 50, inclusive. What is the result?

Using your calculator to find the sum of the first set, the sum of the second set, and then subtracting them would take a long time. Also, punching in those numbers, (it's 252 keys), you're likely to hit a wrong key and to have to start over. The whole process could be very time consuming, and as you can see it's not all that accurate, either. There's a large margin for error. There has to be a better way.

If you stop and work it out you'll realize that each number in the first set is 6 fewer than a corresponding number in the second set (1 and 7, 2 and 8, 3 and 9, etcetera). Since the first set runs from 1 to 44, there must be 44 pairs of numbers, and each pair of numbers has a difference of 6. Therefore the difference between the sums of the first set and the sum of the second set must be 44 × 6, which equals 264, the correct answer. The only part of that question you should have used a calculator for (if you couldn't do it in your head) was the last step, multiplying 44 and 6. Clean, easy, and no time wasted.

The Other Most Common Calculator Mistake

Order of operations: otherwise known as PEMDAS. Test-takers have a habit of forgetting about it as soon as they get a hold of a calculator. If you just punch in the numbers in the order they're in on the page, it doesn't guarantee a correct answer. You have to follow the order of operations. This may seem like a simple error, but it can cost you a lot of points. For a quick refresher, here's the order of operations:

Parentheses

Exponents

Multiplication

Division

Addition

Subtraction

Suppose you wanted to find the value of the fraction $\dfrac{6}{4 \times 9}$ in decimal form. The fraction stands for 6 divided by the product of 4 and 9, or 6 divided by 36, which equals $\dfrac{1}{6}$. If you simply enter the numbers in as they appear on the page, however, you'll end up with 6 divided by 4, times 9, which equals 13.5, not the correct answer.

WRAPPING IT UP

So now you're ready to start practicing. In the following chapters you'll find 18 practice sets designed to help you ace the SAT Math section. The sections are set up by topic, so you can go through them in order or skip around. We recommend you go through all of them. Practice never hurt anyone. Don't forget about the handy reference guide at the back of the book, SAT Math in a Nutshell. It can help you through any rough spots. By the end of this book, you'll be prepared to take on any SAT Math question that may come your way. Just remember—we believe in you, so you should too.

SAT Math Practice

Chapter Three: **Number Operations**

Being able to perform basic number operations is fundamental for SAT Math. These questions specifically test concepts such as finding sums, differences, products, quotients, the order of operations (**P**arentheses, **E**xponents, **M**ultiplication/**D**ivision, **A**ddition/**S**ubtraction), and properties of numbers. The basic properties of number operations are as follows:

Distributive Property

$a(b + c) = ab + ac$

Commutative Property

$ab = ba$ and $a + b = b + a$

Associative Property

$a(bc) = (ab)c$ (for multiplication)

$a + (b + c) = (a + b) + c$ (for addition)

This might seem like a lot, we understand, but RELAX! You know this stuff. These are the building blocks of math—concepts you've been working with for years. So here's your chance to brush up on the easy stuff—the first step to a higher score. For further reading, check out these topics:

1. Number Categories
2. Adding/Subtracting Signed Numbers
3. Multiplying/Dividing Signed Numbers
4. PEMDAS
6. Exponential Growth
7. Union and Intersection of Sets
18. Reducing Fractions
19. Adding/Subtracting Fractions
20. Multiplying Fractions
21. Dividing Fractions
22. Converting Mixed Numbers and Improper Fractions
23. Reciprocals
24. Comparing Fractions
25. Fractions and Decimals

Chapter Three Practice Set
Answer Sheet

1. (A) (B) (C) (D) (E)   9. (A) (B) (C) (D) (E)
2. (A) (B) (C) (D) (E)   10. (A) (B) (C) (D) (E)
3. (A) (B) (C) (D) (E)   11. Grid-in below
4. (A) (B) (C) (D) (E)   12. (A) (B) (C) (D) (E)
5. (A) (B) (C) (D) (E)   13. Grid-in below
6. Grid-in below   14. Grid-in below
7. (A) (B) (C) (D) (E)   15. (A) (B) (C) (D) (E)
8. (A) (B) (C) (D) (E)   16. (A) (B) (C) (D) (E)

6.

11.

13.

14.

PRACTICE SET

Basic

1. Which of the following is less than $\frac{1}{6}$?

    .16666

    (A) 0.1667

    (B) $\frac{3}{18}$

    (C) 0.167

    (D) 0.1666

    (E) $\frac{8}{47}$

2. Which of the following lists three fractions in ascending order?

    (A) $\frac{9}{26}, \frac{1}{4}, \frac{3}{10}$

    (B) $\frac{9}{26}, \frac{3}{10}, \frac{1}{4}$

    (C) $\frac{1}{4}, \frac{9}{26}, \frac{3}{10}$

    (D) $\frac{1}{4}, \frac{3}{10}, \frac{9}{26}$

    (E) $\frac{3}{10}, \frac{9}{26}, \frac{1}{4}$

3. Which of the following is not equal to $\frac{36}{45}$?

    (A) $\frac{4}{5}$

    (B) $\frac{12}{15}$ $\frac{4}{5}$

    (C) $\frac{20}{25}$ $\frac{4}{5}$

    (D) $\frac{24}{35}$

    (E) $\frac{48}{60}$

4. Which of the following is equal to 25(27 + 29 + 31)?

    (A) 25(27 + 29) + 31

    (B) 25(27) + 29 + 31

    (C) 25(27) + (29 + 31)(25)

    (D) 25 + (27)(29)(31)

    (E) 25(27 + 29) + 25(29 + 31)

5. $1.04\overline{)0.079}$ =

    .0759

    (A) $10.4\overline{)0.0079}$

    (B) $104\overline{)0.79}$

    (C) $10.4\overline{)0.79}$

    (D) $0.104\overline{)0.79}$

    (E) $104\overline{)0.0079}$

6. $\dfrac{\frac{12}{1}}{\frac{1}{4}}$ =   48

Medium

7. $\dfrac{7}{5} \times \left(\dfrac{3}{7} - \dfrac{2}{5} \right)$ =

    $\frac{15}{35} - \frac{14}{35}$

    (A) $\frac{1}{165}$

    (B) $\frac{1}{35}$

    (C) $\frac{1}{25}$

    (D) $\frac{9}{15}$

    (E) 1

8. Which of the following is closest in value to the decimal 0.40?

    (A) $\frac{1}{3}$

    (B) $\frac{3}{8}$

    (C) $\frac{1}{2}$

    (D) $\frac{5}{9}$

    (E) $\frac{4}{7}$

9. Set X is the set of all prime numbers, and set Y is the set of all integers from 1 to 10 inclusive. Which of the following is a complete and accurate list of the intersection of X and Y?

    (A) {1,3,5,7}

    (B) {3,5,7}

    (C) {2,3,5,7}

    (D) {1,3,5,7,9}

    (E) {2,3,5,7,9}

10. If the first term in a geometric sequence is 7, and the third term is 63, what is the ninth term?

    (A) 367

    (B) 567

    (C) 2,209

    (D) 45,927

    (E) 165,274

11. The union of sets A, B, and C is {1, 2, 3, 4, 5, 6, 7}, the intersection of Sets A, B, and C is {0}, (empty set) and Set A = {1, 2, 3, 4}. If Set B contains a greater number of elements than does Set C, what is the largest possible value of the sum of the elements of Set B?

12. The first term in a certain geometric sequence is x and the fourth term in the sequence is $27x$, where x is a nonzero number. Which of the following represents the tenth term?

    (A) $26x$

    (B) 27

    (C) $154x$

    (D) $4,327x$

    (E) $19,683x$

13. $[(12-11)-(10-9)]-[(12-11-10)-9]=$

$$\frac{5}{9}, \frac{5}{12}, \frac{23}{48}, \frac{11}{24}, \frac{3}{7}$$

14. What is the positive difference between the largest and smallest of the fractions above?

Hard

15. For which of the following expressions would the value be greater if 160 were replaced by 120?

    I. $1,000 - 160$

    II. $\dfrac{160}{1+160}$

    III. $\dfrac{1}{1-\dfrac{1}{160}}$

    (A) None

    (B) I only

    (C) III only

    (D) I and II

    (E) I and III

16. If w, x, y, and z are all integers greater than 2, which of the following is greatest?

    (A) $x + yz + w$

    (B) $(x + y)z + w$

    (C) $x + y(z + w)$

    (D) $x + (yz + w)$

    (E) $(x + y)(z + w)$

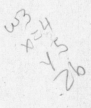

ANSWERS AND EXPLANATIONS

Basic

1. D

We are asked which of the five values is less than $\frac{1}{6}$.

Choice (A): Since $\frac{1}{6} = 0.166\overline{6}$ (the bar indicates that the 6 repeats), $0.1667 > \frac{1}{6}$. No good.

Choice (B): $\frac{3}{18} = \frac{1 \times 3}{6 \times 3} = \frac{1}{6}$. No good.

Choice (C): $0.167 > 0.16\overline{6}$. No good.

Choice (D): 0.1666 is less than $0.16666\overline{6}$. That means it is less than $\frac{1}{6}$, so this is the correct answer.

Choice (E): $\frac{1}{6} = \frac{8}{48}$ and $\frac{8}{47} > \frac{8}{48}$; therefore, $\frac{8}{47} > \frac{1}{6}$.

No good.

2. D

The same three fractions appear in each answer choice, and we need to arrange these in ascending order.

Convert fractions to decimals, using your calculator:

$\frac{1}{4} = 0.25$.

$\frac{3}{10} = 0.3$. This is a little less than $\frac{1}{3}$, but more than $\frac{1}{4}$.

$\frac{9}{26} = 0.346$. This is greater than $\frac{3}{10}$. The correct ascending order is $\frac{1}{4}, \frac{3}{10}, \frac{9}{26}$.

3. D

Each fraction can be reduced to $\frac{4}{5}$ except (D), which cannot be simplified.

4. C

Use the distributive law: $25(27 + 29 + 31) =$
$25(27) + 25(29) + 25(31) =$
$25(27) + (29 + 31)25$.

5. C

To get the same quotient in a division problem, the decimal point must be moved the same number of places in the same direction for both numbers. This is the same as multiplying or dividing both numbers by the same power of 10, which won't change the number of times one goes into the other. Only choice (C) alters both decimal points the same way, multiplying each number by a factor of 10.

6. 48

Turn this division problem into multiplication by applying the "invert and multiply" rule:

$$12 \div \frac{1}{4} = 12 \times \frac{4}{1} = 48$$

Medium

7. C

We could perform the subtraction within the parentheses and then multiply, but it's simpler to use the distributive law.

$$\frac{7}{5} \times \left(\frac{3}{7} - \frac{2}{5} \right) = \frac{7}{5} \times \frac{3}{7} - \frac{7}{5} \times \frac{2}{5}$$

$$= \frac{3}{5} - \frac{14}{25}$$

$$= \frac{3}{5} \times \frac{5}{5} - \frac{14}{25}$$

$$= \frac{15}{25} - \frac{14}{25} = \frac{1}{25}$$

8. B

You can use your calculator to find the decimal equivalent of each answer choice, and then decide which is closest. Or, if you feel comfortable with the relative sizes of the choices, find the two choices that are closest to 0.40—one larger, one smaller, and then find which of those is closer.

Since $0.4 < \frac{1}{2}$, we can eliminate both $\frac{5}{9}$ and $\frac{4}{7}$ (since each is greater than $\frac{1}{2}$, both must be farther from 0.4 than $\frac{1}{2}$). On the other hand, $\frac{3}{8} < 0.4$ (the decimal equivalent of $\frac{3}{8}$ is 0.375), and since $\frac{1}{3} = \frac{3}{9} < \frac{3}{8}$, we can eliminate $\frac{1}{3}$. So it comes down to $\frac{3}{8}$ or $\frac{1}{2}$. Since $\frac{3}{8} = 0.375$, it is 0.025 away from 0.4, which is much closer than $\frac{1}{2}$ (or 0.5, which is 0.1 away). So $\frac{3}{8}$ is the closest.

9. C

Remember that 1 is NOT a prime number and that 2 is prime—in fact, it is the smallest and the only even prime number. Knowing that 2 is prime, you can eliminate (A), (B), and (D). Because 9 is divisible by 3, it is not a prime number, so only (C) remains.

10. D

Before Test Day, practice using the formula for geometric sequences: $a_n = a_1 r^{n-1}$, where r is the ratio between consecutive terms, a_1 is the first term, and a_n is the nth term. Expect it to be a little tricky at first but, like most math, easier over time. Use $a_n = a_1 r^{n-1}$ to solve for r: $63 = 7r^2$, so $9 = r^2$ and $\pm3 = r$. Now solve for a_9: $a_9 = 7(r)^8$. Whether r is 3 or –3, $r^8 = 6{,}561$ and $a_9 = (7)(6{,}561) = 45{,}927$.

11. 18

In some combination, B and C together contain $\{5, 6, 7\}$. Think about the possibilities, given that B contains more elements than C does and that you're asked to maximize the sum of the elements in B. Make $B = \{5, 6, 7\}$ and make C the empty set. Then the sum of the elements of B $= 5 + 6 + 7 = 18$.

12. E

Knowing how to make an educated guess will help you score points on Test Day. Look for oddballs to eliminate, such as (B) here—the only choice without an x in it. Use $a_n = a_1 r^{n-1}$ to solve for r: $27x = xr^3$, so $27 = r^3$ and $r = 3$. Using $r = 3$, solve for a_{10}: $a_{10} = x(3)^9$, so $a_{10} = 19{,}683x$.

13. 18

Follow PEMDAS:

$$[(12 - 11) - (10 - 9)] - [(12 - 11 - 10) - 9]$$
$$= [1 - 1] - [- 9 - 9]$$
$$= 0 - (- 18)$$
$$= 18$$

14. .138 or .139 or $\frac{5}{36}$

With a calculator, convert each fraction to its decimal equivalent. Subtract the smallest from the largest to find the answer: 0.1388. Or you could realize that all the fractions are less than $\frac{1}{2}$ except for $\frac{5}{9}$. So $\frac{5}{9}$ is the largest. The $\frac{5}{12}$ is the fraction farthest away from $\frac{1}{2}$, so it is the smallest.

So $\frac{5}{9} - \frac{5}{12} = \frac{4 \times 5}{4 \times 9} - \frac{3 \times 5}{3 \times 12} = \frac{20 - 15}{36} = \frac{5}{36}$.

Hard

15. E

In statement I, if we were to subtract a smaller number from 1,000, our result would be larger. Since substituting 120 for 160 in this expression would produce a greater result, we can eliminate choices (A) and (C), which do not include statement I.

Statement II is equivalent to $\frac{160}{161}$. If we were to replace

each 160 with 120, our result would be $\frac{120}{1 + 120}$ which

is $\frac{120}{121}$. Which is greater? You can easily find out using

your calculator, but if you prefer, you can think of each

fraction's distance from 1. Both fractions are a tiny bit less

than 1. Imagine a number line; $\frac{160}{161}$ is $\frac{1}{161}$ away from 1,

while $\frac{120}{121}$ is $\frac{1}{121}$ away from 1. Since $\frac{1}{161}$ is less than

$\frac{1}{121}$, that means $\frac{160}{161}$ must be *closer* to 1 than $\frac{120}{121}$.

And that means $\frac{160}{161}$ is a little larger than $\frac{120}{121}$. So if we

did replace 160 with 120, we would get a smaller result.

Eliminate choice (D).

In statement III we're dividing 1 by a fraction, which is the

same as multiplying 1 by the reciprocal of the fraction. In

order to get a *larger* reciprocal, we need to start with a

smaller fraction. Which is smaller, $1 - \frac{1}{160}$ or $1 - \frac{1}{120}$?

$1 - \frac{1}{120}$ is smaller since it is farther to the left from 1

on the number line. By replacing 160 with 120 we get a

smaller fraction in the denominator of our expression and,

therefore, a *larger* reciprocal. That gives the expression a

larger value. So III is part of the correct answer. If this is dif-

ficult to see, we can actually do the math:

$$\frac{1}{1 - \frac{1}{160}} = \frac{1}{\frac{159}{160}} = 1 \times \frac{160}{159} = 1\frac{1}{159}$$

$$\frac{1}{1 - \frac{1}{120}} = \frac{1}{\frac{119}{120}} = 1 \times \frac{120}{119} = 1\frac{1}{119}$$

$$1\frac{1}{119} > 1\frac{1}{159}$$

Statements I and III are larger when 160 is replaced with
120, so the answer is choice (E).

16. E

It's possible to solve this one by picking numbers for the
variables, but it's not necessary. Since all the variables are
greater than 2, multiplying any two of them together will
produce a greater value than either variable alone would
have. If you multiply out each answer choice and eliminate
the parentheses, then you get:

(A) $x + yz + w$
(B) $xz + yz + w$
(C) $x + yz + yw$
(D) $x + yz + w$
(E) $xz + xw + yz + yw$

A piece-by-piece comparison shows that choice (E) must
have the greatest value.

Chapter Four: **Number Properties**

Some math questions test your ability to perform a specific operation, and others test your ability to work through the problem-solving process. This chapter deals with yet another type of math question: one that tests your understanding of the special characteristics of the various classes of numbers. Think of it this way: In the same way that you know certain things about your best friend—that she likes mystery novels and pizza—you need to know that a prime number is a number that is greater than one, and its factors are only one and itself. This is what "characteristics of the various classes of numbers" means: those things that make a class of numbers unique. Here are some more detailed number property topics for further reading:

Chapter Four Practice Set
Answer Sheet

1. Ⓐ Ⓑ Ⓒ Ⓓ Ⓔ
2. Ⓐ Ⓑ Ⓒ Ⓓ Ⓔ
3. Grid-in below
4. Grid-in below
5. Ⓐ Ⓑ Ⓒ Ⓓ Ⓔ
6. Grid-in below
7. Ⓐ Ⓑ Ⓒ Ⓓ Ⓔ
8. Ⓐ Ⓑ Ⓒ Ⓓ Ⓔ
9. Ⓐ Ⓑ Ⓒ Ⓓ Ⓔ
10. Ⓐ Ⓑ Ⓒ Ⓓ Ⓔ
11. Ⓐ Ⓑ Ⓒ Ⓓ Ⓔ

12. Grid-in below
13. Grid-in below
14. Grid-in below
15. Ⓐ Ⓑ Ⓒ Ⓓ Ⓔ
16. Ⓐ Ⓑ Ⓒ Ⓓ Ⓔ
17. Ⓐ Ⓑ Ⓒ Ⓓ Ⓔ
18. Ⓐ Ⓑ Ⓒ Ⓓ Ⓔ
19. Ⓐ Ⓑ Ⓒ Ⓓ Ⓔ
20. Grid-in below
21. Grid-in below
22. Grid-in below

3.

4.

6.

12.

13.

14.

20.

21.

22.

PRACTICE SET

Basic

1. How many odd integers are between $\frac{10}{3}$ and $\frac{62}{3}$?

    (A) 19
    (B) 18
    (C) 10
    (D) 9
    (E) 8

2. If the sum of three different prime numbers is an even number, what is the smallest of the three?

    (A) 2
    (B) 3
    (C) 5
    (D) 7
    (E) It cannot be determined from the information given.

3. If the product of 3 consecutive odd integers is 15, what is the smallest of the three integers?

4. What is the number of distinct prime factors of 200?

5. If the product of three integers is odd, which of the following must be true?

    (A) The sum of any two of the integers is even.
    (B) The product of any two of the integers is even.
    (C) The sum of the three integers is even.
    (D) The average (arithmetic mean) of the three integers is even.
    (E) The median of the three integers is even.

6. What is the greatest integer that will divide evenly into both 36 and 54?

Medium

7. If the integer P leaves a remainder of 4 when divided by 9, all of the following must be true EXCEPT

    (A) The number that is 4 less than P is a multiple of 9.
    (B) The number that is 5 more than P is a multiple of 9.
    (C) The number that is 2 more than P is a multiple of 3.
    (D) When divided by 3, P will leave a remainder of 1.
    (E) When divided by 2, P will leave a remainder of 1.

8. How many three-digit integers can be divided by 2 to produce a new integer with the same tens' digit and units' digit as the original integer?

    (A) 0
    (B) 1
    (C) 2
    (D) 3
    (E) 4

9. On a number line, point B is at a distance of 5 from point C, and point D is at a distance of 7 from point C. What is the distance from point B to point D?

    (A) 2
    (B) 5
    (C) 7
    (D) 12
    (E) It cannot be determined from the information given.

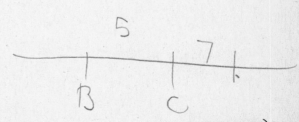

KAPLAN

10. If a and b are integers and the sum of ab and b is odd, which of the following could be true?

    I. a and b are both odd.

    II. a is even and b is odd.

    III. a is odd and b is even.

  (A) I only

  (B) II only

  (C) III only

  (D) I and II

  (E) I and III

11. If a, b, and c are positive integers and a is a factor of b, then which of the following must be true?

  (A) $2a = 4b$

  (B) $bc > ac$

  (C) bc is a multiple of a

  (D) ac is a factor of b

  (E) ab is a multiple of c

12. If $x = 8y$, where y is a prime number greater than 2, how many different positive odd factors does x have?

13. In a certain shop, each customer takes a number to be served. If the first customer of the day took number 14, and the last customer took number 314, how many customers were there that day?

14. What is the smallest integer greater than 1 that leaves a remainder of 1 when divided by any of the integers 6, 8, and 10?

Hard

15. If both the product and sum of four integers are even, which of the following could be the number of even integers in the group?

    I.   0

    II. 2

    III. 4

  (A) I only

  (B) II only

  (C) III only

  (D) II and III only

  (E) I, II, and III

16. How many positive integers less than 60 are equal to the product of a positive multiple of 5 and an even number?

  (A) 4

  (B) 5

  (C) 9

  (D) 10

  (E) 11

17. Which of the following is the greatest integer less than 630,000 that can be written using all of the digits from 1 to 6?

  (A) 629,999

  (B) 654,321

  (C) 624,531

  (D) 621,543

  (E) 625,431

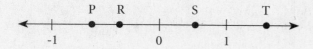

18. Points P, R, S, and T lie on a number line, as illustrated above. Which of the following statements could be true?

    (A) $R \times S = P$
    (B) $P \times R = T$
    (C) $R \times S = T$
    (D) $R \times T = P$
    (E) $P \times T = S$

19. If q, r, and s are distinct positive integers and $q = rs$, then which of the following must be true?

    (A) q is not prime
    (B) r is prime
    (C) s is not a factor of q
    (D) r is a multiple of s
    (E) qr is prime

20. What is the positive difference between the number of distinct prime factors of 15^2 and the number of distinct prime factors of 64^3?

21. In the repeating decimal 0.097531097531…, what is the 44th digit to the right of the decimal point?

22. A wire is cut into 3 equal parts. The resulting segments are then cut into 4, 6, and 8 equal parts, respectively. If each of the resulting segments has an integer length, what is the minimum length of the wire?

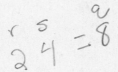

ANSWERS AND EXPLANATIONS

Basic

1. E

We're asked for the number of odd integers between $\frac{10}{3}$ and $\frac{62}{3}$, so let's be more clear about this range. $\frac{10}{3}$ is the same as $3\frac{1}{3}$, and $\frac{62}{3}$ is the same as $20\frac{2}{3}$. We count the odd integers between $3\frac{1}{3}$ and $20\frac{2}{3}$. We can't include 3 since 3 is less than $3\frac{1}{3}$. Similarly, we can't include 21 since it's larger than $20\frac{2}{3}$. This leaves the odd integers of 5, 7, 9, 11, 13, 15, 17, and 19. That's a total of 8.

2. A

If the sum of three numbers is even, either all three are even or only one of the three is even. The sum of three odd numbers can *never* be even, nor can the sum of one odd and two evens. Remember, we're dealing with three different *prime* numbers. There's only one even prime: 2; all the rest are odd. Therefore, only one of our group can be even, and that must be 2. Since 2 is the smallest prime, it must also be the smallest of the three.

3. 1

Trial and error is the best way to find the answer here. Consecutive odd integers include −3, −1, 1, 3, 5, 7, 9, 11..., and so on. 15 is obviously the product of 5 and 3, so we can say that 15 is the product of the three consecutive odd integers 1, 3, and 5, the smallest of which is 1.

4. 2

A prime number is any number that can only be divided by 1 and itself. A composite number (a counting number with more than two factors) can be written as a product of all its prime factors. The distinct prime factors are those prime factors that are different from each other. So then for this problem $200 = 100 \times 2 = (10 \times 10) \times 2 = (5 \times 2) \times (5 \times 2) \times 2$. You find out that 200 has five prime factors (5, 5, 5, 2, and 2), but only two distinct prime factors (5 and 2).

5. A

For the product of three integers to be odd, each integer must itself be odd. The sum of two odds is an even. To make these points more concrete, pick numbers. Say that the three integers are 3, 3, and 3. Only (A) must be true.

6. 18

Check the factors of 36, in descending order, to see which is also a factor of 54. 36 is the largest factor of 36, but it doesn't divide into 54. The next largest factor is 18, and this does divide into 54, so it is also a factor of 54.

Medium

7. E

We need to find the one choice that isn't *always* true. To find it, let's test each choice. Choice (A) is always true: Since $P \div 9$ has a remainder of 4, P is 4 greater than some multiple of 9, so the number 4 less than P is a multiple of 9. And if $P - 4$ is a multiple of 9, then the next multiple of 9 would be $(P - 4) + 9$, or $P + 5$; thus choice (B) is also true. With choice (C), we know that since $P - 4$ is a multiple of 9, it is also a multiple of 3. By adding 3s, we know that $(P - 4) + 3$, or $P - 1$, and $(P - 4) + 3 + 3$, or $P + 2$, are also multiples of 3. Choice (C) must be true. And since $P - 1$ is a multiple of 3, when P is divided by 3, it will have a remainder of 1, and choice (D) is always true.

This leaves only choice (E). In simpler terms, choice (E) states that P is always odd. Since multiples of 9 are alternately odd and even (9, 18, 27, 36...), $P - 4$ could be either even or odd, so P also could be either even or odd. Choice (E) is not always true, so it is the correct answer choice.

If you have trouble thinking this way, try picking a number for P that fits the description ("a remainder of 4 when divided by 9…"). You could pick 13, but if you try 13 in each answer choice, you'll find that all five seem to be true. You'll have to try a different number for P. How about 22? It fits the description, and it disproves the statement in choice (E). Picking numbers is not always the fastest meth-od—sometimes you'll have to try many numbers before you find what you need—but it's a good tactic if you don't know what else to do.

8.   E

Only one digit can be divided by 2 to produce the same digit: 0. If the last two digits in a three-digit number are 0, it's possible to divide by 2 and still have the same last two digits. So the three-digit numbers worth considering are the hundreds: 100, 200, 300, 400, and so on. With a little thought you'll see that some of these don't work either. If the hundreds' digit is an odd number, dividing by 2 leaves a 5 in the tens' place. For example, 500 divided by 2 is 250. Therefore the only numbers that will work are 200, 400, 600, and 800.

9.   E

Do not assume that the points lie on the line in alpha-betical order, since this is not stated. If B and D are on opposite sides of C, then the distance between them is 12. But they could be on the same side, in which case the distance between them would be 2. Since there's no way to tell which is the case, the correct answer is choice (E).

10. B

Pick numbers. Statement I says a and b are both odd. Let $a = 1$ and $b = 3$. Then $ab + b = (1)(3) + 3 = 6$. Since the sum is even, statement I can't be correct. Statement II says a is even and b is odd. Let $a = 2$, and $b = 3$. Then $ab + b = (2)(3) + 3$, or 9. Since the sum is odd, this statement is true. Statement III says a is odd and b is even. Let $a = 3$ and $b = 2$. Then $ab + b = (3)(2) + 2$, or 8, which is not odd. So only statement II works, and choice (B) is indeed correct.

11. C

By definition, bc is a multiple of b. You're given that b is a multiple of a. So bc must be a multiple of a. To see this more concretely, pick numbers. Imagine that a is 4, b is 4, and c is 5:

(A) $2(4) = 4(4)$? No.

(B) $(4)(5) > (4)(5)$? No.

(C) $(4)(5)$ is a multiple of (4)? Yes.

(D) $(4)(5)$ is a factor of (4)? No.

(E) $(4)(4)$ is a multiple of (5)? No.

12. 2

If y is a prime number greater than 2, it must be odd. So it and 1 are the only odd factors of x. You might see this more clearly if you pick numbers. Say $y = 3$. Then $x = 24$. The only odd factors of 24 are 1 and 3.

13. 301

It's tempting to simply subtract the starting number from the final number, but that gives you the difference between the numbers. To find the total number of cus-tomers you need to include the first customer as well, the one who took number 14. For instance, if the first num-ber taken was 2 and the last number taken was 4, three people were served (number 2, number 3, and number 4) not $4 - 2$, or 2. So if the first customer had number 14 and the last 314 there were $314 - 14 + 1 = 301$ customers.

14. 121

We are asked for the smallest integer greater than 1 that leaves a remainder of 1 when divided by 6, 8, and 10. If we find the smallest integer that is a common multiple of these three numbers, we can add 1 to that number to get our answer. To find the least common multiple of 6, 8, and 10, we find the prime factors of each, and eliminate the shared factors.

$$6 = 2 \times 3$$
$$8 = 2 \times 2 \times 2$$
$$10 = 2 \times 5$$

We drop one factor of 2 from 10 and from 6, since they are already present in the factors of 8.

$$2 \times 2 \times 2 \times 3 \times 5 = 120; \ 120 + 1 = 121$$

Hard

15. D

Since these four integers have an even product, at least one of them must be even, so statement I, 0, is impossi-ble. Is it possible for exactly 2 of the 4 to be even? If there are 2 odds and 2 evens, the sum is even, since odd + odd = even, and even + even = even. Also, if there's only 1 even among the integers, the product is even, so state-ment II is possible. Similarly, statement III gives an even product and even sum, so our answer is II and III only.

16. B

Here we want to determine how many numbers between 0 and 60 are even multiples of 5. All even multiples of 5 must be multiples of 10. So the multiples of 10 between 0 and 60 are 10, 20, 30, 40, and 50. That's 5 altogether.

17. E

To arrange the digits into the largest number, you want to put the biggest digits in the highest-value places. For the number to be less than 630,000, it must start with 62. The next largest digit, 5, must go in the thousands' place, and 4 in the hundreds' place. Three goes in the tens' place, and since 2 is already used, 1 is left for the ones' place. This gives us 625,431, answer choice (E).

18. D

Approximate the value of each point and see what happens. P could be around $\frac{-3}{4}$; R might be $\frac{-1}{2}$; S looks like positive $\frac{1}{2}$; and T is about $1\frac{1}{2}$.

Now you can try each answer choice.

(A): $R \times S = P$ becomes $\left(\frac{-1}{2}\right)\left(\frac{1}{2}\right) = -\frac{1}{4} \neq -\frac{3}{4}$.

(B): $P \times R = T$ becomes $\left(\frac{-3}{4}\right)\left(\frac{-1}{2}\right) = \frac{3}{8} \neq 1\frac{1}{2}$.

(C): $R \times S = T$ becomes $\left(\frac{-1}{2}\right)\left(\frac{1}{2}\right) = -\frac{1}{4} \neq 1\frac{1}{2}$.

(D): $R \times T = P$ becomes $\left(\frac{-1}{2}\right)\left(1\frac{1}{2}\right) = -\frac{3}{4} = -\frac{3}{4}$.

(E): $P \times T = S$ becomes $\left(\frac{-3}{4}\right)\left(1\frac{1}{2}\right) = -\frac{9}{8} \neq \frac{1}{2}$.

Choice (D) is correct.

19. A

You know that q is the product of two integers, and that neither of the two integers equals q (because the three integers are distinct). So q is the product of two other numbers—which rules out the possibility that q is prime, because if q were prime, it would be the product of itself

and 1. This is a great question for picking numbers. The values $q = 20$, $r = 4$, and $s = 5$ disprove every choice but (A).

20. 1

$15^2 = (15)(15) = 3(3 \times 5)^2$. So 3 and 5 are the two distinct prime factors of 15^2.

$64^3 = (2 \times 2 \times 2 \times 2 \times 2 \times 2)^3$. So 2 is the single prime factor of 64^3. Don't forget to do the last part of the problem—find the positive difference between the number of distinct prime factors, $2 - 1 = 1$.

21. 9

First we have to identify the pattern. It consists of the same 6 numerals, 0, 9, 7, 5, 3, and 1, in that order, repeating infinitely. Our job is to identify the 44th digit to the right of the decimal point. Since the pattern of 6 numerals will continually repeat, every 6th digit of the digits to the right of the decimal point will be the same, namely the numeral 1. So 1 will be the 6th, 12th, 18th, and 24th (and so on) digit. Since 44 is just 2 more than 42, which is a multiple of 6, the 44th digit will be the digit 2 places to the right of 1. That's 9.

22. 72

Each third of the wire is cut into 4, 6, and 8 parts respectively, and all the resulting segments have integer lengths. This means that each third of the wire has a length that is evenly divisible by 4, 6, and 8. The smallest positive integer divisible by 4, 6, and 8 is 24, so each third of the wire has a minimum length of 24. So the minimum length of the whole wire is three times 24, or 72.

Chapter Five: **Averages**

You hear things about averages all the time and probably don't even realize it. On the news, reporters are always talking about the average employment rate, or how much money a new movie averaged at the box office over the weekend. What this really means is that the sum of the data is being divided by the total number of elements of data. If you have 5 people whose ages are 12, 14, 15, 22, and 34, and you want to find their average age, you add up their ages (which we're sure you've worked out as 97) and then divide that sum by 5 (the number of people, or elements of data). You end up with 19.4, the average age of the 5 people.

But what if you were asked to find the average of a group of averages? Let's say you took 5 exams in social studies over a semester and have an average grade of 90. You also took 6 exams in English with an average grade of 84, a total of 4 science exams with an average grade of 80, and 6 math exams with an average grade of 90. How could you go about finding your average total grade on all of your exams for the semester? Though it might be your first impulse, the wrong way to do it is to add up the average scores and divide by 4.

The correct way to do it is to figure out your total number of points and then divide it by the total number of exams. You know you took 5 exams in social studies, and your average grade was 90, so what number do you have to divide by 5 to get 90? More simply stated, you just multiply the average by the number of elements to get the total number of points, in this case $5 \times 90 = 450$. Do this for each subject and figure out that you got a total of 504 points on your English exams, 320 points on your science exams, and 540 on your math exams. Now that you have the totals, you solve the problem the way you'd solve any other average problem: Add up the data and divide by the number of elements, in this case the total number of exams you took, which is 21.

$$\frac{450 + 504 + 320 + 540}{21} = 86.381, \text{ rounded to the nearest thousandth.}$$

Questions involving averages are quite common on the SAT, so it's a good idea to have a solid grip on this subject. Test makers probably won't ask you about the average loss on long-term mutual fund investments, but they will want to test some basic skills. For further reading on this subject:

37. Average Formula

38. Average of Evenly Spaced Numbers

39. Using the Average to Find the Sum

40. Finding the Missing Number

41. Median and Mode

Chapter Five Practice Set
Answer Sheet

1. Ⓐ Ⓑ Ⓒ Ⓓ Ⓔ
2. Ⓐ Ⓑ Ⓒ Ⓓ Ⓔ
3. Ⓐ Ⓑ Ⓒ Ⓓ Ⓔ
4. Ⓐ Ⓑ Ⓒ Ⓓ Ⓔ
5. Ⓐ Ⓑ Ⓒ Ⓓ Ⓔ
6. Ⓐ Ⓑ Ⓒ Ⓓ Ⓔ
7. Ⓐ Ⓑ Ⓒ Ⓓ Ⓔ
8. Grid-in below
9. Ⓐ Ⓑ Ⓒ Ⓓ Ⓔ

10. Ⓐ Ⓑ Ⓒ Ⓓ Ⓔ
11. Ⓐ Ⓑ Ⓒ Ⓓ Ⓔ
12. Ⓐ Ⓑ Ⓒ Ⓓ Ⓔ
13. Ⓐ Ⓑ Ⓒ Ⓓ Ⓔ
14. Grid-in below
15. Ⓐ Ⓑ Ⓒ Ⓓ Ⓔ
16. Ⓐ Ⓑ Ⓒ Ⓓ Ⓔ
17. Grid-in below
18. Grid-in below

19. Ⓐ Ⓑ Ⓒ Ⓓ Ⓔ
20. Ⓐ Ⓑ Ⓒ Ⓓ Ⓔ
21. Ⓐ Ⓑ Ⓒ Ⓓ Ⓔ
22. Ⓐ Ⓑ Ⓒ Ⓓ Ⓔ
23. Grid-in below
24. Grid-in below
25. Grid-in below

8.   14.   17.   18.

23.   24.   25.

PRACTICE SET

Basic

1. If the average (arithmetic mean) of *a* and −5 is 10, then *a* =
    (A) 25
    (B) 15
    (C) 5
    (D) −5
    (E) −15

2. The average (arithmetic mean) of 6 consecutive integers is $18\frac{1}{2}$. What is the average of the first 5 of these integers?
    (A) $12\frac{1}{2}$
    (B) 15
    (C) 16
    (D) $17\frac{1}{2}$
    (E) 18

NAME	WEIGHT IN POUNDS
Chris	150
Anne	153
Malcolm	154
Paul	157
Sam	151

3. What is the average (arithmetic mean) weight of the five people whose weights are listed in the table above?
    (A) 152
    (B) 153
    (C) $153\frac{1}{2}$
    (D) 154
    (E) 155

4. A certain store stocks 5 different brands of ice cream, and sells a pint of each for $2.75, $3.25, $2.50, $3.25, and $3.00, respectively. What is the positive difference between the mode price and the median price?
    (A) $0.05
    (B) $0.25
    (C) $0.30
    (D) $0.50
    (E) $0.75

5. The average (arithmetic mean) of 3 numbers is 45. If 2 of the numbers are 35 and 45, what is the third number?
    (A) 30
    (B) 40
    (C) 45
    (D) 50
    (E) 55

6. If the average (arithmetic mean) of *b* and 2 is equal to the average of *b*, 3, and 4, what is the value of *b*?
    (A) 2
    (B) 4
    (C) 8
    (D) 10
    (E) 16

7. The average (arithmetic mean) of 30, 50, and 70 is 15 more than the average of 40, 60, and what number?
    (A) 65
    (B) 55
    (C) 35
    (D) 15
    (E) 5

8. A violinist practices 1 hour a day from Monday through Friday. How many hours must she practice on Saturday in order to average 2 hours a day for the 6-day period?

Medium

9. The average (arithmetic mean) of 6 numbers is 6. If 3 is subtracted from each of 4 of the numbers, what is the new average?

    (A) $1\frac{1}{2}$

    (B) 2

    (C) 3

    (D) 4

    (E) $4\frac{1}{2}$

10. What is the average (arithmetic mean) of n, $n + 1$, $n + 2$, and $n + 3$?

    (A) $n + 1$

    (B) $n + 1\frac{1}{2}$

    (C) $n + 2$

    (D) $n + 2\frac{1}{2}$

    (E) $n + 6$

11. The average (arithmetic mean) of two numbers is $3n - 4$. If one of the numbers is n, then the other number is

    (A) $2n - 4$
    (B) $3n - 4$
    (C) $5n - 8$
    (D) $5n + 8$
    (E) $6n - 8$

12. If the average (arithmetic mean) of $x + 2$, $x + 4$, and $x + 6$ is 0, then $x =$

    (A) -4
    (B) -3
    (C) -2
    (D) -1
    (E) 0

13. In a certain class there are 12 boys and 18 girls. If the class average score for an algebra exam is 90 and the boys' average score is 87, what is the girls' average score?

    (A) 88.5
    (B) 91
    (C) 92
    (D) 93
    (E) 94.5

14. What is the sum of the median, mode, and range of the set $\{-1, 0, 1, 1, 2, 0, 0, 2\}$?

15. The average (arithmetic mean) of a set of 4 numbers is 8.75. When a fifth number is introduced to the set, the average of the set becomes 8. What is the fifth number?

    (A) -3
    (B) 5
    (C) 8.375
    (D) 8.6
    (E) 10.3

16. If the sum of m integers is 0, which of the following must be true?

    I. $m - 1$ is an odd number.
    II. $m + 1$ is an even number.
    III. The average (arithmetic mean) of the m integers is 0.

    (A) I only
    (B) II only
    (C) III only
    (D) I and III
    (E) II and III

17. Jerry's average (arithmetic mean) score on the first three of four tests is 85. If Jerry wants to raise his average by 2 points, what score must he earn on the fourth test?

KAPLAN

18. In a certain course, Lily received an average (arithmetic mean) score of 82 for her first 2 tests, 76 for her third test, and 92 for her fourth test. What grade must she receive on her next test if she wants an average (arithmetic mean) of 86 for all 5 tests?

Hard

19. 15 movie theaters average 600 customers per theater per day. If 6 of the theaters close down but the total theater attendance stays the same, what is the average daily attendance per theater among the remaining theaters?

    (A) 500
    (B) 750
    (C) 1,000
    (D) 1,200
    (E) 1,500

20. The average (arithmetic mean) of 6 positive numbers is 5. If the average of the least and greatest of these numbers is 7, what is the average of the other 4 numbers?

    (A) 3
    (B) 4
    (C) 5
    (D) 6
    (E) 7

21. If the average of $27 - x$, $x - 8$, and $3x + 11$ is y, what is the average of $2y$ and $\frac{2y}{3}$?

    (A) $4x + 40$

    (B) $x + 10$

    (C) $\frac{8x + 80}{3}$

    (D) $\frac{4x + 40}{3}$

    (E) $\frac{2x + 20}{3}$

22. If the average (arithmetic mean) of t and s is 25 and the average of r and s is 40, what is the value of $r - t$?

    (A) 65
    (B) 32.5
    (C) 30
    (D) 15
    (E) It cannot be determined from the information given.

23. George drives the first 30 miles of a trip at a constant rate of 40 miles per hour. If he drives the remaining 75 miles of the trip at a constant rate of 50 miles per hour, what is his average speed for the entire trip?

24. If the average (arithmetic mean) of 18 consecutive odd integers is 534, what is the least of these integers?

25. If the average (arithmetic mean) of a, b, and 7 is 13, what is the average of $a + 3$, $b - 5$, and 6?

ANSWERS AND EXPLANATIONS

Basic

1. A

We can plug everything we are given into the standard formula for an average of two numbers and then solve for a. Since we know the average of −5 and a is 10:

$$\frac{\text{Sum of terms}}{\text{Number of terms}} = \text{Average of terms}$$

$$\frac{-5 + a}{2} = 10$$

$$-5 + a = 20$$

$$a = 20 + 5$$

$$a = 25$$

A much faster method is to balance the numbers: Since −5 is 15 less than the average, 10, a must be 15 more than the average, or 10 + 15 = 25.

2. E

The average of evenly spaced numbers is the middle number. The average of 6 such numbers lies halfway between the third and fourth numbers. Since $18\frac{1}{2}$ is the average, the third number must be 18 and the fourth number 19. The 6 numbers are: 16, 17, 18, 19, 20, 21. Since the first 5 numbers are also evenly spaced, their average is be the middle (third) number, 18.

3. B

To find the average, add the weights and divide by the number of people.

$$\text{Average} = \frac{150 + 153 + 154 + 157 + 151}{5}$$

$$= \frac{765}{5} = 153$$

4. B

The mode of a group of terms is the value that occurs most frequently. The only price that occurs more than once is $3.25, so it is the mode price. The median is the middle term in a group arranged in numerical order. If the prices are listed in either ascending or descending order, the third and middle term is $3.00. So the difference between the mode and median prices is $3.25−$3.00 = $0.25.

5. E

The average (arithmetic mean) of a set of numbers is the sum of the numbers divided by the number of numbers in the set. Let the unknown number $= x$. Then $\frac{x + 35 + 45}{3}$ = 45. This simplifies to $x + 80 = 135$, or $x = 55$.

6. C

The first thing we need to do is translate "the arithmetic mean of b and 2 equals the arithmetic mean of b, 3, and 4," from English to math. This sentence means $\frac{b + 2}{2} = \frac{b + 3 + 4}{3}$. We can cross multiply and simplify to get $3(b + 2) = 2(b + 7)$. This is the same as $3b + 6 = 2b + 14$. Subtract $(6 + 2b)$ from both sides to get $b = 8$, choice (C).

We could also use Backsolving on this problem, by finding the mean of each answer choice and 2 and each answer choice, 3, and 4, and seeing whether the two quantities are equal.

7. E

The average of 30, 50, and 70 is $\frac{30 + 50 + 70}{3} = \frac{150}{3}$ = 50. 50 is 15 more than 35. $35 = \frac{40 + 60 + x}{3}$, so 105 = 40 + 60 + x. x = 5.

8. 7

To average 2 hours a day over 6 days, the violinist must practice 2×6, or 12 hours. From Monday through Friday, the violinist practices 5 hours, 1 hour each day. To total 12 hours, she must practice $12 - 5$, or 7, hours on Saturday.

Medium

9. D

If 6 numbers have an average of 6, their sum is 6×6, or 36. To subtract 3 from 4 of the numbers, we subtract 4×3, or 12, from the sum. The new sum is $36 - 12$, or 24; the new average is $\frac{24}{6}$, or 4.

10. B

Don't let the n variables bother you; the arithmetic performed is the same.

Method I:

Add the terms and divide by the number of terms. Since each term contains n, we can ignore the n and add it back at the end. Without the ns, we get $\frac{0 + 1 + 2 + 3}{4} = \frac{6}{4} = 1\frac{1}{2}$.

The average is $n + 1\frac{1}{2}$.

Method II:

These are just evenly spaced numbers (regardless of what n is). Since there are 4 of them, the average is midway between the second and third terms: midway between $n + 1$ and $n + 2$, or $n + 1\frac{1}{2}$.

11. C

This can be done two ways. In the first method, we can use the average formula and label the other number x:

$$\frac{(n + x)}{2} = 3n - 4$$

$$n + x = 2(3n - 4)$$

$$n + x = 6n - 8$$

$$x = 6n - 8 - n$$

$$x = 5n - 8$$

A second way to do this is to pick numbers. Let's say that n is 10. Then $3n - 4$ is $3(10) - 4$ or 26. If the average of 10 and some number is 26, then since 10 is 16 less than 26, the other number must be 16 more than 26. So, the other number must be 42. Plug in 10 for n in each answer choice to see which one gives us 42. If more than one answer choice gives us 42, we have to try another number. Choice (A) gives us 16; no good. Choice (B) gives us 26; no good. Choice (C) works, since 5 times 10, minus 8 is 42. Choice (D) gives us 58 and choice (E) gives us 52. Since only choice (C) gave us 42, this must be correct.

12. A

The fastest way to solve this problem is to recognize that $x + 2$, $x + 4$, and $x + 6$ are evenly spaced numbers, so that the average equals the middle value, $x + 4$. We're told that the average of these values is zero, so:

$$x + 4 = 0$$

$$x = -4$$

13. C

The class average is equal to the number of boys times the boys' average, plus the number of girls times the girls' average, divided by the total number of students. Let $x =$ the girls' average.

$$\frac{12(87) + 18(x)}{30} = 90$$

Cross multiplying:

$$12(87) + 18(x) = 30(90)$$

$$1{,}044 + 18x = 2{,}700$$

$$18x = 1{,}656$$

$$x = 92$$

14. 3.5

The mode of the set (the element in the set that occurs most often) is 0. The range (the difference between the largest and smallest elements in the set) is $2 - (-1) = 3$. The median (the middle element when numbers are sorted in the set) is 0.5 because $\frac{0 + 1}{2} = 0.5$. The sum of these 3 measures is $0 + 3 + 0.5 = 3.5$.

15. B

This question involves two separate but related applications of the average formula. First use the formula to determine the sum of the four original numbers in the set: $8.75 = \frac{sum}{4}$, so the sum is $8.75 \times 4 = 35$. Now ask yourself what would have to be added to this sum to bring the average to 8. Remember that the introduction of an additional number brings the number of numbers to 5: $8 = \frac{35 + n}{4 + 1}$, so $40 = 35 + n$, and $n = 5$.

16. C

If you know that a group of integers add up to zero, what else do you know about the group? Since III appears in three choices, start with it. If the sum of a group of integers is zero, must the average of the group also be zero? Yes. The average is the sum of the numbers divided by the number of numbers. If the sum of the numbers is zero, the average must be zero, because zero divided by anything is zero. So the answer must be (C), (D), or (E). Now evaluate I or II. In I, if $m - 1$ is odd, m itself must be even. Must there be an even number of integers in order

for the sum of the integers to be zero? No. For example, $(-3) + (-3) + (6) = 0$. Now eliminate (D). II essentially says that m is odd. Must that be true? No, as $(-6) + (6) = 0$ shows. I and II are sometimes true, but III must be true.

17. 93

Jerry's average score is 85. His total number of points for the 3 tests is the same as if he had scored 85 on each of the tests: $85 + 85 + 85$, or 255. He wants to average 87 over 4 tests, so his total must be $87 + 87 + 87 + 87 = 348$. The difference between his total score after 3 tests and the total that he needs after 4 tests is $348 - 255$, or 93. Jerry needs a 93 to raise his average over the 4 tests to 87.

Another way of thinking about the problem is to "balance" the average around 87. Imagine Jerry has 3 scores of 85. Each of the first 3 is 2 points below the average of 87. So together, the first 3 tests are a total of 6 points below the average. To balance the average at 87, the score on the fourth test will have to be 6 points more than 87, or 93.

18. 98

Plug the information about Lily's first 4 test grades into the average formula to find what grade on a fifth test would result in an overall average of 86. Lily averaged 82 on her first and second tests. This is mathematically equivalent to her scoring 82 on each of these 2 tests. Let $x =$ the fifth test grade.

$$86 = \frac{76 + 92 + 2(82) + x}{5}$$

$$86 = \frac{332 + x}{5}$$

$$430 = 332 + x$$

$$98 = x$$

 KAPLAN

Hard

19. C

The key to this problem is that the total theater attendance stays the same after 6 theaters close. No matter how many theaters there are:

Total attendance = (number of theaters) × (average attendance).

We know that originally there are 15 theaters, and they average 600 customers per day. Plug these values into the formula above to find the total theater attendance:

Total attendance = (15) × (600) = 9,000.

Even after the 6 theaters close, the total attendance remains the same. Now, though, the number of theaters is only 9:

New average attendance

$$= \frac{\text{Total attendance}}{\text{New number of theaters}}$$

$$= \frac{9,000}{9}$$

$$= 1,000$$

20. B

We can't find individual values for any of these 6 numbers. However, with the given information we can find the sum of the 6 numbers, and the sum of just the largest and smallest. Subtracting the sum of the smallest and largest from the sum of all 6 will leave us with the sum of the 4 others, from which we can find *their* average.

The sum of all 6 numbers = (average of all 6 numbers) × (number of values) = 5 × 6, or 30.

The sum of the greatest and smallest = (average of greatest and smallest) × 2 = 7 × 2 = 14.

The sum of the other 4 numbers = (the sum of all 6) − (the sum of the greatest and smallest) = (30 − 14) = 16.

Since the sum of the other 4 numbers is 16, their average is $\frac{16}{4}$, or 4.

21. D

In terms of y, the average of $2y$ and $\frac{2y}{3}$ is

$$\frac{2y + \frac{2y}{3}}{2} = \frac{\frac{6y}{3} + \frac{2y}{3}}{2}$$

$$= \frac{8y}{3} \times \frac{1}{2}$$

$$= \frac{8y}{6}$$

$$= \frac{4y}{3}$$

Next, solve for y as the average of $27 - x$, $x - 8$, and $3x + 11$:

$$y = \frac{27 - x + x - 8 + 3x + 11}{3}$$

$$y = \frac{30 + 3x}{3}$$

$$y = \frac{3(x + 10)}{3}$$

$$y = x + 10$$

Plug this into $\frac{4y}{3}$:

$$= \frac{4(x + 10)}{3}$$

$$= \frac{4x + 40}{3}$$

22. C

If the average of r and s is 40, $r + s = 80$. If the average of t and s is 25, $t + s = 50$. Subtract the equation $t + s = 50$ from the equation $r + s = 80$:

$$r + s = 80$$
$$- (t + s = 50)$$
$$\overline{ r - t = 30}$$

KAPLAN

23. 46.6 or 46.7

To find the average speed for the entire trip, divide the total distance traveled by the total amount of time traveled. Use the formula:

$$\text{Rate} \times \text{Time} = \text{Distance}$$

to find out how much time each part of the trip took. To drive 30 miles at 40 miles per hour would take $40 \times \text{Time} = 30$,

$$\text{Time} = \frac{30}{40} = \frac{3}{4} \text{ hour.}$$

To drive 75 miles at 50 miles per hour would take

$$50 \times \text{Time} = 75,$$

$$\text{Time} = \frac{75}{50} = 1\frac{1}{2} \text{ hours.}$$

So the average speed:

$$= \frac{30 + 75 \text{ miles}}{\frac{3}{4} + 1\frac{1}{2} \text{ hours}} = 46\frac{2}{3} \text{ miles per hour.}$$

24. 517

The average of a group of evenly spaced numbers is equal to the middle number. In this problem, there is an even number of terms, 18, so the average is midway between the 2 middle numbers, the 9th and 10th terms. This tells us that the 9th consecutive odd integer here will be the first odd integer less than 534, which is 533. Once we have the 9th term, we can count backward to find the first.

10th: 535, Average: 534, 9th: 533, 8th: 531, 7th: 529, 6th: 527, 5th: 525, 4th: 523, 3rd: 521, 2nd: 519, 1st: 517.

25. 12

We need to find the average of $a + 3$, $b - 5$, and 6. If we could determine their sum, then all we'd need to do is divide this sum by 3 to find their average. Well, we don't know a and b, but we can determine their sum. We are given the average of a, b, and 7. The sum of these 3 values is the average times the number of terms, or $13 \times 3 = 39$. If $a + b + 7 = 39$, then $a + b = 39 - 7$, or $a + b = 32$. Remember, we're asked for the average of $a + 3$, $b - 5$, and 6. The sum of these expressions can be rewritten as $a + b + 3 - 5 + 6$, or, as $a + b + 4$.

If $a + b = 32$, then $a + b + 4 = 32 + 4$, or 36. Therefore, the sum is 36 and the number of terms is 3, so the average is $\frac{36}{3}$, or 12.

Chapter Six: **Ratios and Rates**

The tricky thing about ratios is that they tend to disguise themselves, or at least change their appearance enough to make them a little confusing. A ratio is just two numbers being compared. Whereas a fraction is usually a comparison between a part and a whole, a ratio can be a comparison of a part to a whole, or other combinations of elements, like a part to a part. Let's take the ratio of "three to four." It can also be written *3 to 4*, *3:4*, or even, *3/4*. Ratios also relate to percents and decimals. The decimal 1.2, when representative of a ratio, means 12 things for every 10 things.

A rate is a ratio that is a comparison of two different things with different units, like miles per hour. The word *per* is always a good indicator that you're dealing with a rate. A particularly common rate question tests your knowledge of the *distance formula*, which is expressed as $d = r \times t$. Let's say Superguy and Batfellow, two superheroes, leave their secret hideouts at the exact same time, headed for the same crime scene. If Superguy is flying 2 miles per second and Batfellow is running 3 miles per second, how far has each of them made it after 30 minutes of travel?

To start out with, let's convert miles per second to miles per hour. There are 3,600 seconds in an hour, so if Superguy flies 2 miles in a second, then in an hour he will fly 2 × 3,600 seconds, or 7,200 miles per hour. In the same fashion, Batfellow will run 3 × 3,600 seconds, or 10,800 miles per hour. So how far will the superheroes get after 30 minutes of travel? If Superguy flies 7,200 miles in an hour, then he flies 3,600 miles every half hour, and if Batfellow runs 10,800 miles every hour, he runs 5,400 miles every half hour. For further reading on ratios, rates, and all their many components:

32. Setting up a Ratio

33. Part-to-Part Ratios and Part-to-Whole Ratios

34. Solving a Proportion

35. Rate

36. Average Rate

Chapter Six Practice Set
Answer Sheet

1. Ⓐ Ⓑ Ⓒ Ⓓ Ⓔ   9. Grid-in below   17. Ⓐ Ⓑ Ⓒ Ⓓ Ⓔ   25. Ⓐ Ⓑ Ⓒ Ⓓ Ⓔ

2. Ⓐ Ⓑ Ⓒ Ⓓ Ⓔ   10. Ⓐ Ⓑ Ⓒ Ⓓ Ⓔ   18. Ⓐ Ⓑ Ⓒ Ⓓ Ⓔ   26. Ⓐ Ⓑ Ⓒ Ⓓ Ⓔ

3. Ⓐ Ⓑ Ⓒ Ⓓ Ⓔ   11. Ⓐ Ⓑ Ⓒ Ⓓ Ⓔ   19. Grid-in below   27. Ⓐ Ⓑ Ⓒ Ⓓ Ⓔ

4. Ⓐ Ⓑ Ⓒ Ⓓ Ⓔ   12. Ⓐ Ⓑ Ⓒ Ⓓ Ⓔ   20. Grid-in below   28. Grid-in below

5. Ⓐ Ⓑ Ⓒ Ⓓ Ⓔ   13. Ⓐ Ⓑ Ⓒ Ⓓ Ⓔ   21. Grid-in below   29. Ⓐ Ⓑ Ⓒ Ⓓ Ⓔ

6. Ⓐ Ⓑ Ⓒ Ⓓ Ⓔ   14. Ⓐ Ⓑ Ⓒ Ⓓ Ⓔ   22. Ⓐ Ⓑ Ⓒ Ⓓ Ⓔ   30. Grid-in below

7. Ⓐ Ⓑ Ⓒ Ⓓ Ⓔ   15. Ⓐ Ⓑ Ⓒ Ⓓ Ⓔ   23. Ⓐ Ⓑ Ⓒ Ⓓ Ⓔ   31. Ⓐ Ⓑ Ⓒ Ⓓ Ⓔ

8. Ⓐ Ⓑ Ⓒ Ⓓ Ⓔ   16. Ⓐ Ⓑ Ⓒ Ⓓ Ⓔ   24. Grid-in below   32. Grid-in below

9.   19.   20.   21.

24.   28.   30.   32.

PRACTICE SET

Basic

1. A subway car passes 3 stations every 10 minutes. At this rate, how many stations will it pass in 1 hour?

    (A) 2
    (B) 12
    (C) 15
    (D) 18
    (E) 30

2. On a certain street map, $\frac{3}{4}$ inch represents one mile. What distance, in miles, is represented by $1\frac{3}{4}$ inches?

    (A) $1\frac{1}{2}$

    (B) $1\frac{3}{4}$

    (C) $2\frac{1}{3}$

    (D) $2\frac{1}{2}$

    (E) $5\frac{1}{4}$

3. The Greenpoint factory produced $\frac{2}{5}$ of the Consolidated Brick Company's bricks in 1991. If the Greenpoint factory produced 1,400 tons of bricks in 1991, what was the Consolidated Brick Company's total output that year, in tons?

    (A) 700
    (B) 2,100
    (C) 2,800
    (D) 3,500
    (E) 7,000

4. The ratio of $3\frac{1}{4}$ to $5\frac{1}{4}$ is equivalent to the ratio of

    (A) 3 to 5
    (B) 13 to 21
    (C) 5 to 7
    (D) 7 to 5
    (E) 5 to 3

5. If a car travels $\frac{1}{100}$ of a kilometer each second, how many kilometers does it travel per hour?

    (A) $\frac{3}{5}$

    (B) $3\frac{3}{5}$

    (C) 36

    (D) 72

    (E) 100

6. Fred can vacuum 144 square feet of carpet in 5 minutes. At this rate, how long would it take him to vacuum 2,880 square feet of carpet?

    (A) 20 minutes
    (B) 40 minutes
    (C) 50 minutes
    (D) 100 minutes
    (E) 140 minutes

7. A printing press produces 4,440 posters per hour. At this rate, in how many minutes can the printing press produce 370 posters?

    (A) 0.12
    (B) 5
    (C) 12
    (D) 50
    (E) 720

8.   A certain box contains baseballs and golf balls. If the ratio of baseballs to golf balls is 2:3, and there are 30 baseballs in the box, how many golf balls are in the box?

   (A) 15
   (B) 18
   (C) 20
   (D) 36
   (E) 45

9.   After spending $\frac{5}{12}$ of his salary, a man has $140 left. What is his salary, in dollars?

Medium

10.   At garage A, it costs $8.75 to park a car for the first hour and $1.25 for each additional hour. At garage B, it costs $5.50 for the first hour and $2.50 for each additional hour. What is the difference between the cost of parking a car for 5 hours at garage A and parking it for the same length of time at garage B ?

   (A) $1.50
   (B) $1.75
   (C) $2.25
   (D) $2.75
   (E) $3.25

11.   If a kilogram is equal to approximately 2.2 pounds, which of the following is the best approximation of the number of kilograms in 1 pound?

   (A) $\frac{11}{5}$

   (B) $\frac{5}{8}$

   (C) $\frac{5}{11}$

   (D) $\frac{1}{3}$

   (E) $\frac{1}{5}$

12.   If the ratio of boys to girls in a class is 5 to 3, which of the following could not be the number of students in the class?

   (A) 32
   (B) 36
   (C) 40
   (D) 48
   (E) 56

13.   If a tree grew 5 feet in n years, what was the average rate, in inches per year, at which the tree grew during those years?

   (A) $60n$

   (B) $\frac{5}{n}$

   (C) $\frac{5}{12n}$

   (D) $\frac{12n}{5}$

   (E) $\frac{60}{n}$

14.   If a man earns $200 for his first 40 hours of work in a week and then is paid $1\frac{1}{2}$ times his regular hourly rate for any additional hours, how many hours must he work to make $230 in a week?

   (A) 4
   (B) 5
   (C) 6
   (D) 44
   (E) 45

15. In a certain class, 3 out of 24 students are in student organizations. What is the ratio of students in student organizations to students not in student organizations?

(A) $\frac{1}{8}$

(B) $\frac{1}{7}$

(C) $\frac{1}{6}$

(D) $\frac{1}{5}$

(E) $\frac{1}{4}$

16. A student's grade in a course is determined by 4 quizzes and 1 exam. If the exam counts twice as much as each of the quizzes, what fraction of the final grade is determined by the exam?

(A) $\frac{1}{6}$

(B) $\frac{1}{5}$

(C) $\frac{1}{4}$

(D) $\frac{1}{3}$

(E) $\frac{1}{2}$

17. The cost of 4 sweatshirts is n dollars. At this rate, what is the cost, in dollars, of 40 sweatshirts?

(A) $\frac{10n}{4}$

(B) $\frac{n}{40}$

(C) $\frac{40}{n}$

(D) $10n$

(E) $40n$

18. If 1 "triminute" is equivalent to 3 minutes, how many triminutes are equivalent to 2.5 hours?

(A) 50

(B) 150

(C) 250

(D) 300

(E) 450

19. In a local election, votes were cast for Mr. Dyer, Ms. Frau, and Mr. Borak in the ratio of 4:3:2. If there were no other candidates and none of the 1,800 voters cast more than one vote, how many votes did Ms. Frau receive?

20. Ms. Smith recently drove a total of 700 miles on a business trip. If her car averaged 35 miles per gallon of gasoline and gasoline cost $1.25 per gallon, what was the cost in dollars of the gasoline for the trip?

21. If cement, gravel, and sand are to be mixed in the ratio of 3:5:7 respectively, and 5 tons of cement are available, how many tons of the mixture can be made? (Assume that enough gravel and sand are available to use all the available cement.)

Hard

22. A student finishes the first half of an exam in $\frac{2}{3}$ of the time it takes him to finish the second half. If the entire exam takes him an hour, how many minutes does he spend on the first half of the exam?

(A) 20

(B) 24

(C) 27

(D) 36

(E) 40

KAPLAN

23. John buys R pounds of cheese to feed N people at a party. If $N + P$ people come to the party, how many more pounds of cheese must John buy in order to feed everyone at the original rate?

    (A) $\dfrac{NP}{R}$

    (B) $\dfrac{N}{RP}$

    (C) $\dfrac{N+P}{R}$

    (D) $\dfrac{P}{NR}$

    (E) $\dfrac{PR}{N}$

24. Phil is making a 40-kilometer canoe trip. If he travels at 30 kilometers per hour for the first 10 kilometers, and then at 15 kilometers per hour for the rest of the trip, how many minutes longer will it take him than if he makes the entire trip at 20 kilometers per hour?

25. A sporting goods store ordered an equal number of white and yellow tennis balls. The tennis ball company delivered 30 extra white balls, making the ratio of white balls to yellow balls 6:5. How many tennis balls did the store originally order?

    (A) 120
    (B) 150
    (C) 180
    (D) 300
    (E) 330

26. If x oranges cost the same as y peaches and peaches cost 39 cents each, how many dollars does each orange cost?

    (A) $\dfrac{39x}{100y}$

    (B) $\dfrac{39y}{100x}$

    (C) $\dfrac{3,900}{xy}$

    (D) $\dfrac{39y}{x}$

    (E) $\dfrac{39x}{y}$

27. If $\dfrac{1}{2}$ of the number of white mice in a certain laboratory is $\dfrac{1}{8}$ of the total number of mice, and $\dfrac{1}{3}$ of the number of gray mice is $\dfrac{1}{9}$ of the total number of mice, then what is the ratio of the number of white mice to the number of gray mice?

    (A) 16:27
    (B) 2:3
    (C) 3:4
    (D) 4:5
    (E) 8:9

28. Joe makes lemonade by mixing $\dfrac{2}{3}$ of a cup of powdered lemonade mix with 2 quarts of water. How many cups of powdered lemonade mix would Joe have to mix with 11 quarts of water to make properly concentrated lemonade?

29. On a certain college faculty, $\frac{4}{7}$ of the professors are male, and the ratio of the number of tenured to untenured professors is 2:5. If $\frac{1}{5}$ of the male professors are tenured, then what fraction of the female professors are untenured?

    (A) $\frac{1}{7}$

    (B) $\frac{1}{3}$

    (C) $\frac{2}{5}$

    (D) $\frac{3}{5}$

    (E) $\frac{2}{3}$

30. Angelica drove 100 miles to Baxterville at an average speed of 50 miles per hour. She then increased her average speed by 20 percent and drove 30 miles to Center City. What was her average speed for the entire journey, in miles per hour?

31. A baseball player runs from first base to second base at an average speed of f meters per minute and from second base to third base at an average speed of $f + 4$ meters per minute. If the distance d, in meters, from first base to second base is the same as the distance from second base to third base, which of the following represents the average speed at which the player runs from first-to-second-to-third base?

    (A) $\frac{f^2 - 4f}{f + 4}$

    (B) $\frac{2f^2 + 8f}{f + 2}$

    (C) $\frac{f^2 + 8f}{f + 4}$

    (D) $\frac{f^2 + 4f}{2(f + 2)}$

    (E) $\frac{f^2 + 4f}{(f + 2)}$

32. An oculist charges $30 for an eye examination, frames, and glass lenses, but $42 for an eye examination, frames, and plastic lenses. If the plastic lenses cost four times as much as the glass lenses, how much do the glass lenses cost?

ANSWERS AND EXPLANATIONS

Basic

1. D

Since there are 60 minutes in an hour, the subway will pass $\frac{60}{10}$ or 6 times as many stations in 1 hour as it passes in 10 minutes. In 10 minutes it passes 3 stations; in 60 minutes it must pass 6×3 or 18 stations.

2. C

In this question, the ratio is implied: For every $\frac{3}{4}$ inch of map there is 1 real mile, so the ratio of inches to the miles they represent is always $\frac{3}{4}$ to 1. Therefore, we can set up the proportion:

$$\frac{\#\text{ of inches}}{\#\text{ of miles}} = \frac{\frac{3}{4}}{1} = \frac{3}{4}$$

Now $1\frac{3}{4}$ inches $= \frac{7}{4}$ inches.

Set up a proportion:

$$\frac{\frac{7}{4}\text{ inches}}{\#\text{ of miles}} = \frac{3}{4}$$

Cross multiply:

$$\frac{7}{4} \times 4 = 3 \times \#\text{ of miles}$$

$$7 = 3 \times \#\text{ of miles}$$

$$\frac{7}{3} = \#\text{ of miles}$$

or $2\frac{1}{3} = \#$ of miles

3. D

Method I:

If $\frac{2}{5}$ of Consolidated's output (the bricks produced by the Greenpoint factory) was 1,400 tons, $\frac{1}{5}$ must have been half as much, or 700 tons. The entire output for 1991 was $\frac{5}{5}$ or five times as much: 5×700 or 3,500 tons.

Method II:

We are asked for total output, so let's call the total output T. We are told that 1,400 tons represents $\frac{2}{5}$ of T or $\frac{2}{5}T$, so we can set up the following equation:

$$\frac{2}{5}T = 1,400$$

Multiply both sides by $\frac{5}{2}$ to solve for T:

$$\frac{5}{2} \times \frac{2}{5}T = 1,400 \times \frac{5}{2}$$

$$T = \frac{1,400 \times 5}{2} = 700 \times 5 = 3,500$$

4. B

We are asked which of 5 ratios is equivalent to the ratio of $3\frac{1}{4}$ to $5\frac{1}{4}$. Since the ratios in the answer choices are expressed in whole numbers, turn this ratio into whole numbers:

$$3\frac{1}{4} : 5\frac{1}{4} = \frac{13}{4} : \frac{21}{4} = \frac{\frac{13}{4}}{\frac{21}{4}} = \frac{13}{4} \times \frac{4}{21} = \frac{13}{21}$$

or 13:21.

5. C

Find the number of seconds in an hour, and then multiply this by the distance the car is traveling each second. There are 60 seconds in a minute and 60 minutes in 1 hour; therefore, there are 60 × 60, or 3,600, seconds in an hour. In one second the car travels $\frac{1}{100}$ kilometers; in 1 hour the car will travel $3,600 \times \frac{1}{100}$, or 36 kilometers.

6.   D

Set up as a proportion:

$$\frac{144 \text{ square feet}}{5 \text{ minutes}} = \frac{2,880 \text{ square feet}}{x \text{ minutes}} \text{ or } \frac{144}{5} = \frac{2,880}{x}.$$

Multiply both sides by 5x to get $144x = 2,880(5)$, then divide by 144 to get $x = \frac{2,880(5)}{144} = 100$.

7.   B

If the printing press produces 4,440 posters per hour, it produces $\frac{4,440}{60} = 74$ posters per minute. To find out how long it will take to produce 370 posters, set up the equation 370 posters $= x$ minutes × 74 posters per minute. Divide both sides by 74 posters per minute to find that x = 5 minutes.

8.   E

We can express the ratio of baseballs to the golf balls as $\frac{2}{3}$. Since we know the number of baseballs, we can set up a proportion: $\frac{2}{3} = \frac{30}{x}$, where x is the number of golf balls. To solve, we cross multiply, and get $2x = 90$, or $x = 45$.

9.   240

If the man has spent $\frac{5}{12}$ of his salary, he still has $1 - \frac{5}{12}$, or $\frac{7}{12}$ of his salary. So $140 represents $\frac{7}{12}$ of his salary.

Set up a proportion, using S to represent his salary:

$$\frac{7}{12} = \frac{140}{S}$$

Cross multiply:

$$7S = 12 \times 140$$
$$S = \frac{12 \times 140}{7}$$
$$S = 240$$

Medium

10.   B

We need to compute the cost of parking a car for 5 hours at each garage. Since the 2 garages have a split-rate system of charging, the cost for the first hour is different from the cost of each remaining hour.

The first hour at garage A costs $8.75

The next 4 hours cost 4 × $1.25 = $5.00

The total cost for parking at garage A = $8.75 + $5.00 = $13.75

The first hour at garage B costs $5.50

The next 4 hours cost 4 × $2.50 = $10.00

The total cost for parking at garage B = $5.50 + $10.00 = $15.50

So the difference in cost = $15.50 − $13.75 = $1.75.

11.   C

Here you can set up a direct proportion:

$$\frac{1 \text{ kilogram}}{2.2 \text{ pounds}} = \frac{x \text{ kilograms}}{1 \text{ pound}}$$

Cross multiply (the units drop out):

$$1(1) = 2.2x$$
$$x = \frac{1}{2.2} = \frac{10}{22} = \frac{5}{11}$$

If you have trouble setting up the proportion, you could use the answer choices to your advantage and take an educated guess. Since 2.2 pounds equals a kilogram, 1 pound must be a little less than $\frac{1}{2}$ kilogram. Of the possible answers, $\frac{11}{5}$ and $\frac{5}{8}$ are greater than $\frac{1}{2}$; $\frac{1}{3}$ and $\frac{1}{5}$ are too small. But $\frac{5}{11}$ is just under $\frac{1}{2}$, and so it should be the correct answer.

12. B

The ratio 5 boys to 3 girls tells you that for every 5 boys in the class there must be 3 girls in the class. So the total number of students in the class must be a multiple of 8, since the smallest possible total is 5 + 3, or 8. Since 36 is not divisible by 8, 36 cannot be the total number of students.

13. E

First find the rate at which the tree grew, in feet per year.

It grew 5 feet in n years, so it grew at an average rate of $\frac{5 \text{ feet}}{n \text{ years}}$.

But we were asked for the average amount it grew in inches per year, so we must convert. There are 12 inches in a foot, so the following can be set up.

$$\frac{5 \text{ feet}}{n \text{ years}} \times \frac{12 \text{ inches}}{1 \text{ foot}} = \frac{60 \text{ inches}}{n \text{ years}} = \frac{60}{n} \text{ inches per year.}$$

This is the average amount the tree grew in 1 year.

If the presence of the variable confuses you, another approach is to pick a number for n. The tree grew 5 feet in n years, so if we let $n = 5$, then the tree grew 5 feet in 5 years, or an average of 1 foot per year. 1 foot = 12 inches, so the tree grew an average of 12 inches a year. Now plug in our value of 5 for n in each answer choice and see which ones give a value of 12.

Choice (A): $60n = 60 \times 5 \neq 12$. Discard.

Choice (B): $\frac{5}{n} = \frac{5}{5} \neq 12$. Discard.

Choice (C): $\frac{5}{12n} = \frac{5}{12 \times 5} \times 5 \neq 12$. Discard.

Choice (D): $\frac{12n}{5} = \frac{12 \times 5}{5} = 12$. Hold onto.

Choice (E): $\frac{60}{n} = \frac{60}{5} = 12$. Hold onto.

We now have two possibilities. Therefore we must try another value for n to distinguish between the two. If $n = 10$ then the tree grew 5 feet in 10 years, or $\frac{1}{2}$ foot a year, which is 6 inches a year. In this case,

Choice (D): $\frac{12n}{5} = \frac{120}{5} \neq 6$. Discard.

Choice (E): $\frac{60}{n} = \frac{60}{10} = 6$. Okay.

(E) is the only answer choice that works in both cases.

14. D

To learn the man's overtime rate of pay, we have to figure out his regular rate of pay. Divide the amount of money made, $200, by the time it took to make it, 40 hours:

$200 \div 40$ hours = $5 per hour. That is the normal rate. The man is paid $1\frac{1}{2}$ times his regular rate during overtime, so when working more than 40 hours he makes $\frac{3}{2} \times \$5$ per hour = $7.50 per hour. Now we can figure out how long it takes the man to make $230. It takes him 40 hours to make the first $200. The last $30 are made at the overtime rate. Since it takes the man one hour to make

$7.50 at this rate, we can figure out the number of extra hours by dividing $30 by $7.50 per hour. $30 ÷ $7.50 per hour = 4 hours. The total time needed is 40 hours plus 4 hours, or 44 hours.

15. B

Since 3 out of 24 students are in student organizations, the remaining 24 − 3, or 21, students are not in student organizations. Therefore, the ratio of students in organizations to students not in organizations is

$$\frac{\text{\# in organizations}}{\text{\# not in organizations}} = \frac{3}{21} = \frac{1}{7}$$

16. D

The grade is decided by 4 quizzes and 1 exam. Since the exam counts twice as much as each quiz, the exam equals two quizzes, so we can say the grade is decided by the equivalent of 4 quizzes and 2 quizzes, or 6 quizzes. The exam equals two quizzes, so it represents $\frac{2}{6}$, or $\frac{1}{3}$, of the grade.

17. D

If 4 sweatshirts cost n dollars, then 40 sweatshirts cost 10 times that much, or $10n$. You could also solve this problem by picking numbers. Let $n = 12$. Thus, 4 sweatshirts cost 12 dollars and 1 sweatshirt costs 3 dollars. 40 sweatshirts cost 40 × 3 dollars, or 120 dollars. Plug in 12 for n in the answer choices to see which yields 120. 10 × n = 10 × 12 = 120.

18. A

First we need to know how many minutes are in two and a half hours. Since there are 60 minutes in an hour, there are 60 × 2.5 = 150 minutes in 2.5 hours. Since there are three minutes in every "triminute", we can divide the number of minutes in 2.5 hours by 3 to get the number of triminutes in 2.5 hours. 150 ÷ 3 = 50, choice (A). We can write this whole sequence down as one equation:

$$2.5 \text{ hours} \times \frac{60 \text{ minutes}}{1 \text{ hour}} \times \frac{1 \text{ triminute}}{3 \text{ minutes}} = 50 \text{ triminutes}$$

Notice how all the units neatly cancel out.

This problem could also be answered by Backsolving. Let's start by trying choice (C), 250 triminutes. 250 triminutes times 3 minutes per triminute equals 750 minutes. 750 minutes divided by 60 minutes per hour equals 12.5 hours, not 2.5. Eliminate choice (C) and try something smaller. Choice (B) gives us 7.5 hours, still too many. At this point, we know the answer must be choice (A), and this proves to be correct. 50 triminutes times 3 minutes per triminute equals 150 minutes; 150 minutes divided by 60 minutes per hour equals 2.5 hours, exactly what we're looking for.

19. 600

The ratio of parts is 4:3:2, making a total of 9 parts. Since 9 parts are equal to 1,800 votes, each part represents $\frac{1,800}{900}$, or 200 votes. Since Ms. Frau represents 3 parts, she received a total of 3 × 200, or 600 votes. (Another way to think about it: Out of every 9 votes, Ms. Frau gets 3, which is $\frac{3}{9}$ or $\frac{1}{3}$ of the total number of votes. $\frac{1}{3}$ of 1,800 is 600.)

We could also have solved this algebraically by setting up a proportion, with F as Ms. Frau's votes:

$$\frac{3}{9} = \frac{F}{1,800}$$

$$\frac{3}{9} \times 1,800 = F$$

$$600 = F$$

20. 25

If Ms. Smith's car averages 35 miles per gallon, she can go 35 miles on 1 gallon. To go 700 miles she will need $\frac{700}{35}$, or 20 gallons of gasoline. The price of gasoline was $1.25 per gallon, so she spent 20 × $1.25, or $25, for her trip.

21. 25

The ratio of cement to gravel to sand is 3:5:7. For every 3 portions of cement we put in, we get $3 + 5 + 7$, or 15, portions of the mixture. So the recipe gives us $\frac{15}{3}$, or 5, times as much mixture as cement. We have 5 tons of cement available, so we can make 5×5, or 25, tons of the mixture.

Hard

22. B

The time it takes to complete the entire exam is the sum of the time spent on the first half of the exam and the time spent on the second half. We know the time spent on the first half is $\frac{2}{3}$ of the time spent on the second half. If S represents the time spent on the second half, then the total time spent is $\frac{2}{3}S + S$, or $\frac{5}{3}S$. We know this total time is 1 hour, or 60 minutes. So we can set up a simple equation and solve for S.

$$\frac{5}{3}S = 60$$

$$\frac{3}{5} \times \frac{5}{3}S = \frac{3}{5} \times 60$$

$$S = 36$$

So the second half takes 36 minutes. The first half takes $\frac{2}{3}$ of this, or 24 minutes. (You could also find the first half by subtracting 36 minutes from the total time, 60 minutes.)

23. E

If John buys R pounds for N people, he is planning on feeding his guests cheese at a rate of $\frac{R \text{ pounds}}{N \text{ people}} = \frac{R}{N}$ pounds per person.

How much additional cheese must John buy for the extra P people? If John is buying $\frac{R}{N}$ pounds of cheese for each person, he will need $P \times \frac{R}{N}$, or $\frac{PR}{N}$ pounds for the extra P people. We can check our answer by seeing if the units cancel out:

$$P \text{ people} \times \frac{R \text{ pounds}}{N \text{ people}} = \frac{PR}{N} \text{ pounds}$$

Another approach: Get rid of all those variables by picking numbers. Say John buys 10 pounds of cheese for 5 people (that is, $R = 10$ and $N = 5$). Then everyone gets 2 pounds of cheese. Also say 7 people come, 2 more than expected (that is, $P = 2$). Then he needs 14 pounds to have enough for everybody to consume 2 pounds of cheese. Since he already bought 10 pounds, he must buy an additional 4 pounds. Therefore, an answer choice that equals 4 when we substitute 10 for R, 5 for N, and 2 for P is possibly correct:

Choice (A): $\frac{(5)(2)}{10} \neq 4$. Discard.

Choice (B): $\frac{5}{(10)(2)} \neq 4$. Discard.

Choice (C): $\frac{5 + 2}{10} \neq 4$. Discard.

Choice (D): $\frac{2}{(5)(10)} \neq 4$. Discard.

Choice (E): $\frac{(2)(10)}{5} = 4$. Correct.

Since only choice (E) gives us 4, that must be the correct answer.

24. 20

First find how long the trip takes him at each of the 2 different rates, using the formula time $= \dfrac{\text{distance}}{\text{rate}}$. He travels the first 10 km at 30 km per hour, so he takes $\frac{10}{30} = \frac{1}{3}$ hour for this portion of the journey.

He travels the remaining 30 km at 15 km per hour, so he takes $\frac{30}{15} = 2$ hours for this portion of the journey.

So the whole journey takes him $2 + \frac{1}{3} = 2\frac{1}{3}$ hours. Now we need to compare this to the amount of time it would take to make the same trip at a constant rate of 20 km per hour. If he traveled the whole 40 km at 20 km per hour, it would take $\frac{40}{20} = 2$ hours.

This is $\frac{1}{3}$ hour, or 20 minutes, shorter.

25. D

We can solve this algebraically. Let the number of yellow balls received be x. Then the number of white balls received is 30 more than this, or $x + 30$.

So $\dfrac{\text{\# of white balls}}{\text{\# of yellow balls}} = \dfrac{6}{5} = \dfrac{x + 30}{x}$

Cross multiply: $\qquad 6x = 5(x + 30)$

Solve for x: $\qquad 6x = 5x + 150$

$\qquad\qquad\qquad x = 150.$

Since the number of white balls ordered equals the number of yellow balls ordered, the total number of balls ordered is $2x$, which is 2×150, or 300.

26. B

Since the question asks for the answer in dollars, start by converting cents to dollars. There are 100 cents in a dollar, so 39 cents $= \dfrac{39}{100}$ dollars. Since each peach costs $\dfrac{39}{100}$ dollars, y peaches cost $\dfrac{39}{100}y$ dollars. If x oranges cost as

much as y peaches, x oranges also cost $\dfrac{39}{100}y$ dollars, or $\dfrac{39y}{100}$ dollars. Then one orange costs $\dfrac{1}{x}$ as much, or $\dfrac{39y}{100x}$ dollars.

This is an ideal problem to solve by picking numbers. Let's say that 5 oranges and 10 peaches cost the same; that is, $x = 5$ and $y = 10$. If peaches are 39 cents each, 10 of them will cost \$3.90, so that's the cost of 5 oranges. That means each orange costs $\dfrac{\$3.90}{5}$ or \$0.78. We try our numbers in each answer choice:

Choice (A): $\dfrac{(39)(5)}{(100)(10)} = \dfrac{195}{1,000}$. Discard.

Choice (B): $\dfrac{(39)(10)}{(100)(5)} = \dfrac{390}{500} = \dfrac{39}{50} = 0.78$. This may be our answer.

Choice (C): $\dfrac{3,900}{(5)(10)} = \dfrac{3,900}{50} = 78$. This is 78 dollars, not 78 cents. Discard.

Choice (D): $\dfrac{39(10)}{5} = \dfrac{390}{5} = 78$. Again, discard.

Choice (E): $\dfrac{(39)(5)}{10} = \dfrac{195}{10} = 19.5$. Again, discard.

Since only choice (B) produced the correct result, it must be correct.

27. C

In this question we cannot determine the number of white mice or gray mice, but we can determine their ratio.

Method I:

Since $\frac{1}{2}$ of the number of white mice makes up $\frac{1}{8}$ of the total number of mice, the total number of white mice must be double $\frac{1}{8}$ of the total number of mice, or $\frac{1}{4}$ of the total number of mice. Algebraically, letting W be the number of white mice and T the total number of mice, if $\frac{1}{2} \times W = \frac{1}{8} \times T$, then $W = \frac{1}{4} \times T$. So $\frac{1}{4}$ of the total number of mice are white. Similarly, since $\frac{1}{3}$ of the number of gray mice is $\frac{1}{9}$ of the total number of mice, $3 \times \frac{1}{9}$ of all the mice, or $\frac{1}{3}$ of all the mice, are gray. Therefore, the ratio of the number of white mice to the number of gray mice is $\frac{1}{4} : \frac{1}{3}$, which is the same as $\frac{3}{12} : \frac{4}{12}$, or 3:4.

Method II:

Pick numbers. Whenever a problem gives us information about ratios and asks us to determine some other ratio, we can *pick a value* for one of the quantities and solve for the ratio based on this value. The result will be the same no matter what value we pick.

In this case, we can pick a number for the total number of mice. Pick one that will facilitate calculations. Let's try 72, since it's a multiple of all the denominators of the fractions in the ratios (2, 3, 8, and 9). Now we can get values for the number of white mice and gray mice by using the given information. For the white mice, we have:

$\frac{1}{2}$ the # of white mice $= \frac{1}{8}$ the total # of mice

$= \frac{1}{8} \times 72 = 9.$

If 9 is $\frac{1}{2}$ of the number of white mice, there must be 2×9, or 18, white mice altogether. As for the gray mice, the following applies.

$\frac{1}{3}$ the number of gray mice $= \frac{1}{9}$ the total # of mice

$= \frac{1}{9} \times 72 = 8.$

If 8 is $\frac{1}{3}$ of the number of gray mice, there must be 3×8, or 24, gray mice altogether. The ratio of white mice to gray mice, then, is 18:24, or 3:4.

28. $\frac{11}{3}$ **or 3.66 or 3.67**

If $\frac{2}{3}$ of a cup of powdered lemonade mix is needed for 2 quarts of water, $\frac{1}{3}$ cup of the mix is needed for 1 quart of water. 11 quarts, then, would take $11 \times \frac{1}{3}$ cups of powdered lemonade, which can be gridded as $\frac{11}{3}$, or gridded as a decimal.

29. D

Pick a total number of professors. Because you'll be dealing with fifths and sevenths of the total, pick a number—say, 35—that's divisible by both 5 and 7. Because the question includes so many data, bring order to the complex situation by setting up a grid:

	Male	Female	Total
Tenured			
Untenured			
Total			

If $\frac{4}{7}$ of the faculty are male, the male total is $\frac{4}{7} \times 35 = 20$, and the female total must therefore be 15. If the ratio of tenured to untenured professors is 2:5, $\frac{2}{7}$ of the faculty, or 10 professors, must be tenured, and the remaining $\frac{5}{7}$ or 25 must be untenured:

	Male	Female	Total
Tenured			10
Untenured			25
Total	20	15	

The key piece of data that enables you to complete the grid is the fact that $\frac{1}{5}$ of the males—that is, $\frac{1}{5} \times 20 = 4$—is tenured:

	Male	Female	Total
Tenured	4		10
Untenured			25
Total	20	15	

You're now in a position to complete the grid:

	Male	Female	Total
Tenured	4	6	10
Untenured	16	9	25
Total	20	15	

Now focus on exactly what's asked: the fraction of female professors that are untenured is $\frac{9}{15} = \frac{3}{5}$.

30. 52

Beware! Average speed for the journey is not the same as the average of her speeds on the 2 parts of her trip. Her average speed is the total distance she traveled divided by the total time she spent traveling. For the first part of her journey, she traveled 100 miles at a rate of 50 miles per hour. Therefore, it took her 2 hours to drive to Baxterville. During the second part of her journey, she increased her speed by 20 percent. 20 percent of 50 is 10, so she was traveling at $50 + 10 = 60$ miles per hour. At a rate of 60 miles per hour, she would have traveled 30 miles in 30 minutes.

We can summarize this information in a chart to make it easier to follow:

	To Baxterville	To Center City	Total
distance (miles)	100 miles	30 miles	130 miles
time (hours)	2 hr.	1/2 hr.	2.5 hr.
rate (miles/hour)	50 mph	60 mph	

Since the average speed is the total distance traveled over the total time spent traveling, Angelica's average speed is 130 miles per 2.5 hours, or 52 miles per hour.

31. E

Pick numbers. Say $f = 4$ and $d = 16$. Then the time it took to get from first to second is $\frac{16}{4}$ minutes and the time it took to get from second to third is $\frac{16}{8} = 2$ minutes. Average speed is $\frac{\text{total distance}}{\text{total time}} = \frac{16 + 16}{4 + 2} = \frac{32}{6} = \frac{16}{3}$. Which choice has a value of $\frac{16}{3}$ when $f = 4$ and $d = 16$?

Only (E).

32. 4

In each case the examination and the frames are the same; the difference in cost must be due to the difference in the costs of the lenses. Since plastic lenses cost 4 times as much as glass lenses, the *difference* in cost must be 3 times the cost of the glass lenses.

$$\begin{aligned} \text{Difference in cost} &= \text{Cost of plastic} - \text{Cost of glass} \\ &= 4(\text{cost of glass}) - 1(\text{cost of glass}) \\ &= 3(\text{cost of glass}) \end{aligned}$$

The difference in cost is $42 - 30$, or $12. Since this is 3 times the cost of the glass lenses, the glass lenses must cost $\frac{\$12}{3}$, or $4.

Chapter Seven: **Percents**

Not only are percents a common occurrence on the SAT (in fact, the test makers love them), they're also common in daily life. These two reasons alone are enough for you to know that percents are a concept you're going to need to understand. A percentage is really just a ratio, but it's always a ratio of some number out of 100. Instead of saying that in the year 2000, 35 out of 100 people in New York State were employed in the professional, education, health, or social service industries, we could just say that 35 percent (or 35%) of people in New York State were employed in those industries. A percent, like any ratio, can be written as a decimal (0.35), a fraction $\left(\dfrac{35}{100} \right)$, or a percent (35%).

We can find the percent of any number by changing the percent to a decimal (moving the decimal point two places to the left) and multiplying by the given number. To find 30 percent of 400, start by changing the 30 percent to a decimal (.30). Then multiply .30 × 400 to get 120. 30 percent of 400 is 120. So how would you reverse that formula if you were trying to find what percent of 200 that 30 is? Divide 30 by 200, which is .15, and then convert the decimal to a percent. This tells you that 30 is 15 percent of 200. Unsure about that? Let's check it. 15 percent changed to a decimal is .15. Multiply .15 and 200 and you get 30. For further reading on percents:

28. Percent Formula

29. Percent Increase

30. Finding the Original Whole

31. Combined Percent Increase and Decrease

Chapter Seven Practice Set
Answer Key

1. Ⓐ Ⓑ Ⓒ Ⓓ Ⓔ   15. Ⓐ Ⓑ Ⓒ Ⓓ Ⓔ
2. Ⓐ Ⓑ Ⓒ Ⓓ Ⓔ   16. Ⓐ Ⓑ Ⓒ Ⓓ Ⓔ
3. Ⓐ Ⓑ Ⓒ Ⓓ Ⓔ   17. Ⓐ Ⓑ Ⓒ Ⓓ Ⓔ
4. Ⓐ Ⓑ Ⓒ Ⓓ Ⓔ   18. Ⓐ Ⓑ Ⓒ Ⓓ Ⓔ
5. Ⓐ Ⓑ Ⓒ Ⓓ Ⓔ   19. Ⓐ Ⓑ Ⓒ Ⓓ Ⓔ
6. Ⓐ Ⓑ Ⓒ Ⓓ Ⓔ   20. Grid-in below
7. Ⓐ Ⓑ Ⓒ Ⓓ Ⓔ   21. Ⓐ Ⓑ Ⓒ Ⓓ Ⓔ
8. Ⓐ Ⓑ Ⓒ Ⓓ Ⓔ   22. Ⓐ Ⓑ Ⓒ Ⓓ Ⓔ
9. Ⓐ Ⓑ Ⓒ Ⓓ Ⓔ   23. Ⓐ Ⓑ Ⓒ Ⓓ Ⓔ
10. Ⓐ Ⓑ Ⓒ Ⓓ Ⓔ   24. Ⓐ Ⓑ Ⓒ Ⓓ Ⓔ
11. Grid-in below   25. Ⓐ Ⓑ Ⓒ Ⓓ Ⓔ
12. Ⓐ Ⓑ Ⓒ Ⓓ Ⓔ   26. Ⓐ Ⓑ Ⓒ Ⓓ Ⓔ
13. Ⓐ Ⓑ Ⓒ Ⓓ Ⓔ   27. Grid-in below
14. Ⓐ Ⓑ Ⓒ Ⓓ Ⓔ   28. Grid-in below

11.   20.   27.   28.

PRACTICE SET

Basic

1. If 48 of the 60 seats on a bus were occupied, what percent of the seats were not occupied?

    (A) 12%
    (B) 20%
    (C) 25%
    (D) 60%
    (E) 80%

2. 4 people shared a taxi to the airport. The fare was $36.00, and they gave the driver a tip equal to 25 percent of the fare. If they equally shared the cost of the fare and tip, how much did each person pay?

    (A) $9.00
    (B) $9.75
    (C) $10.25
    (D) $10.75
    (E) $11.25

3. In a certain class, if Edie's average rose from 72 to 84, by what percent did her average increase?

    (A) 12%

    (B) $14\frac{2}{7}\%$

    (C) $16\frac{2}{3}\%$

    (D) $66\frac{2}{3}\%$

    (E) $85\frac{5}{7}\%$

4. If 60 percent of W equals 20 percent of T, what percent of T is W?

    (A) 12%

    (B) $33\frac{1}{3}\%$

    (C) 60%

    (D) 120%

    (E) $133\frac{1}{3}\%$

5. 36 percent of 18 is 18 percent of what number?

    (A) 9
    (B) 24
    (C) 36
    (D) 40
    (E) 48

6. A closet contains 24 pairs of shoes. If 25 percent of those pairs of shoes are black, how many pairs are NOT black?

    (A) 4
    (B) 6
    (C) 12
    (D) 18
    (E) 20

7. What is the percent discount on a jacket marked down from $120 to $100?

    (A) $16\frac{2}{3}\%$

    (B) 20%

    (C) 30%

    (D) $33\frac{1}{3}\%$

    (E) 40%

8. A survey found that 80 percent of the apartments in City G have smoke alarms installed. Of these, 20 percent have smoke alarms that are not working. What percent of the apartments in City G were found to have working smoke alarms?

    (A) 60%

    (B) 64%

    (C) $66\frac{2}{3}$%

    (D) 70%

    (E) 72%

9. What percent of 40 is 8?

    (A) 5%
    (B) 10%
    (C) 20%
    (D) 22.5%
    (E) 30%

10. When Joe started his exercise program, he could do 12 pushups in a minute. After he had been practicing for two weeks, he could do 21 pushups in a minute. By what percent did Joe's rate of doing pushups increase?

    (A) 9%
    (B) 21%
    (C) 42%
    (D) 57%
    (E) 75%

11. What is 10 percent of 20 percent of 30?

Medium

12. Bob took 20 math tests last year. If he failed 6 of them, what percent of the math tests did he pass?

    (A) $37\frac{1}{2}$%

    (B) 60%

    (C) $62\frac{1}{2}$%

    (D) $66\frac{2}{3}$%

    (E) 70%

13. In a certain box of gloves, 12 pairs are size 7 and 24 pairs are size 6. If all the gloves in the box are either size 6 or size 7, what percent of the gloves in the box are size 6?

    (A) $33\frac{1}{3}$%

    (B) 50%

    (C) $66\frac{2}{3}$%

    (D) 75%

    (E) 200%

14. If 65 percent of x is 195, what is 75 percent of x?

    (A) 215
    (B) 225
    (C) 235
    (D) 250
    (E) 260

15. A 25-ounce solution is 20 percent alcohol. If 50 ounces of water are added to it, what percent of the new solution is alcohol?

    (A) 5%

    (B) $6\frac{2}{3}\%$

    (C) 10%

    (D) $13\frac{1}{3}\%$

    (E) 20%

16. A store sells a watch for a profit of 25 percent of the wholesale cost. What percent of the selling price of the watch is the store's profit?

    (A) 12.5%
    (B) 20%
    (C) 25%
    (D) 50%
    (E) 75%

17. In 2002, 30 percent of the 200 apartment units on a certain street were condominiums. By 2003, the total number of units on the street had increased by 25 percent, and 40 percent of units were condominiums. What was the percent increase of condominiums during this period.

    (A) $10\frac{1}{5}\%$

    (B) 30%

    (C) $33\frac{1}{3}\%$

    (D) 40%

    (E) $66\frac{2}{3}\%$

18. What is 0.02 percent of 2.5 percent of 0.8?

    (A) 0.0004
    (B) 0.00004
    (C) 0.000004
    (D) 0.0000004
    (E) 0.00000004

19. The price of a newspaper rises from 5 cents to 15 cents. What is the increase in price?

    (A) 50%
    (B) 75%
    (C) 100%
    (D) 150%
    (E) 200%

20. After getting a 20 percent discount, Jerry paid $100 for a bicycle. How much, in dollars, did the bicycle originally cost?

Hard

21. A stock decreases in value by 20 percent. By what percent must the stock price increase to reach its former value?

    (A) 15%
    (B) 20%
    (C) 25%
    (D) 30%
    (E) 40%

22. The population of a certain town increases by 50 percent every 50 years. If the population in 1950 was 810, in what year was the population 160?

    (A) 1650
    (B) 1700
    (C) 1750
    (D) 1800
    (E) 1850

KAPLAN

23. A man bought 10 crates of oranges for a total cost of $80. If he lost 2 of the crates, at what price would he have to sell each of the remaining crates in order to earn a total profit of 25 percent of the total cost?

    (A) $10.00
    (B) $12.50
    (C) $15.00
    (D) $100.00
    (E) $120.00

24. In a certain school, 50 percent of all male students and 60 percent of all female students play a varsity sport. If 40 percent of the students at the school are male, what percent of the students DO NOT play a varsity sport?

    (A) 44%
    (B) 50%
    (C) 55%
    (D) 56%
    (E) 60%

25. The quantities a, b, and c are positive and ab equals $\frac{c}{4}$. If a is increased by 50 percent and b is decreased by 25 percent, then, in order for the equation to remain true, c must be

    (A) decreased by 25%

    (B) decreased by $12\frac{1}{2}$%

    (C) increased by $12\frac{1}{2}$%

    (D) increased by 25%

    (E) increased by 50%

26. The number that is 400 percent greater than 15 is what percent greater than 150 percent of 30?

    (A) 15%

    (B) 25%

    (C) $33\frac{1}{3}$%

    (D) $66\frac{2}{3}$%

    (E) $166\frac{2}{3}$%

27. If increasing 20 by P percent gives the same result as decreasing 60 by P percent, what is P percent of 70?

28. A baseball team won 45 percent of the first 80 games it played. How many of the remaining 82 games will the team have to win in order to win exactly 50 percent of all the games it plays?

ANSWERS AND EXPLANATIONS

Basic

1. B

If 48 out of 60 seats on a bus were occupied, then

60 − 48, or 12, seats were not occupied. Remember,

percent $= \dfrac{\text{part}}{\text{whole}} \times 100\%$, the percent of seats not occu-

pied $= \dfrac{12}{60} \times 100\%$, or $\dfrac{1}{5} \times 100\% = 20\%$. So choice

(B) is correct.

2. E

The total cost of the taxi ride equals $36.00 + (25\%$ of

$36.00), or $36.00 + (\dfrac{1}{4} \times \$36.00) = \$36.00 + \$9.00 =$

$45.00. If four people split the cost equally, then each per-

son paid $\dfrac{\$45.00}{4}$, or $11.25 each. So choice (E) is correct.

3. C

Percent increase $= \dfrac{\text{amount of increase}}{\text{original whole}} \times 100\%$. So if

Edie's average rose from 72 to 84, the amount of the

increase is 84 − 72, or 12. The percent increase $=$

$\dfrac{12}{60} \times 100\%$, or $16\dfrac{2}{3}\%$, and choice (C) is correct.

4. B

The question asks us to find W as a percent of T.

$\quad$ 60% of W = 20% of T

$\quad$ $.6W = .2T$

Now solve for W:

$\quad W = \dfrac{.2T}{.6}$

$\quad W = \dfrac{1}{3}T$

$\dfrac{1}{3}$ is $33\dfrac{1}{3}\%$, so W is $33\dfrac{1}{3}\%$ of T.

5. C

This question involves a principle that appears frequently
on the SAT: a percent of $b = b$ percent of a. You can
show that with the following example:

36% of $18 \quad = \dfrac{36}{100} \times 18$

$\quad = \dfrac{18}{100} \times 36$

$\quad = 18\%$ of 36

The answer here is 36.

6. D

If 25 percent of the shoes are black, then 100% − 25%,

or 75 percent of the shoes are not black. 75 percent of

$24 = \dfrac{3}{4} \times 24 = 18$.

7. A

The percent discount equals the amount of discount divided by the original price (not the final price). The amount
of discount is $120 − $100, or $20. The original price was
$120.

Percent discount $= \dfrac{20}{120} \times 100\% = \dfrac{1}{6} \times 100\% =$

$16\dfrac{2}{3}\%$.

8. B

If 20 percent of the apartments with smoke alarms were

found to have smoke alarms that are not working, then

the remaining 80 percent of the apartments with smoke

alarms have smoke alarms that are working. Since 80 per-

cent of all apartments in the city have smoke alarms, and

80 percent of these have working smoke alarms, 80 percent of 80 percent of all the apartments in the city have working smoke alarms. Converting to fractions, 80 percent of 80 percent $= \frac{8}{10} \times \frac{8}{10} = \frac{64}{100}$ is 64%.

Alternatively, since we are working with percents only, try picking numbers. Let the number of apartments in City G be 100. If 80 percent of these have smoke alarms, then 80 percent of 100, or 80, apartments have smoke alarms. If 20 percent of these do not work, then 80 percent do work.

Eighty percent of 80 is $\frac{8}{10} \times 80 = 64$ apartments. If 64 of the 100 apartments in City G have working smoke alarms, then we come up with $\frac{64}{100}$ or 64 percent, that have working smoke alarms.

9. C

Find 8 percent of 40 by comparing the ratio of 8 and 40 to the ratio of x and 100. The variable x will be the percent of 40 that 8 is. $\frac{8}{40} = \frac{x}{100}$. Therefore, $40x = 800$ and $x = 20$.

10. E

First determine how much Joe's rate of doing pushups increased. He could do 12 pushups per minute at the beginning of his exercise program, and 21 pushups per minute at the end, so his rate of doing pushups increased by $21 - 12 = 9$. Since we're trying to figure out by what percent his rate of doing pushups increased from what it was at the beginning, we need to find what percent 9 is of 12.

Percent change $\frac{\text{actual change}}{\text{original amount}} = \frac{9}{12} = .75$, so Joe's rate of doing pushups increased by 75%.

11. .6 OR 3/5

You are asked for 10% of 20 percent of 30. You can simply multiply this through on a calculator:

10% = 0.1; 20% = 0.2

So 10 percent of 20 percent of 30 becomes 0.1 × 0.2 × 30 = 0.6.

Medium

12. E

You can assume Bob either passed or failed each test; there's no third possibility. If Bob failed 6 tests out of 20, he passed the other 14. Bob passed $\frac{14}{20}$ of the tests. To convert $\frac{14}{20}$ to a percent, multiply numerator and denominator by 5; this will give us a fraction with a denominator of 100: $\frac{14}{20} \times \frac{5}{5} = \frac{70}{100}$ or 70%. (Or realize that since $\frac{1}{20} = 5\%$, $\frac{14}{20}$ must be 14 times as big, or $14 \times 5\%$, or 70%.) Bob passed 70 percent of his tests.

13. C

First, you have to identify the part and the whole. You're asked what percent of the gloves in the box are size 6, so the part is the number of size 6 gloves, and the whole is the total number of gloves. You're told there are 12 size 7 pairs and 24 size 6 pairs, for a total of 36 pairs. Of those 36 pairs, 24 pairs are size 6, so $\frac{24}{36}$ are size 6. $\frac{24}{36} = \frac{2}{3}$, or $66\frac{2}{3}\%$.

14. B

You first need to find what x is. If 65% of $x = 195$, then

$$(0.65)(x) = 195$$

$$x = \frac{195}{0.65} = 300$$

75% of 300 = 0.75 × 300 = 225

15. B

You're asked what percent of the new solution is alcohol. The part is the number of ounces of alcohol; the whole is the total number of ounces of the new solution. There were 25 ounces originally. Then 50 ounces were added, so there are 75 ounces of new solution. How many ounces are alcohol? 20 percent of the original 25-ounce solution was alcohol. 20 percent is $\frac{1}{5}$, so $\frac{1}{5}$ of 25, or 5 ounces are alcohol. Now you can find the percent of alcohol in the new solution:

$$\% \text{ of alcohol} = \frac{\text{alcohol}}{\text{total solution}} \times 100\%$$

$$= \frac{5}{75} \times 100\%$$

$$= \frac{20}{3}\% = 6\frac{2}{3}\%$$

16. B

The easiest approach is to pick a sample value for the wholesale cost of the watch, and from that, work out the profit and selling price. As usual with percent problems, it's simplest to pick 100. If the watch cost the store $100, then the profit will be 25% of $100, or $25. The selling price equals the cost to the store plus the profit: $100 + $25, or $125.

The profit represents $\frac{25}{125}$ or $\frac{1}{5}$ of the selling price.

The percent equivalent of $\frac{1}{5}$ is 20%.

17. E

In 2002, 30 percent of 200 or (.3)(200) = 60 units were condominiums. By 2003, the number of units had risen by 25 percent—that is, to (1.25)(200) = 250. Of these, 40 percent or (.4)(250) = 100, were condominiums. The percent increase from 60 to 100 is

$$\frac{\text{actual change}}{\text{original amount}} = \frac{40}{60} = \frac{2}{3} = 66\frac{2}{3}\%.$$

18. C

First convert the percents to decimals: 0.02% = 0.0002 and 2.5% = 0.025. Now use your calculator: (0.0002)(0.025)(0.8) = 0.000004.

19. E

$$\text{Percent increase} = \frac{\text{Amount of increase}}{\text{original whole}} \times 100\%$$

The original whole is the price before the increase. The amount of increase is the difference between the increased price and the original price. So the amount of increase is 15¢ − 5¢ = 10¢.

$$\% \text{ increase} = \frac{10¢}{5¢} \times 100\% = 2 \times 100\% = 200\%.$$

20. 125

The bicycle was discounted by 20 percent; this means that Jerry paid (100% − 20%), or 80 percent, of the original price. Jerry paid $100, so you have the percent and the part and need to find the whole. Now plug the numbers into the percent formula:

Percent × Whole = Part

$$80\% \times \text{Whole} = \$100$$

$$0.8 \times \text{Whole} = \$100$$

$$\text{Whole} = \frac{\$100}{.8}$$

$$\text{Whole} = \$125$$

The bicycle originally sold for $125.

Hard

21. C

The key is: While the value of the stock decreases and increases by the same amount, it doesn't decrease and increase by the same percent. When the stock first decreases, that amount of change is part of a larger whole. If the stock were to increase to its former value, that same amount of change would be a larger percent of a smaller whole.

Pick a number for the original value of the stock, such as $100. (Since it's easy to take percents of 100, it's usually best to choose 100.) The 20 percent decrease represents $20, so the stock decreases to a value of $80. Now in order for the stock to reach the value of $100 again, there must be a $20 increase. What percent of $80 is $20?

It's $\frac{\$20}{\$80} \times 100\%$, or $\frac{1}{4} \times 100\%$, or 25%.

22. C

Since the population increases by 50 percent every 50 years, the population in 1950 was 150 percent, or $\frac{3}{2}$, of the 1900 population. This means the 1900 population was $\frac{2}{3}$ of the 1950 population. Similarly, the 1850 population was $\frac{2}{3}$ of the 1900 population, and so on. You can just keep multiplying by $\frac{2}{3}$ until you get to a population of 160.

$$1950: 810 \times \frac{2}{3} = 540 \text{ in } 1900$$

$$1900: 540 \times \frac{2}{3} = 360 \text{ in } 1850$$

$$1850: 360 \times \frac{2}{3} = 240 \text{ in } 1800$$

$$1800: 240 \times \frac{2}{3} = 160 \text{ in } 1750$$

The population was 160 in 1750.

Another approach is to work forward from the population of 160 until reaching 810; then determine how far back the population of 160 must have been. During each 50-year period, the population increases by 50 percent, or by $\frac{1}{2}$.

$$160: 160 + \frac{1}{2}(160) = 240$$

$$240: 240 + \frac{1}{2}(240) = 360$$

$$360: 360 + \frac{1}{2}(360) = 540$$

$$540: 540 + \frac{1}{2}(540) = 810$$

So, if the population was 810 in 1950, it must have been 540 in 1900, 360 in 1850, 240 in 1800, and 160 in 1750.

23. B

The man paid $80 for 10 crates of oranges, and then lost 2 crates. That leaves him with 8 crates. You want to find the price per crate that will give him an overall profit of 25 percent. 25 percent, or $\frac{1}{4}$, of $80 is $20. So to make a 25 percent profit, he must bring in $80 + $20, or $100, in sales receipts. If he has 8 crates, that means that each crate must sell for $\frac{\$100}{8}$, or $12.50.

24. A

First find what percent of the whole population does play a varsity sport. We can do this by finding out what percent of all students are male students who play a varsity sport, and what percent of all students are female students who play a varsity sport, and then summing these values. 40 percent of all students are male, so 60 percent of the students are female.

First, what percent of all students are males who play a varsity sport? 50 percent of the males play a varsity sport; that is, 50 percent (or half) of 40 percent = $.5 \times .4 = .20$ = 20 percent of all the students.

Now for the women. 60 percent of the females play a varsity sport; that is, 60 percent of 60 percent = $.6 \times .6 = .36$ = 36% of all the students.

Sum the percents of the males and females who play a varsity sport: 20% + 36% = 56% of the total student population.

The percent of all students who DO NOT play a varsity sport is 100% − 56% = 44%.

25. C

You have the equation $ab = \frac{c}{4}$. Increasing a by 50 percent is the same as multiplying a by $\frac{3}{2}$. Decreasing b by 25 percent is the same as multiplying b by $\frac{3}{4}$. Performing both these operations gives $\frac{3}{2}a \times \frac{3}{4}b = \frac{9}{8}ab$.

Therefore, ab has increased by $\frac{1}{8}$. If ab increases by $\frac{1}{8}$, then in order for the equation to remain true, $\frac{c}{4}$ must also be increased by $\frac{1}{8}$. If $\frac{c}{4}$ is increased by $\frac{1}{8}$, c is also increased by $\frac{1}{8}$.

An increase of $\frac{1}{8}$ is the same as an increase of $12\frac{1}{2}\%$.

You can make this a lot less algebraic by picking numbers. We'll pick values for a and b, which will yield a particular value for c (since its value is determined by a and b). Then you will make the described changes to a and b, and see what change this gives for c.

Since a, b, and c are positive numbers, say a is 2 and b is 4.

$$ab = \frac{c}{4}$$
$$c = 4ab$$
$$c = 4(2)(4) = 32$$

If a is increased by 50 percent, it becomes $2 + 1$, or 3. Since b is decreased by 25 percent, it becomes $4 - 1$, or 3. The relationship between a, b, and c remains the same, but we'll use capital letters to denote the new values:

$$AB = \frac{C}{4}$$
$$C = 4AB$$
$$C = 4(3)(3) = 36$$

Therefore, C increases from 32 to 36, which is a change of 4. The percent increase is then $\frac{4}{32} \times 100\% = 12\frac{1}{2}\%$.

26. D

The number that is 400 percent greater than 15 is 500 percent of 15, or $5 \times 15 = 75$. 150 percent of 30 means $(1.5)(30) = 45$. So 75 is what percent greater than 45?

$$\text{Percent change} = \frac{\text{actual change}}{\text{original amount}} = \frac{30}{45} = \frac{2}{3} = 66\frac{2}{3}\%.$$

27. 35

Increasing 20 by P percent means adding P percent of 20 to 20, so we can write "increasing 20 by P percent gives the same result as decreasing 60 by P percent" as

$$20\left(1 + \frac{P}{100}\right) = 60\left(1 - \frac{P}{100}\right) \text{ or } 20 + \frac{20P}{100} = 60 - \frac{60P}{100}.$$

This equation simplifies to $\frac{80P}{100} = 40$. Therefore, $P = 50$.

Now we need to find P percent of 70, which is $0.5(70)$ or 35.

28. 45

In their season, the baseball team plays $80 + 82$, or 162 games. To win exactly 50 percent or $\frac{1}{2}$ of their games, they must win 81 games. They have won 45 percent of their first 80 games. Since $45\% \times 80 = \frac{9}{20} \times 80 = 36$, they have won 36 games. To finish with 81 wins, they must win $81 - 36$, or 45, of the remaining games.

KAPLAN

Chapter Eight: **Powers and Roots**

Powers, or exponents, are just a way of telling you that a specific number is being multiplied by itself a certain number of times. The normal-sized number—the one being multiplied—is the base, and the tiny number is the exponent. The exponent tells us how many times to multiply the base by itself. For example, 2^4 actually means $2 \times 2 \times 2 \times 2$, (which, as we're sure you've figured out, equals 16). This is referred to as "two to the fourth power," or "two to the power of four." When a number is raised to the second power, it is called the "square of that number," or said number *squared*. When a number is raised to the third power, the same rules apply, but this time it is *cubed*. It's easy to remember cubed in terms of geometric area and volume. Area deals with a two-dimensional object and gives an answer in terms of square units. Volume deals with a three-dimensional object and gives an answer in terms of cubic units.

Though the *square root* of a number may sound intimidating, it's just the inverse of the square of that number. When we say *inverse,* we mean an opposite operation, like addition and subtraction. Finding the square root and squaring a number, like addition and subtraction, are inverse operations. So the square root of a number (x) is always going to be the number that gives you (x) when the number is squared. Sounds confusing?

Let's take 16. What number multiplied by itself will give you 16? The correct answer is 4. This means the square root of 16 is 4. Incidentally, 16 is a *perfect square*. A perfect square is a whole number whose square root is also a whole number. Of course not all numbers are perfect squares, but every positive number does have a square root. Here are some key concepts the test makers love to include:

44. Multiplying and Dividing Powers

45. Raising Powers to Powers

46. Simplifying Square Roots

47. Adding and Subtracting Roots

48. Multiplying and Dividing Roots

49. Negative Exponents and Rational Exponents

68. Radical Equations

Chapter Eight Practice Set Answer Sheet

1. Ⓐ Ⓑ Ⓒ Ⓓ Ⓔ   11. Ⓐ Ⓑ Ⓒ Ⓓ Ⓔ
2. Ⓐ Ⓑ Ⓒ Ⓓ Ⓔ   12. Ⓐ Ⓑ Ⓒ Ⓓ Ⓔ
3. Ⓐ Ⓑ Ⓒ Ⓓ Ⓔ   13. Ⓐ Ⓑ Ⓒ Ⓓ Ⓔ
4. Ⓐ Ⓑ Ⓒ Ⓓ Ⓔ   14. Ⓐ Ⓑ Ⓒ Ⓓ Ⓔ
5. Ⓐ Ⓑ Ⓒ Ⓓ Ⓔ   15. Grid-in below
6. Ⓐ Ⓑ Ⓒ Ⓓ Ⓔ   16. Grid-in below
7. Ⓐ Ⓑ Ⓒ Ⓓ Ⓔ   17. Ⓐ Ⓑ Ⓒ Ⓓ Ⓔ
8. Grid-in below   18. Ⓐ Ⓑ Ⓒ Ⓓ Ⓔ
9. Ⓐ Ⓑ Ⓒ Ⓓ Ⓔ   19. Ⓐ Ⓑ Ⓒ Ⓓ Ⓔ
10. Ⓐ Ⓑ Ⓒ Ⓓ Ⓔ   20. Grid-in below

8.   15.   16.   20.

PRACTICE SET

Basic

1. $2^4 \times 4^3 =$

    (A) 8^{12}

    (B) 8^7

    (C) 6^7

    (D) 2^{10}

    (E) 2^7

2. $6\sqrt{9} \times 2\sqrt{16} =$

    (A) 72

    (B) 144

    (C) 288

    (D) 864

    (E) 1,728

3. If $x = 9a^2$ and $a > 0$, then $\sqrt{x} =$

    (A) $-3a$

    (B) $3a$

    (C) $9a$

    (D) $3a^2$

    (E) $81a^4$

4. Which of the following is NOT equal to 0.0675?

    (A) 67.5×10^{-3}

    (B) 6.75×10^{-2}

    (C) 0.675×10^{-1}

    (D) 0.00675×10^2

    (E) 0.0000675×10^3

5. If $x^{-3} = 27$, $x =$

    (A) -3

    (B) $-\dfrac{1}{3}$

    (C) $\dfrac{1}{3}$

    (D) 3

    (E) 9

6. If $n^{-4} = \dfrac{1}{28,561}$, what is the value of n?

    (A) $\dfrac{1}{169}$

    (B) $-\dfrac{1}{13}$

    (C) $\dfrac{1}{28,561}$

    (D) $\dfrac{1}{13}$

    (E) 13

7. If $m^{\frac{3}{2}} = 8$, what is the value of m?

    (A) 2

    (B) 4

    (C) 6

    (D) 10

    (E) $16\sqrt{2}$

8. $\dfrac{4^3 - 4^2}{2^2} =$

KAPLAN

Medium

9. If q is an odd integer greater than 1, what is the value of $(-1)^q + 1$?

   (A) -2
   (B) -1
   (C) 0
   (D) 2
   (E) It cannot be determined from the information given.

10. If $x > 0$, then $(4^x)(8^x) =$

    (A) 2^{9x}
    (B) 2^{8x}
    (C) 2^{6x}
    (D) 2^{5x}
    (E) 2^{4x}

11. If $\dfrac{\sqrt{n}}{3}$ is an even integer, which of the following could be the value of n?

    (A) 27
    (B) 48
    (C) 81
    (D) 121
    (E) 144

12. Which of the following is equal to 8^5?

    I. $2^5 \times 4^5$
    II. 2^{15}
    III. $2^5 \times 2^{10}$

    (A) II only
    (B) I and II only
    (C) I and III only
    (D) II and III only
    (E) I, II, and III

13. If $2\sqrt{c} + 3 = 5$, what is the value of c?

    (A) 0
    (B) 1
    (C) $\sqrt{2}$
    (D) 2
    (E) 3

14. If $\sqrt{x + y} = 5x$, what is the value of y in terms of x?

    (A) $25x$
    (B) $5x^2$
    (C) $25x^2$
    (D) $25x^2 - x$
    (E) 25

15. If $s^2 t^{-2} = 1$ and $st = -4$, what is the value of $s + t$?

16. If $x = 2$, then $3^x + (x^3)^2 =$

Hard

17. If $xyz \neq 0$, then $\dfrac{x^2 y^6 z^{10}}{xy^3 z^5} =$

    (A) $xy^2 z^2$
    (B) $xy^3 z^5$
    (C) $x^2 y^2 z^2$
    (D) $x^2 y^3 z^5$
    (E) $x^3 y^9 z^{15}$

18. If $x^a x^b = 1$ and $x \neq \pm 1$, then $a + b =$

    (A) x
    (B) -1
    (C) 0
    (D) 1
    (E) It cannot be determined from the information given.

19. What is the remainder when $2x^3 - x^2 + 3x - 4$ is divided by $x + 2$?

    (A) −34
    (B) −30
    (C) 0
    (D) 13
    (E) 30

20. If $5^n > 10,000$ and n is an integer, what is the smallest possible value of n?

ANSWERS AND EXPLANATIONS

Basic

1. D

To multiply 2 numbers with the same base, add the 2 exponents. Here, we have 2 different bases, 2 and 4. We must rewrite 1 of the numbers so that the bases are the same. Since $4 = 2^2$, we can easily rewrite 4^3 as a power of 2: $4^3 = (2^2)^3$. To raise a power to an exponent, multiply the exponents, so $(2^2)^3 = 2^6$.

Therefore, $2^4 \times 4^3 = 2^4 \times 2^6$

$$= 2^{4+6}$$

$$= 2^{10}$$

2. B

The expression $6\sqrt{9} \times 2\sqrt{16}$ can be simplified by taking the square roots of 9 and 16, respectively:

$$6\sqrt{9} \times 2\sqrt{16} =$$

$$(6 \times 3) \times (2 \times 4) = 18 \times 8 = 144$$

So choice (B) is correct.

3. B

We can find the value of $\sqrt{x}$ by substituting $9a^2$ for x.

$$\sqrt{x} = \sqrt{9a^2}$$

$$= \sqrt{9} \times \sqrt{a^2}$$

$$= 3a$$

Note: We could do this only because we know that $a > 0$. The radical sign ($\sqrt{}$) refers to the positive square root of a number.

4. D

To multiply or divide a number by a power of 10, we move the decimal point to the right or left, respectively, the same number of places as the number of zeros in the power of 10. Multiplying by a negative power of 10 is the same as dividing by a positive power. For instance: $3 \times 10^{-2} = \frac{3}{10^{-2}}$. Keeping this in mind, let's go over the choices one by one. Remember: We are looking for the choice that is *not* equal to 0.0675.

Choice (A): $67.5 \times 10^{-3} = 0.0675$. No good.

Choice (B): $6.75 \times 10^{-2} = 0.0675$. No good.

Choice (C): $0.675 \times 10^{-1} = 0.0675$. No good.

Choice (D): $0.00675 \times 10^2 = 0.675$.

$0.675 \neq 0.0675$, so this is the correct answer.

Let's go over choice (E) for practice.

Choice (E): $0.0000675 \times 10^3 = 0.0675$. No good.

5. C

An easy way to manage negative exponents is to think of the negative sign as meaning "one, over", as in $x^{-3} = \frac{1}{x^3}$. Also, remember that this problem could also be back-solved if the following algebraic solution seems too complicated.

$$x^{-3} = 27$$

$$\frac{1}{x^3} = 27$$

$$27x^3 = 1$$

$$x^3 = \frac{1}{27}$$

$$x = \frac{1}{3}$$

6. E

Remember that backsolving is an alternative to the following algebraic solution in questions such as this one.

$$n^{-4} = \frac{1}{n^4} = \frac{1}{28{,}561}$$

$$n^4 = \sqrt[4]{28{,}561}$$

$$n = 28{,}561$$

$$n = 13$$

7. B

$$m^{\frac{3}{2}} = 8$$

$$\sqrt[2]{m^3} = 8$$

$$m^3 = 64$$

$$m = 4$$

8. 12

If you use a calculator on this question, be very careful to follow the order of operations. In this case, remember to find the values of the exponential terms first.

A different approach: When you divide powers with the same base, keep the base and subtract the exponent of the denominator from the exponent of the numerator. First get everything in the same base. Since $2^2 = 4 = 4^1$, then

$$\frac{4^3 - 4^2}{2^2} = \frac{4^3 - 4^2}{4^1}$$

$$= \frac{4^3}{4^1} - \frac{4^2}{4^1}$$

$$= 4^{3-1} - 4^{2-1}$$

$$= 4^2 - 4^1$$

$$= 16 - 4$$

$$= 12$$

Medium

9. C

The product of two negatives is positive, and the product of three negatives is negative. In fact, if we have any odd number of negative terms in a product, the result will be negative; any even number of negative terms gives a positive product. Since q is odd, we have an odd number of factors of -1. Therefore, the product is -1. Adding 1 to -1, we get 0.

10. D

Remember the rules for operations with exponents. First you have to get both powers in terms of the same base so you can combine the exponents. Note that the answer choices all have base 2. Start by expressing 4 and 8 as powers of 2:

$$(4^x)(8^x) = (2^2)^x \times (2^3)^x$$

To raise a power to an exponent, multiply the exponents:

$$(2^2)^x = 2^{2x}$$

$$(2^3)^x = 2^{3x}$$

To multiply powers with the same base, add the exponents:

$$2^{2x} \times 2^{3x} = 2^{(2x+3x)}$$

$$= 2^{5x}$$

11. E

If $\dfrac{\sqrt{n}}{3}$ is an even integer, then $\sqrt{n}$ must be a multiple of 2 and 3 and therefore n must be a perfect square and an even multiple of 3. Looking at the answer choices, you can immediately eliminate choices (A) and (B) because they are not perfect squares. Out of the remaining choices, only choice (E), 144, is both a perfect square and an even multiple of 3. Check it to make sure it works. If $n = 144$, then $\dfrac{\sqrt{144}}{3} = \dfrac{12}{3} = 4$. So 144 fits the given conditions, and choice (E) is correct.

12. E

You can easily raise 8 to the 5th power using your calculator and see that it equals 32,768. Plugging each of the 3 statements into your calculator, being wary of the order of operations, you will see that each statement also equals 32,768. So answer choice (E) is correct.

Alternatively, look at this question as a good review of the rules for the product of exponential expressions. In order to make the comparisons easier, transform 8^5 and each of the 3 options so that they have a common base. Since 2 is the smallest base among the expressions to be compared, let it be your common base. Since $8^5 = (2^3)^5 = 2^{3 \times 5} = 2^{15}$, look for options equivalent to 2^{15}.

I: $2^5 \times 4^5 = 2^5 \times (2^2)^5 = 2^5 \times 2^{2 \times 5} = 2^5 \times 2^{10}$
$= 2^{5+10} = 2^{15}$. Okay.

II: 2^{15}. Okay.

III: $2^5 \times 2^{10} = 2^{5+10} = 2^{15}$. Okay.

Again, all three are equivalent to 2^{15} or 8^5.

13. B

Be careful when squaring both sides of an equation. It is usually easier to simplify the equation as much as you can before squaring both sides. Also, remember that $0^2 = 0$ and $1^2 = 1$. Finally, note that backsolving is a great alternative strategy for this question.

$2\sqrt{c} + 3 = 5$

$2\sqrt{c} = 2$

$\sqrt{c} = 1$

$c = 1^2 = 1$

14. D

Know how to make an educated guess. In this case, eliminate oddballs, such as 25—the only choice without a variable in it.

$\sqrt{x + y} = 5x$

$x + y = 25x^2$

$y = 25x^2 - x$

15. 0

First, solve one equation for s in terms of t:

$st = -4$, so $s = \dfrac{-4}{t}$

Then plug this into the second equation:

$s^2 t^{-2} = \dfrac{s^2}{t^2} = \dfrac{\left(\dfrac{-4}{t}\right)}{t^2} = \dfrac{\dfrac{16}{t^2}}{t^2} = \dfrac{16}{t^4} = 1$

$16 = t^4$

$t = 2$ or $t = -2$

Then plug the value of t back into the first equation to find the value of s:

$s = \dfrac{-4}{2} = -2$ or $s = \dfrac{-4}{-2} = 2$

So either $s = 2$ and $t = -2$, or $s = -2$ and $t = 2$. In either case, $s + t = 2 + -2 = 0$.

16. 73

Substitute 2 for x, and then solve by following PEMDAS.

$3x + (x^3)^2 = 3^2 + (2^3)^2$

$x = 3^2 + 8^2$

$= 9 + 64$

$= 73$

Hard

17. B

First break up the expression to separate the variables, transforming the fraction into a product of three simpler fractions:

$$\frac{x^2 y^6 z^{10}}{xy^3 z^5} = \left(\frac{x^2}{x}\right)\left(\frac{y^6}{y^3}\right)\left(\frac{z^{10}}{z^5}\right)$$

Now carry out each division by keeping the base and subtracting the exponents.

$$\frac{x^2}{x} = x^{2-1} = x$$

$$\frac{y^6}{y^3} = y^{6-3} = y^3$$

$$\frac{z^{10}}{z^5} = z^{10-5} = z^5$$

The answer is the product of these three terms, or $xy^3 z^5$.

18. C

We are told that $x^a x^b = 1$. Since $x^a x^b = x^{a+b}$, we know that $x^{a+b} = 1$. If a power is equal to 1, either the base is 1 or -1, or the exponent is 0. Since we are told $x \neq 1$ or -1, the exponent must be 0; therefore, $a + b = 0$.

19. B

Questions such as this look intimidating on first blush, but are much less so once you realize that they follow the same basic patterns and rules as do arithmetic long division questions:

$$
\begin{array}{r}
2x^2 - 5x + 13 \\
x + 2 \overline{\smash{)}\, 2x^3 - x^2 + 3x - 4} \\
\underline{2x^3 + 4x^2} \\
-5x^2 + 3x \\
\underline{-5x^2 - 10x} \\
13x - 4 \\
\underline{13x + 26} \\
-30
\end{array}
$$

20. 6

Use your calculator to test values of n. Raise 5 to successive exponents to see which is the smallest power such that $5^n > 10{,}000$. Alternatively, try approximating to find n. $5^2 = 25$, $5^3 = 125$, so $5^3 > 100$.

Then $5^4 > 100 \times 5$, or $5^4 > 500$

$5^5 > 500 \times 5$, or $5^5 > 2{,}500$

$5^6 > 2{,}500 \times 5$, or $5^6 > 12{,}500$

5^6 must be greater than 10,000, but 5^5 clearly is much less than 10,000. So, in order for 5^n to be greater than 10,000, n must be at least 6.

Chapter Nine: **Graphs**

You're likely to find a few graphs on the SAT. Remember, a graph is just a visual interpretation of given data, whether it's a table, pie chart, line graph, or bar graph. The question will be asking you to get some sort of information from the graph. The best strategy you've got is to *read everything carefully*. Having said that, don't get bogged down by extraneous data (the data that won't help you answer the question). The test makers put tricky, misleading information into questions to try and trap you. It also helps to know your terminology so that when you see words like *vertex*, *y-axis*, or *peak*, you'll be prepared.

Chapter Nine Practice Set
Answer Sheet

1. Ⓐ Ⓑ Ⓒ Ⓓ Ⓔ   7. Ⓐ Ⓑ Ⓒ Ⓓ Ⓔ

2. Ⓐ Ⓑ Ⓒ Ⓓ Ⓔ   8. Ⓐ Ⓑ Ⓒ Ⓓ Ⓔ

3. Ⓐ Ⓑ Ⓒ Ⓓ Ⓔ   9. Ⓐ Ⓑ Ⓒ Ⓓ Ⓔ

4. Grid-in below   10. Ⓐ Ⓑ Ⓒ Ⓓ Ⓔ

5. Ⓐ Ⓑ Ⓒ Ⓓ Ⓔ   11. Ⓐ Ⓑ Ⓒ Ⓓ Ⓔ

6. Ⓐ Ⓑ Ⓒ Ⓓ Ⓔ   12. Ⓐ Ⓑ Ⓒ Ⓓ Ⓔ

4.

	/	/	
·	·	·	·
	0	0	0
1	1	1	1
2	2	2	2
3	3	3	3
4	4	4	4
5	5	5	5
6	6	6	6
7	7	7	7
8	8	8	8
9	9	9	9

PRACTICE SET

Basic

Questions 1 and 2 refer to the following table.

LUNCHEON SPECIALS

MEAL	PRICE
Hamburger	$3.00
Chicken	$2.75
Tuna Salad	$2.50
Pasta Salad	$2.25
Pizza	$1.50

1. If the table above represents the luncheon prices at a certain cafeteria, what is the average (arithmetic mean) price for a meal at this cafeteria?

    (A) $2.40
    (B) $2.50
    (C) $2.60
    (D) $2.70
    (E) $2.80

2. If three people each ordered a different meal, which of the following could not be the total cost of the meals, excluding tax?

    (A) $7.50
    (B) $7.00
    (C) $6.75
    (D) $6.25
    (E) $6.00

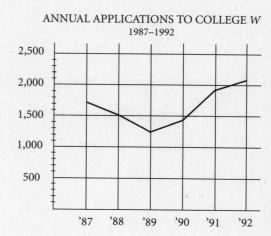

ANNUAL APPLICATIONS TO COLLEGE *W*
1987–1992

3. The graph above represents the number of applications submitted to College *W* each year for a 6-year period. If applications increase by approximately the same percent from 1992 to 1993 as they decreased from 1988 to 1989, approximately how many applications will College *W* receive in 1993?

    (A) 2,100
    (B) 2,300
    (C) 2,520
    (D) 2,625
    (E) 2,800

KAPLAN

DISTRIBUTION OF GRADES FOR MATH EXAM

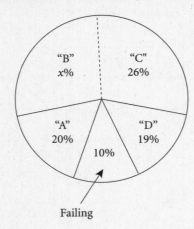

"B" x%   "C" 26%

"A" 20%   "D" 19%

10%

Failing

4. If 180 students passed the test, how many received a grade of B?

ANNUAL TOURISM REVENUE IN CITY X
1986–1992

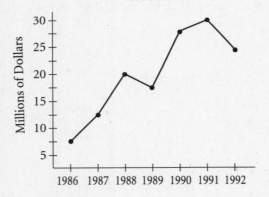

5. The graph above represents the annual revenue from tourism in City X over a 7-year period. During which of the following periods was the change in tourism revenues greatest?

(A) 1986–1987
(B) 1987–1988
(C) 1989–1990
(D) 1990–1991
(E) 1991–1992

6. By what percent did tourism revenues decrease from 1988 to 1989?

(A) 10%

(B) $12\frac{1}{2}$%

(C) 25%

(D) $37\frac{1}{2}$%

(E) 50%

MAJORS OF JUNIOR CLASS AT COLLEGE *W*

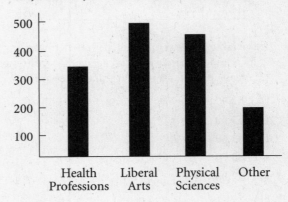

7. If the graph above represents the majors of the entire junior class, what is the ratio of juniors majoring in Physical Sciences to all juniors enrolled?

(A) 3:7
(B) 5:13
(C) 1:3
(D) 3:10
(E) 3:26

AMOUNT IN DOLLARS CONTRIBUTED BY A SCHOOL TO FIVE STUDENT ORGANIZATIONS

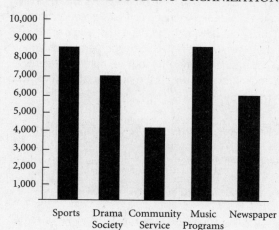

8. How much more money did the school contribute to the drama society than to the community service organization?

    (A) $4,000
    (B) $3,500
    (C) $3,000
    (D) $2,500
    (E) $2,000

9. If the school provided 80 percent of the budget of the newspaper, what was the newspaper's total budget?

    (A) $4,800
    (B) $6,800
    (C) $7,200
    (D) $7,500
    (E) $8,750

Questions 10 – 12 refer to the following tables:

Number of Sandwiches Ordered			
Department	Ham and Cheese	Vegetable	Roast Beef
Human Resources	3	1	2
Engineering	2	2	5
Customer Service	4	2	0

Cost of Sandwiches			
Store	Ham and Cheese	Vegetable	Roast Beef
Dave's	$2.00	$1.50	$3.00
Joe's	$1.50	$2.00	$3.50

10. A company decided to order sandwiches for the company picnic. The tables above show how many of each type of sandwich each department in the company ordered, along with the cost of each type of sandwich from two sandwich shops. If the Engineering department ordered its sandwiches from Dave's, how much would it spend?

    (A) $10.00
    (B) $10.50
    (C) $11.00
    (D) $22.00
    (E) $24.50

11. If the company ordered sandwiches for all 3 departments from Joe's, how much would it spend?

    (A) $40.00
    (B) $46.50
    (C) $48.00
    (D) $52.00
    (E) $56.50

12. How much money would the company save if it ordered sandwiches for all 3 departments from Dave's instead of Joe's?

    (A) $0.00
    (B) $0.50
    (C) $1.50
    (D) $4.65
    (E) $46.50

KAPLAN

ANSWERS AND EXPLANATIONS

Basic

1. A

To find the average price for a meal, use the formula:

$$\text{average} = \frac{\text{sum of terms}}{\text{number of terms}}$$

$$= (\$3.00 + \$2.75 + \$2.50 + \$2.25 + \$1.50) \div 5$$

$$= \$12.00 \div 5$$

$$= \$2.40$$

2. E

The 3 lowest-priced meals—pizza at $1.50, pasta salad at $2.25, and tuna salad at $2.50—total $6.25. So it is not possible that a combination of 3 different meals could cost less than $6.25. Since choice (E), $6.00, is less than this, it could not be the total cost of 3 different meals.

3. C

The number of applications received in a particular year is represented as the vertical distance from the bottom of the graph to the line above that year. In 1988 College W received 1,500 applications, and in 1989 only 1,200. This is a decrease of 300 applications, so from 1988 to 1989 applications decreased by $\frac{300}{1,500} = \frac{1}{5} = 20\%$. (Remember, when figuring a percent increase/decrease, put the amount of change over the original amount, in this case 1,500; if you put it over the amount you end up with, you'd get $\frac{300}{1,200} = \frac{1}{4} = 25\%$, and you'd answer the problem incorrectly.) In 1992 College W received 2,100 applications. If between 1992 and 1993, applications increased by the same percent that they decreased between 1988 and 1989, it would be an increase of $2,100 \times 20\% = 420$. So in 1993 College W will receive $2,100 + 420 = 2,520$ applications.

4. 50

In a pie chart, the whole pie represents a total quantity, while each slice represents a part or percent of that whole. So finding out how many students received a grade of B on the test is a percent problem: The percent of students who received a B, times the total number of students who took the exam, equals the number of students who received a B.

The "B" slice is identified as x percent, so you need to solve for x. All the slices together must equal 100 percent of the pie, so $20\% + 26\% + 19\% + 10\% + x\% = 100\%$, $75\% + x\% = 100\%$, $x\% = 25\%$. So 25%, or $\frac{1}{4}$, times the total number of students who took the exam will give you the answer you need. You aren't given the total number of students, but you are told that 180 students passed the exam. Since only 10 percent failed the test, 90 percent passed it. So $180 = 90\%$, or $\frac{9}{10}$ of the total number of students, $180 \times \frac{10}{9} =$ the total number of students = 200. Now you can solve the problem: $\frac{1}{4} \times 200 = 50$, so 50 students received a grade of B.

5. C

The amount of tourism revenue generated in a certain year is represented as the vertical distance from the bottom of the graph to the point above that year. The key along the vertical axis tells you that the income is measured in millions of dollars. Looking at the graph you can see that the greatest change in revenue occurs between 1989 and 1990, when it jumps from $17.5 million to $27.5 million, for an increase of $10 million.

6. B

Revenue dropped from 20 million dollars in 1988 to 17.5 million dollars in 1989. This is a decrease of 2.5 million dollars. To find what percent decrease this is, use the formula:

$$\text{Percent} = \frac{\text{part}}{\text{whole}}$$

$$= \frac{2.5}{20}$$

$$= 0.125$$

To convert this decimal to a percent, multiply by 100 percent:

$0.125 \times 100\% = 12.5\%$, answer choice (B).

7. D

On this bar graph, the number of students choosing a particular major is represented as the vertical distance from the bottom of the graph to the top of the bar above that major. Find the number of majors in Physical Sciences by reading off the graph; 450 juniors are majoring in Physical Sciences. Next find the total number of students by adding all the bars. That is 350 in Health Professions, plus 500 in Liberal Arts, plus 450 in Physical Sciences, plus 200 in other majors for a total of 1,500 juniors.

The ratio of juniors majoring in Physical Sciences, to all juniors is then $\frac{450}{1500} = \frac{3}{10}$, or 3:10.

8. C

You need to find the amount of money the school contributed to the drama society and subtract from that the amount of money the school contributed to the community service organization. Since the bars in this graph are drawn vertically, the height of each shows its value. The bar for the drama society is $7,000, while the bar for the community service organization is $4,000: $7,000 − $4,000 = $3,000.

9. D

Looking at the bar for the newspaper, you'll see that the newspaper received $6,000 from the school. If this represents 80 percent or $\frac{4}{5}$ of its total budget, $\frac{4}{5} \times$ newspaper's total budget = $6,000, so the newspaper's total budget = $\frac{5}{4} \times \$6,000 = \$7,500$.

10. D

You only need one line from each table to find the answer to this question. Multiply the cost of each type of sandwich from Dave's by the number of that type of sandwich the engineering department ordered, then add those numbers to get the total cost: 2($2.00) + 2($1.50) + 5($3.00) = $4.00 + $3.00 + $15.00 = $22.00.

11. C

Read the question carefully to find out what information you need. In this case, you'll need to find the total number of each type of sandwich ordered, then multiply that by the cost of that type of sandwich at Joe's:

Ham and Cheese: 3 + 2 + 4 = 9

Vegetable: 1 + 2 + 2 = 5

Roast Beef : 2 + 5 + 0 = 7

Total Cost: 9($1.50) + 5($2.00) + 7($3.50) = $13.50 + $10.00 + $24.50 = $48.00

12. C

In addition to finding the cost of ordering all the sandwiches from Joe's, you also need to find the cost of ordering all the sandwiches from Dave's, then find the difference between them. Find the cost of ordering all the sandwiches from Dave's the same way you found the cost of ordering all the sandwiches from Joe's. Total cost at Dave's: 9($2.00) + 5($1.50) + 7($3.00) = $18.00 + $7.50 + $ 21.00 = $46.50

Difference: $48.00 − $46.50 = $1.50

KAPLAN

Chapter Ten: **Basic Algebra**

Algebra is a mathematical language used to solve problems. The algebraic language takes an unknown item and represents it as a variable. In any algebra question you'll find all the same elements you'll find in a question dealing with number operations (multiplication, addition, fractions, factoring). The difference with algebra is how it's written and solved. Algebra uses symbols called *variables* (usually letters like *x* or *n*), numbers that stand to the left of variables (*coefficients*), and numbers that stand alone (*constants*).

One key component of algebra is the equation. An equation is a statement in algebra that says two expressions are equivalent. Solving an equation is like solving a puzzle or playing a strategy game. The object of the game is to find an appropriate number value for the variable(s). Like any game, algebra has rules. The rules state that an algebraic equation is like a set of scales that you have to keep balanced at all times. If you want to balance a set of scales, whatever you do to one side you must do to the other. For instance, you have to add or take away the same amount from both sides. The same goes for an algebraic equation.

If the problem is $x + 13 = 45$ and you subtract 13 from the left side (to isolate the variable on one side of the equation), then to balance the equation, you must subtract 13 from 45 on the right side. You're left with *x* on the left side by itself and 32 on the right side, so $x = 32$. This is overly simplistic, we know, but it's a basic example of what you might find on the test. For further reading on this topic:

50. Determining Absolute Value

51. Evaluating an Expression

52. Adding and Subtracting Monomials

53. Adding and Subtracting Polynomials

54. Multiplying Monomials

55. Multiplying Binomials (FOIL)

56. Multiplying Other Polynomials

57. Factoring Out a Common Divisor

58. Factoring the Difference of Squares

59. Factoring the Square of a Binomial

60. Factoring Other Polynomials (Reverse FOIL)

61. Simplifying an Algebraic Equation

62. Solving a Linear Equation

63. Solving "In Terms Of"

Chapter Ten Practice Set
Answer Key

1. Ⓐ Ⓑ Ⓒ Ⓓ Ⓔ
2. Ⓐ Ⓑ Ⓒ Ⓓ Ⓔ
3. Ⓐ Ⓑ Ⓒ Ⓓ Ⓔ
4. Ⓐ Ⓑ Ⓒ Ⓓ Ⓔ
5. Ⓐ Ⓑ Ⓒ Ⓓ Ⓔ
6. Ⓐ Ⓑ Ⓒ Ⓓ Ⓔ
7. Grid-in below
8. Grid-in below
9. Grid-in below
10. Grid-in below
11. Grid-in below

12. Ⓐ Ⓑ Ⓒ Ⓓ Ⓔ
13. Ⓐ Ⓑ Ⓒ Ⓓ Ⓔ
14. Ⓐ Ⓑ Ⓒ Ⓓ Ⓔ
15. Ⓐ Ⓑ Ⓒ Ⓓ Ⓔ
16. Ⓐ Ⓑ Ⓒ Ⓓ Ⓔ
17. Ⓐ Ⓑ Ⓒ Ⓓ Ⓔ
18. Ⓐ Ⓑ Ⓒ Ⓓ Ⓔ
19. Ⓐ Ⓑ Ⓒ Ⓓ Ⓔ
20. Ⓐ Ⓑ Ⓒ Ⓓ Ⓔ
21. Ⓐ Ⓑ Ⓒ Ⓓ Ⓔ
22. Grid-in below

23. Grid-in below
24. Ⓐ Ⓑ Ⓒ Ⓓ Ⓔ
25. Ⓐ Ⓑ Ⓒ Ⓓ Ⓔ
26. Ⓐ Ⓑ Ⓒ Ⓓ Ⓔ
27. Grid-in below
28. Grid-in below
29. Ⓐ Ⓑ Ⓒ Ⓓ Ⓔ
30. Grid-in below
31. Grid-in below

7. 8. 9. 10. 11. 22.

23. 27. 28. 30. 31.

PRACTICE SET

Basic

1. If $x = -3$, what is the value of the expression $x^2 + 3x + 3$?

   (A) -21

   (B) -15

   (C) -6

   (D) 3

   (E) 21

2. Let $<<x>> = 2x - 1$ for all positive integers. If $<<x>> = 15$, then $x =$

   (A) 6

   (B) 7

   (C) 8

   (D) 15

   (E) 16

3. $5z^2 - 5z + 4 - z(3z - 4) =$

   (A) $2z^2 - z + 4$

   (B) $2z^2 - 9z + 4$

   (C) $5z^2 - 8z + 8$

   (D) $5z^2 - 8z$

   (E) $2z^2 - 5z$

4. If $a = 2$, $b = -1$, and $c = 1$, which of the following must be true?

   I. $a + b + c = 2$

   II. $2a + bc = 4$

   III. $4a - b + c = 8$

   (A) I only

   (B) III only

   (C) I and II only

   (D) I and III only

   (E) I, II, and III

5. If $y \neq z$, then $\dfrac{xy - zx}{z - y} =$

   (A) x

   (B) 1

   (C) 0

   (D) -1

   (E) $-x$

6. For any number w, let $\# w \#$ be defined by the equation $\# w \# = -[w^2(w - 1)]$. What is the value of $\# -1 \#$?

   (A) -2

   (B) -1

   (C) 0

   (D) 1

   (E) 2

7. If $3 + x = 8$, what is the value of $5x$?

8. If $2(x - 40) = 3(x - 30)$, what is the value of x?

9. If $a = -1$ and $b = -2$, then $2a^2 - 2ab + b^2 =$

10. If $\dfrac{3}{a} = \dfrac{5}{4}$, what is the value of a?

11. If $q \times 34 \times 36 \times 38 = 17 \times 18 \times 19$, then $q =$

Medium

12. Which of the following is equivalent to $3x^2 + 18x + 27$?

   (A) $3(x^2 + 6x + 3)$

   (B) $3(x + 3)(x + 6)$

   (C) $3(x + 3)(x + 3)$

   (D) $3x(x + 6 + 9)$

   (E) $3x^2 + x(18 + 27)$

13. $(a^2 + b)^2 - (a^2 - b)^2 =$

    (A) $-4a^2b$

    (B) 0

    (C) $(2ab)2$

    (D) $4a^2b$

    (E) b^2

14. If $z \neq 0$, $x = \dfrac{4}{z}$, and $yz = 8$, then $\dfrac{x}{y} =$

    (A) 0.5

    (B) 1

    (C) 2

    (D) 16

    (E) 32

15. If $abc \neq 0$, then $\dfrac{a^2bc + ab^2c + abc^2}{abc} =$

    (A) $a + b + c$

    (B) $a + b + cabc$

    (C) $a^3b^3c^3$

    (D) $3abc$

    (E) $2abc$

16. If $x \blacklozenge y = (x - y)^2$ for all integers, which of the following must be true?

    I. $x \blacklozenge y = y \blacklozenge x$

    II. $x \blacklozenge y = x \blacklozenge (-y)$

    III. $x \blacklozenge (-y) = (-x) \blacklozenge y$

    (A) I only

    (B) III only

    (C) I and II

    (D) I and III

    (E) II and III

17. If $x = 4$, what is $3y(4 - 2x)$ in terms of y?

    (A) $-12y$

    (B) $-6y$

    (C) $-8y - 2$

    (D) $12y - 4$

    (E) 12

18. If $1 = |x|$, then x is

    (A) -1

    (B) 0

    (C) 1

    (D) -1 or 1

    (E) 0 or 1

19. If $3n - 1 = 8 + 2m$, what is the value of $5(3n - 2m)$?

    (A) 2

    (B) 5

    (C) 11

    (D) 45

    (E) 90

20. If $|2x + 9| = 33$, $x =$

    (A) -21

    (B) -12

    (C) -12 or -21

    (D) 12 or -21

    (E) 12

21. If $x = -|6|^2 - |-4 + 7| \times 7$, then $x =$

    (A) -74

    (B) -57

    (C) -23

    (D) 15

    (E) 36

22. If the product of 4, 5, and q is equal to the product of 5, p, and 2, and $pq \neq 0$, what is the value of $\frac{p}{q}$?

23. If $x = 2$ and $y = 3$, then $\dfrac{xy}{\dfrac{1}{x} + \dfrac{1}{y}} =$

Hard

24. The expression $\dfrac{3}{x-1} - 6$ will equal 0 when x equals which of the following?

    (A) -3

    (B) $-\dfrac{2}{3}$

    (C) $\dfrac{1}{2}$

    (D) $\dfrac{3}{2}$

    (E) 3

25. If $x > 1$ and $\dfrac{a}{b} = 1 - \dfrac{1}{x}$, then $\dfrac{b}{a} =$

    (A) x

    (B) $x - 1$

    (C) $\dfrac{x-1}{x}$

    (D) $\dfrac{x}{x-1}$

    (E) $\dfrac{1}{x}$

26. If the numerical values of $(m + n)^2$ and $(m - n)^2$ are equal, then which of the following must be true?

    I. $m + n = 0$

    II. $m - n = 0$

    III. $mn = 0$

    (A) I only

    (B) II only

    (C) III only

    (D) I and II only

    (E) I, II, and III

27. If $a > 0$, $b > \dfrac{1}{4}$, and $a + 2b = 1$, what is one possible value for a?

28. If $|q + 17| = |q - 17|$, and q is a real number, what is the value of q?

29. If $0 < x < 1$ and $0 < y < 1$, which of the following CANNOT be true?

    (A) $xy > 0$

    (B) $xy > 1$

    (C) $xy > \dfrac{1}{2}$

    (D) $x - y > 0$

    (E) $x + y > 0$

30.   B E E
    $\underline{+ \text{S E A}}$
      I D E A

    In the correctly worked addition problem above, A, B, D, E, I, and S each represent a different digit. What is the smallest possible value of D?

31. If $xy = 8$ and $x^2 + y^2 = 16$, then $(x + y)^2 =$

ANSWERS AND EXPLANATIONS

Basic

1. D

You want to find the value of the expression when x is -3, so plug in -3 for each x:

$$x^2 + 3x + 3 = (-3)^2 + 3(-3) + 3 = 9 + (-9) + 3 = 3$$

2. C

To solve for x, replace $<<x>>$ with the equivalent expression $2x - 1$ and set it equal to 15:

$$
\begin{aligned}
<<x>> &= 15 \\
2x - 1 &= 15 \\
2x &= 16 \\
x &= 8
\end{aligned}
$$

3. A

Before you can carry out any other operations, you have to remove the parentheses. That's what "P" stands for in PEMDAS, an acronym for the order of operations in a mathematical expression: **P**arentheses, **E**xponents, **M**ultiplication, **D**ivision, **A**ddition, **S**ubtraction (see the SAT Math in a Nutshell section). Here you can use the distributive law:

$$
\begin{aligned}
z(3z - 4) &= z \times 3z - z \times 4 \\
&= 3z^2 - 4z
\end{aligned}
$$

But there's more to do—you're *subtracting* this whole expression from $5z^2 - 5z + 4$. Since subtraction is the inverse operation of addition, you must change the signs of $3z^2 - 4z$.

$$
\begin{aligned}
5z^2 - 5z + 4 - (3z^2 - 4z) \\
= 5z^2 - 5z + 4 - 3z^2 + 4z
\end{aligned}
$$

Finally, combining like terms gives us:

$$
\begin{aligned}
5z^2 - 5z + 4 - 3z^2 + 4z \\
= (5z^2 - 3z^2) + (-5z + 4z) + 4 \\
= 2z^2 - z + 4
\end{aligned}
$$

4. A

Substitute $a = 2$, $b = -1$, and $c = 1$ into the statements.

Statement I:
$$
\begin{aligned}
a + b + c &= 2 + (-1) + 1 \\
&= 2
\end{aligned}
$$

Statement I is true, so eliminate choice (B).

Statement II:
$$
\begin{aligned}
2a + bc &= 2(2) + (-1)(1) \\
&= 4 - 1 \\
&= 3
\end{aligned}
$$

Statement II is false, so eliminate choices (C) and (E).

Statement III:
$$
\begin{aligned}
4a - b + c &= 4(2) - (-1) + 1 \\
&= 8 + 1 + 1 \\
&= 10
\end{aligned}
$$

Statement III is false and the correct answer is choice (A).

5. E

Whenever you are asked to simplify a fraction that involves binomials, your first thought should be: Factor! Since x is in both terms of the numerator, we can factor out x and get

$$xy - zx = x(y - z)$$

Performing this operation on the original fraction, you find that

$$\frac{xy - zx}{z - y} = \frac{x(y - z)}{z - y}$$

Rewriting $(z - y)$ as $-1(y - z)$, you get:

$$\frac{x(y - z)}{-1(y - z)}$$

Now cancel $y - z$ from the top and bottom:

$$\frac{x}{-1} = -x$$

Note: There is a reason that you are told that $y \neq z$; otherwise you could have zero in the denominator, and the expression could be undefined.

KAPLAN

6. E

Plug (-1) into the expression $-[w^2(w-1)]$ and simplify:

$$-[(-1)^2((-1)-1)]$$

Negative 1, squared, equals positive 1, so this equals:

$$-[1(-1-1)]$$
$$= -[1(-2)]$$
$$= -(-2) = 2$$

7. 25

Subtract 3 from both sides of the given equation to find $x = 8 - 3 = 5$. Note that the question asks for the value of $5x$, not x. $5x = 5(5) = 25$.

8. 10

If $2(x - 40) = 3(x - 30)$, then $2x - 80 = 3x - 90$. Add $90 - 2x$ to both sides of this equation to find $10 = x$.

9. 2

Plug in -1 for each a and -2 for each b:

$$2a^2 - 2ab + b^2 = 2(-1)^2 - 2(-1)(-2) + (-2)^2$$
$$= 2 - 4 + 4$$
$$= 2$$

10. 2.4 or 12/5

Cross multiply, and then divide both sides by 5:

$$\frac{3}{a} = \frac{5}{4}$$

$$3 \times 4 = 5a$$

$$12 = 5a$$

$$a = \frac{12}{5} \text{ or } 2.4$$

11. 1/8 or .125

Don't multiply anything out! With such a bizarre-looking expression, there's usually a shortcut. Notice that each of the numbers on the right side is a factor of a number on the left side. So divide each side of the equation by $34 \times 36 \times 38$ to isolate q:

$$q = \frac{17 \times 18 \times 19}{34 \times 36 \times 38}$$

$$q = \frac{17}{34} \times \frac{18}{36} \times \frac{19}{38}$$

$$q = \frac{1}{2} \times \frac{1}{2} \times \frac{1}{2}$$

$$= \frac{1}{8} \text{ or } .125$$

Medium

12. C

First factor out the number (3) common to all terms:

$$3x^2 + 18x + 27 = 3(x^2 + 6x + 9)$$

This is not an answer choice, so you must factor the polynomial.

$x^2 + 6x + 9$ is of the form $a^2 + 2ab + b^2$, with $a = x$ and $b = 3$.

So, $x^2 + 6x + 9 = (x + 3)^2$ or $(x + 3)(x + 3)$.

Therefore, $3x^2 + 18x + 27 = 3(x + 3)(x + 3)$.

An alternative method would be to multiply out the answer choices, and see which matches $3x^2 + 18x + 27$.

Choice (A): $3(x^2 + 6x + 3) = 3x^2 + 18x + 9$. Reject.

Choice (B): $3(x + 3)(x + 6) = 3(x^2 + 6x + 3x + 18)$. Using FOIL:

$$= 3(x^2 + 9x + 18)$$
$$= 3x^2 + 27x + 3(18). \text{ Reject.}$$

Choice (C): $3(x + 3)(x + 3) = 3(x^2 + 3x + 3x + 9)$. Using FOIL:

$$= 3(x^2 + 6x + 9)$$
$$= 3x^2 + 18x + 27. \text{ Correct.}$$

13. D

Multiply out each part of the expression using FOIL.

$$(a^2 + b)^2 = (a^2 + b)(a^2 + b)$$
$$= a^4 + a^2b + ba^2 + b^2$$
$$= a^4 + 2a^2b + b^2$$
$$(a^2 - b)^2 = (a^2 - b)(a^2 - b)$$
$$= (a^2)^2 + a^2(-b) + (-b)a^2 + (-b)^2$$
$$= a^4 - 2a^2b + b^2$$

So, $(a^2 + b)^2 - (a^2 - b)^2$

$$= (a^4 + 2a^2b + b^2) - (a^4 - 2a^2b + b^2)$$
$$= a^4 + 2a^2b + b^2 - a^4 + 2a^2b - b^2$$
$$= 2a^2b + 2a^2b$$
$$= 4a^2b$$

14. A

Rearrange the first equation:

$$x = \frac{4}{z}.$$

Multiply both sides by z:

$$xz = 4.$$

So $xz = 4$ and $yz = 8$. That is:

$$\frac{xz}{yz} = \frac{4}{8}.$$
$$\frac{x}{y} = \frac{4}{8} = \frac{1}{2}, \text{ or } 0.5.$$

15. A

The expression has three terms in the numerator, and a single term, abc, in the denominator. Since the three terms in the numerator each have abc as a factor, abc can be factored out from both numerator and denominator, and the expression can be reduced to a simpler form.

$$\frac{a^2bc + ab^2c + abc^2}{abc}$$

$$= \frac{a(abc) + b(abc) + c(abc)}{abc}$$

$$= \frac{(a + b + c)(abc)}{abc}$$

$$= a + b + c$$

16. D

Consider each statement separately. Statement I claims $(x - y)^2 = (y - x)^2$. For any two integers, $y - x$ is the same as $-(x - y)$. So the statement claims that the squares of two integers with the same absolute value, but different signs equal each other. This is true, and can be shown by picking numbers. Therefore statement I must be true.

Statement II claims $(x - y)^2 = [x - (-y)]^2$, which equals $(x + y)^2$. Clearly $x - y$ can have a totally different value from $x + y$, so statement II doesn't have to be true. (You can pick numbers to show this.)

Statement III claims $[x - (-y)]^2 = (-x - y)^2$. That is $(x + y)^2 = [-(x + y)]^2$. The expression being squared in the right-hand side is the negative of the expression being squared on the left-hand side. As before, squaring two numbers with identical absolute values produces the same result. So statement III must be true. That makes choice (D) the right answer.

17. A

Plug $x = 4$ into the expression.

$$3y(4 - 2x) = 3y(4 - 2[4]) = 3y(4 - 8) = 3y(-4) = -12y$$

18. D

Every positive number is the absolute value of two numbers: itself and its negative. Remember that absolute value is always positive because it represents a distance: the distance of a number from zero on the number line. In this case, the numbers whose distance from zero on the number line is one, are 1 and −1.

19. D

You don't need to find n or m. First add 1 to both sides, giving you $3n = 9 + 2m$. Then subtract $2m$ from both sides and re-express the given equation as $3n - 2m = 9$. Then substitute 9 for $3n - 2m$ in the expression $5(3n - 2m)$ to find that $5(9) = 45$.

20. D

If $|2x + 9| = 33$, then $2x + 9 = 33$ or $2x + 9 = -33$, so $2x = 24$ or $2x = -42$, and $x = 12$ or $x = -21$.

21. B

In addition to keeping careful track of the absolute values in this question, remember to follow order of operations.

$$x = -|6|^2 - |-4 + 7| \times 7$$

$$x = -36 - |3| \times 7$$

$$x = -36 - 21$$

$$x = -57$$

22. 2

You're told that $4 \times 5 \times q = 5 \times p \times 2$. The number 5 is a common factor so you can cancel it from each side. You are left with $4q = 2p$ or $2q = p$. Dividing both sides by q in order to get the quotient $\frac{p}{q}$ on one side, you find $\frac{p}{q} = 2$.

23. 36/5 or 7.2

Plug in the given values:

$$\frac{xy}{\frac{1}{x} + \frac{1}{y}} = \frac{2 \times 3}{\frac{1}{2} + \frac{1}{3}}$$

$$= \frac{6}{\frac{3}{6} + \frac{2}{6}}$$

$$= \frac{6}{\frac{5}{6}}$$

$$= 6 \times \frac{6}{5}$$

$$= \frac{36}{5} \text{ or } 7.2$$

Hard

24. D

You are asked to find x when $\frac{3}{x - 1} - 6 = 0$. Clear the denominator by multiplying both sides by $x - 1$.

$$\frac{3}{x - 1}(x - 1) - 6(x - 1) = 0(x - 1)$$

$$3 - 6(x - 1) = 0$$

$$3 - 6x + 6 = 0$$

$$9 - 6x = 0$$

$$9 - 6x + 6x = 0 + 6x$$

$$9 = 6x$$

$$\frac{9}{6} = \frac{6x}{6}$$

$$\frac{3}{2} = x$$

So answer choice (D) is correct. You can check your answer by plugging $\frac{3}{2}$ into the original equation.

25. D

Since $\frac{b}{a}$ is the reciprocal of $\frac{a}{b}$, $\frac{b}{a}$ must be the reciprocal of $1 - \frac{1}{x}$ as well. Combine the terms in $1 - \frac{1}{x}$ and then find its reciprocal.

$$\frac{a}{b} = 1 - \frac{1}{x} = \frac{x}{x} - \frac{1}{x} = \frac{x - 1}{x}$$

Therefore, $\frac{b}{a} = \frac{x}{x - 1}$.

KAPLAN

26. C

You want to know which of the options must be true, given that $(m + n)^2 = (m - n)^2$.

First, expand the expressions.

$$(m + n)^2 = m^2 + 2mn + n^2$$
$$(m - n)^2 = m^2 - 2mn + n^2$$

Since these two expressions are equal, write:

$$m^2 + 2mn + n^2 = m^2 - 2mn + n^2$$

You have m^2 and n^2 on each side of the equal sign. Subtract these from both sides to leave:

$$2mn = -2mn$$

$$mn = -mn$$

Zero is the only number for which this is true, so $mn = 0$.

This shows statement III is certainly correct so eliminate choices (A), (B), and (D), but what about choice (E) that states I, II, and III must be true?

The key word in this problem is "must." If $m = 0$ and $n = -6$, for example, then $mn = 0$ and the given squared expressions are equal. But $m + n = 0 + -6 = -6$, not zero. Likewise, $m - n = 0 - -6 = 6$, not zero. So I and II need not be true, and III is the only correct statement.

27. $0 < a < 1/2$

We know that b is greater than $\frac{1}{4}$ (and therefore positive) and that $a + 2b = 1$, so a and b must both be fractions between 0 and 1. We can narrow down a even more by noting that b is always more than $\frac{1}{4}$, so $2b$ must be more than $\frac{1}{2}$. Since $a + 2b = 1$ and $2b$ is more than $\frac{1}{2}$, a must be less than $\frac{1}{2}$. You can grid a fraction between 0 and $\frac{1}{2}$, such as $\frac{1}{3}$ or $\frac{3}{8}$, or you can grid a decimal such as 0.25 or 0.4.

28. 0

There are four possibilities to deal with:

Possibility 1:

$$q + 17 = q - 17$$
$$q + 34 = q$$
$$34 = 0$$

This is not possible, so there are no real values of q that fulfill this possibility.

Possibility 2:

$$-(q + 17) = q - 17$$
$$-q - 17 = q - 17$$
$$0 = 2q$$
$$0 = q$$

Possibility 3, $q + 17 = -(q - 17)$, functions similarly to Possibility 2.

Possibility 4, $-(q + 17) = -(q - 17)$, functions similarly to Possibility 1.

29. B

Since there are variables in the answer choices, picking numbers is a good strategy for solving this question. Try to pick numbers to prove that each answer choice can be true. For instance, $x = .8$ and $y = .7$ demonstrates that all answer choices except (B) can be true. Furthermore, (B) cannot be true, since x and y must both be positive fractions less than 1, so xy will always be less than 1.

30. 2

The first thing to notice about this problem is that $E + A$ equals either A or $10 + A$. Since each letter represents only one digit, $E + A$ must equal A, since E cannot be 10. Therefore, $E = 0$. If we plug this into the problem, we get:

$$
\begin{array}{r}
B\ 0\ 0 \\
+\ S\ 0\ A \\
\hline
I\ D\ 0\ A
\end{array}
$$

so

$$
\begin{array}{r}
B \\
+\ S \\
\hline
I\ D
\end{array}
$$

So I must be 1, and B plus S must be 12 or more (since if $B + S$ were 10 or 11, the second letter in the answer would be E or I, not D). Therefore, the smallest possible value of D is 2. Note that there are several different possibilities for A, B, and S, but we don't need to find these to solve the problem.

31. 32

First, multiply out $(x + y)^2$ using the FOIL method: $(x + y)^2 = x^2 + 2xy + y^2$.

Regroup the terms:

$$= (x^2 + y^2) + 2(xy)$$

Plug in the given values:

$$= 16 + 2(8) = 32.$$

KAPLAN

Chapter Eleven: **Advanced Algebra**

Try not to be intimidated by advanced algebra problems. Most of the time, they're simply testing your ability to use multiple variables or algebraic strategies. If you know the basics, you'll be fine. Equations and expressions in advanced algebra still contain variables and numbers, they are just more advanced or require a different skill set.

Take *polynomials* for example. A polynomial is a mathematical expression containing two or more algebraic terms, each consisting of a constant multiplied by one or more variables raised to a non-negative power. Polynomial expressions often look like this: $ax^2 + bx + c$. The degree of a polynomial is equal to the value of the highest power of a variable with a non-zero coefficient. What is the degree of the polynomial $x^4 + 4x^3 + 5x^2 + 4x + 4$? The value of the highest power of a variable with a non-zero coefficient here is 4, on x^4. It is implied, even though x doesn't have a "visible" coefficient, that the coefficient is 1. Unless otherwise noted, it is always assumed that the coefficient of any variable is 1.

Another important skill is factoring. Factoring polynomial expressions is very similar to factoring whole numbers. To factor a polynomial, there are basically three steps. First, identify and factor out common factors of all the coefficients. Then, identify and factor out variables appearing in all the terms. Finally, factor the remaining piece, if possible. The expression $x^2 - 2x - 8$, when approached with the three-step method, factors out to $(x + 2)\ (x - 4)$. If you are ever unsure about whether you've factored correctly, check your work by multiplying the factors using the FOIL (**F**irst, **I**nside, **O**utside, **L**ast) method. For further reading on advanced algebra topics:

65. Solving a Quadratic Equation

66. Solving a System of Equations

68. Solving an Inequality

69. Function Notation and Evaluation

70. Direct and Inverse Variation

71. Domain and Range of a Function

Chapter Eleven Practice Set
Answer Sheet

1. (A) (B) (C) (D) (E)   10. (A) (B) (C) (D) (E)   19. (A) (B) (C) (D) (E)
2. (A) (B) (C) (D) (E)   11. (A) (B) (C) (D) (E)   20. (A) (B) (C) (D) (E)
3. (A) (B) (C) (D) (E)   12. (A) (B) (C) (D) (E)   21. (A) (B) (C) (D) (E)
4. (A) (B) (C) (D) (E)   13. (A) (B) (C) (D) (E)   22. (A) (B) (C) (D) (E)
5. (A) (B) (C) (D) (E)   14. (A) (B) (C) (D) (E)   23. Grid-in below
6. (A) (B) (C) (D) (E)   15. Grid-in below   24. (A) (B) (C) (D) (E)
7. Grid-in below   16. (A) (B) (C) (D) (E)   25. (A) (B) (C) (D) (E)
8. Grid-in below   17. Grid-in below   26. Grid-in below
9. Grid-in below   18. Grid-in below

PRACTICE SET

Basic

1. If $a < b$ and $b < c$, which of the following must be true?

    (A) $b + c < 2a$

    (B) $a + b < c$

    (C) $a - b < b - c$

    (D) $a + b < 2c$

    (E) $a + c < 2b$

2. If $13 + a = 25 + b$, then $b - a =$

    (A) 38

    (B) 12

    (C) 8

    (D) −12

    (E) −38

3. If $m > 1$ and $mn - 3 = 3 - n$, then $n =$

    (A) 6

    (B) $\dfrac{6}{m + 1}$

    (C) $\dfrac{6}{m - 1}$

    (D) $\dfrac{6}{1 - m}$

    (E) $-\dfrac{6}{m + 1}$

4. If $r \neq -s$ and $a = \dfrac{r - s}{r + s}$, then $a + 1 =$

    (A) $\dfrac{2r}{r + s}$

    (B) $\dfrac{r - s + 1}{r + s}$

    (C) $\dfrac{2r - 2s}{r + s}$

    (D) $\dfrac{2s}{r + s}$

    (E) $\dfrac{1 - r + s}{r + s}$

5. If $a > b > c$, which of the following cannot be true?

    (A) $b + c < a$

    (B) $2a > b + c$

    (C) $2c > a + b$

    (D) $ab > bc$

    (E) $a + b > 2b + c$

6. If $|a - b| > 0$, which of the following CANNOT be true?

    I. $a > b$

    II. $a < b$

    III. $a = b$

    (A) I only

    (B) II only

    (C) III only

    (D) I and III only

    (E) II and III only

7. If $3m < 48$ and $2m > 24$, what is a possible value for m?

8. If $y^2 + cy - 35 = 0$ and −7 is one solution of the equation, what is the value of c?

Medium

9. If $a + b = 6$, $b + c = -3$, and $a + c = 5$, what is the value of $a + b + c$?

10. If $a < b < c < 0$, which of the following expressions is the greatest?

    (A) $\dfrac{a}{b}$

    (B) $\dfrac{b}{c}$

    (C) $\dfrac{c}{a}$

    (D) $\dfrac{a}{c}$

    (E) It cannot be determined from the information given.

KAPLAN

11. If $y \neq -1$ and $x = \dfrac{1}{y+1}$ then, in terms of x, $y =$

   (A) $x - 1$

   (B) $\dfrac{1}{x} + 1$

   (C) $\dfrac{1}{x+1}$

   (D) $\dfrac{1}{x} - 1$

   (E) $\dfrac{1}{x-1}$

12. Let $\boxed{x} = \dfrac{x^2 + 1}{2}$ and $\bigcirc\!\!\!\!y = \dfrac{3y}{2}$, for all integers x and y. If $m = \bigcirc\!\!\!\!2$, $\boxed{m}$ is equal to which of the following?

   (A) $\dfrac{13}{8}$

   (B) $\dfrac{5}{2}$

   (C) $\dfrac{15}{4}$

   (D) 5

   (E) $\dfrac{37}{2}$

13. If $6a = 2b = 3c$, what is the value of $9a + 5b$, in terms of c?

   (A) $10c$
   (B) $12c$
   (C) $15c$
   (D) $18c$
   (E) $24c$

14. If $x \neq -y$ and $\dfrac{x^2 - y^2}{x + y} = 13$, then $x - y =$

   (A) $\sqrt{13}$
   (B) 7
   (C) 13
   (D) 169
   (E) It cannot be determined from the information given.

15. If $|\,r - 6\,| < 3$, what is one possible value of r?

16. If $\dfrac{x^2 - 4}{x + 2} = 6$, and $x \neq -2$, what is the value of x?

   (A) -8
   (B) -2
   (C) 2
   (D) 6
   (E) 8

17. If $-4 < m < 6$ and $-3 < n < 5$, then what is the greatest possible value of $n - m$ that will fit in the grid (four grid-in spaces)?

18. If $2x + y = -8$ and $-4x + 2y = 16$, what is the value of y?

19. For all $x \neq \pm \dfrac{1}{2}$, $\dfrac{2x^2 + 5x - 3}{4x^2 - 1} =$

   (A) $\dfrac{2x - 3}{2x + 1}$

   (B) $\dfrac{x - 3}{2x + 1}$

   (C) $\dfrac{2x + 3}{2x - 1}$

   (D) $\dfrac{x + 3}{2x + 1}$

   (E) $\dfrac{x - 3}{2x - 1}$

Hard

20. If $x^2 - 9 < 0$, which of the following is true?

    (A) $x < -3$

    (B) $x > 3$

    (C) $x > 9$

    (D) $x < -3$ or $x > 3$

    (E) $-3 < x < 3$

21. If $x^2 - 2x - 15 = (x + r)(x + s)$ for all values of x, one possible value for $r - s$ is

    (A) 8

    (B) 2

    (C) -2

    (D) -3

    (E) -5

22. If $n > 4$, which of the following is equivalent to

    $$\frac{n - 4\sqrt{n} + 4}{\sqrt{n} - 2}?$$

    (A) $\sqrt{n}$

    (B) $2\sqrt{n}$

    (C) $\sqrt{n} + 2$

    (D) $\sqrt{n} - 2$

    (E) $n + \sqrt{n}$

23. If $f(x) = |x^2 + 2x + 1|$, what is the value of $f(-4)$?

24. If $f(x) = \dfrac{1}{x^2}$, what is the domain of $f(x)$?

    (A) all real numbers

    (B) all positive numbers

    (C) all real numbers except zero

    (D) all integers

    (E) all integers except zero

25. The number of foxes on Example Island varies directly as the number of rabbits on the island varies, according to the equation $f = kr$, where f is the number of foxes, r is the number of rabbits, and k is a constant. If there are 10 foxes on the island when there are 300 rabbits, how many foxes would there be if there were 750 rabbits?

    (A) 2.5

    (B) 15

    (C) 25

    (D) 150

    (E) 250

26. If x can be expressed as y^2, where y is a positive integer, then let $* x * = \dfrac{y^3}{2}$. For example, since $9 = 3^2$, $* 9 * = \dfrac{3^3}{2} = \dfrac{27}{2} = 13.5$. If $* m * = 4$, what is the value of $* 4m *$?

ANSWERS AND EXPLANATIONS

Basic

1. D

We're given two inequalities here: $a < b$ and $b < c$, which we can combine into one, $a < b < c$. We need to go through the answer choices to see which must be true.

Choice (A): $b + c < 2a$. Since c is greater than a and b is greater than a, the sum of b and c must be greater than twice a. For instance, if $a = 1$, $b = 2$, and $c = 3$, then $b + c = 5$ and $2a = 2$, so $b + c > 2a$. Choice (A) is never true.

Choice (B): $a + b < c$. This may or may not be true, depending on the actual values of a, b, and c. If $a = 1$, $b = 2$, and $c = 4$, then $a + b < c$. However, if $a = 2$, $b = 3$, $c = 4$, then $a + b > c$. So choice (B) is also no good.

Choice (C): $a - b < b - c$. This choice is easier to evaluate if we simplify it by adding $(b + c)$ to both sides.

$$a - b + (b + c) < b - c + (b + c)$$
$$c + a < 2b$$

Like choice (B), this can be true, but can also be false, depending on the values of a, b, and c. If $a = -1$, $b = 2$, and $c = 3$, then $c + a < 2b$. But if $a = 1$, $b = 2$, and $c = 4$, then $c + a > 2b$. Choice (C) is no good.

Choice (D): $a + b < 2c$. We know that $a < c$ and $b < c$. If we add these inequalities we'll get $a + b < c + c$, or $a + b < 2c$. This statement is always true, so it must be the correct answer.

At this point on the real exam, you should proceed to the next problem. Just for discussion, however:

Choice (E): $a + c < 2b$. This is the same inequality as choice (C). That was no good, so this isn't either.

2. D

You can't find the value of either variable alone, but you don't need to. Rearranging the equation, you get:

$$13 + a = 25 + b$$
$$13 = 25 + b - a$$
$$13 - 25 = b - a$$
$$b - a = -12$$

3. B

We need to isolate n on one side of the equation, and whatever's left on the other side will be an expression for n in terms of m.

$$mn - 3 = 3 - n$$

First, get every n on one side.

$$n + mn - 3 = 3 - n + n$$
$$mn + n - 3 = 3$$
$$mn + n = 6$$

Then isolate n by factoring and dividing.

$$n(m + 1) = 6$$

$$\frac{n(m + 1)}{m + 1} = \frac{6}{m + 1}$$

$$n = \frac{6}{m + 1}$$

4. A

Since $a = \dfrac{r - s}{r + s}$, then $a + 1 = \dfrac{r - s}{r + s} + 1$. To simplify this expression, you make $r + s$ the common denominator:

$$\frac{r - s}{r + s} + 1$$

$$= \frac{r - s}{r + s} + \frac{r + s}{r + s}$$

$$= \frac{r - s + r + s}{r + s}$$

$$= \frac{2r}{r + s}$$

5. C

We are told $a > b > c$, and asked which of the answer choices cannot be true. If we can find just one set of values a, b, and c, where $a > b > c$, that makes the answer choice true, then that answer choice can be eliminated.

Choice (A): $b + c < a$. This inequality can be true if a is sufficiently large relative to b and c. For example, if $a = 10$, $b = 3$, and $c = 2$, $a > b > c$ still holds, and $b + c < a$. No good.

Choice (B): $2a > b + c$. This is always true because a is greater than either b or c. So $a + a = 2a$ must be greater than $b + c$. For instance, $2(4) > 3 + 2$.

Choice (C): $2c > a + b$. This inequality can never be true. The sum of two smaller numbers (two c's) can never be greater than the sum of two larger numbers (a and b). This is the correct answer.

You would stop here if this were the real exam. But let's go over choices (D) and (E) for the sake of discussion.

Choice (D): $ab > bc$. This will be true when the numbers are all positive. Try $a = 4$, $b = 3$, and $c = 2$.

Choice (E): $a + b > 2b + c$. Again, this can be true if a is large relative to b and c. Try $a = 10$, $b = 2$, and $c = 1$.

6. C

That $|a - b| > 0$ doesn't mean $a - b > 0$. It's also possible that $-(a - b) > 0$. If the absolute value of the difference between a and b is greater than 0, that means that either $a > b$ or $a < b$, so both I and II can be true. If $a = b$, then $|a - b|$ is equal to 0, not greater than 0, so III cannot be true.

7. $12 < m < 16$

If $3m < 48$, then $m < \dfrac{48}{3}$ or $m < 16$. And if $2m > 24$, then $m > \dfrac{24}{2}$ or $m > 12$. Thus, m has any value between 12 and 16, or $12 < m < 16$.

8. 2

Since -7 is a solution to the given equation, plug it in for y to find the value of c:

$$(-7)^2 + c(-7) - 35 = 0$$
$$49 - 7c - 35 = 0$$
$$14 - 7c = 0$$
$$14 = 7c$$
$$2 = c$$

Medium

9. 4

The easiest way to solve is to realize that all three equations can simply be added together:

$$a + b = 6$$
$$b + c = -3$$
$$\underline{a + c = 5}$$
$$2a + 2b + 2c = 8$$
$$2(a + b + c) = 8$$
$$a + b + c = 4$$

10. D

Since the quotient of two negatives is always positive and all the variables are negative, all these expressions are positive. To maximize the value of this quotient, we need a numerator with the largest possible absolute value and a denominator with the smallest possible absolute value. This means the negative numerator farthest from zero and the negative denominator closest to zero. Choice (D), $\dfrac{a}{c}$, fits the bill perfectly.

You can also pick numbers for a, b, and c to verify this relationship. If you try -1 for c, -2 for b, and -3 for a, you'll find that $\dfrac{a}{c}$ is the largest fraction.

KAPLAN

11. D

To solve the question you must get y alone on one side of the equation. Since $x = \frac{x}{1}$, you can invert both sides of the equation:

$$x = \frac{1}{y+1}$$

$$\frac{1}{x} = \frac{y+1}{1} = y+1$$

$$\frac{1}{x} - 1 = y$$

12. D

We're given two new symbols, and we need to complete several steps. The trick is figuring out where to start. We are asked to find $\boxed{m}$. In order to do this, we must first find the value of m. Since m is equal to $\bigcirc{2}$ we can find m by finding the value of $\bigcirc{2}$, and we can find $\bigcirc{2}$ by substituting 2 for y in the equation given for $\bigcirc{y}$. The equation becomes:

$$\bigcirc{2} = \frac{3(2)}{2}$$

$$\bigcirc{2} = 3$$

Since $m = \bigcirc{2}$, m is also equal to 3, and $\boxed{m} = \boxed{3}$.

We find $\boxed{3}$ by substituting 3 for x in the equation given for $\boxed{x}$:

$$\boxed{3} = \frac{3^2 + 1}{2}$$

$$= \frac{9+1}{2}$$

$$= \frac{10}{2}$$

$$= 5$$

So $\boxed{m} = 5$

13. B

You can think of the given information as two separate equations: $6a = 3c$, and $2b = 3c$. Perhaps the easiest way to proceed is to get values for a and b and then multiply. If:

$$6a = 3c$$

then $$a = \frac{3c}{6} = \frac{c}{2}$$

So $$9a = \frac{9c}{2}$$

Likewise, if:

$$2b = 3c$$

then $$b = \frac{3c}{2}.$$

So $$5b = 5\left(\frac{3c}{2}\right) = \frac{15c}{2}.$$

$$9a + 5b = \frac{9c}{2} + \frac{15c}{2} = \frac{24c}{2} = 12c$$

14. C

There are a few common quadratic expressions that occasionally appear on the SAT. If you learn to recognize them, a problem like this is easy. Any expression in the form $a^2 - b^2$, which is referred to as "the difference of two squares," can be factored into $(a + b)(a - b)$.

The numerator of the given fraction is in this form, so you can rewrite the fraction as $\frac{(x + y)(x - y)}{x + y}$.

Cancel a factor of $(x + y)$ from numerator and denominator, leaving $x - y$. So $x - y = 13$.

15. $3 < r < 9$

It's a good idea to "reality-check" your answer before filling in the answer grid. Try plugging your answer back into the original inequality to make sure it fulfills that condition.

$$r - 6 < 3$$

$$r < 9$$

and:

$$-(r - 6) < 3$$

$$-r + 6 < 3$$

$$-r < -3$$

$$r > 3$$

Remember to change the direction of the inequality sign when multiplying by -1. So all values of r that are greater than 3 and less than 9 satisfy this inequality.

16. E

If you see something complex in an SAT question, try to simplify it. This equation can be easily simplified by first factoring the numerator of the fraction on the left side.

$$\frac{x^2 - 4}{x + 2} = \frac{(x + 2)(x - 2)}{x + 2}$$

The factors $(x + 2)$ will cancel to leave $x - 2 = 6$, so $x = 8$. Backsolving would also work well for this problem—just try the answer choices to see which will work.

17. 8.99

Since inequalities deal with a range of values, you need to determine which parts of the range will yield the maximum value. The maximum value of $n - m <$ (the upper bound of n minus the lower bound of m): $n - m < 5 - (-4)$, or $n - m < 9$. Therefore, the greatest value for $n - m$ that will fit in the grid is 8.99.

18. 0

To solve for y, make the x terms drop out. The first equation involves $2x$, while the second involves $-4x$, so multiply both sides of the first equation by 2.

$$2(2x + y) = 2(-8)$$

$$4x + 2y = -16$$

Adding the corresponding sides of this equation and the second equation together gives:

$$4x + 2y = -16$$

$$\underline{+ (-4x + 2y = 16)}$$

$$4x + 2y - 4x + 2y = -16 + 16$$

$$4y = 0$$

$$y = 0$$

An alternative method is to solve the first equation for x in terms of y and then substitute this expression into the second equation.

$$2x + y = -8$$

$$2x = -8 - y$$

$$x = \frac{-8 - y}{2}$$

Now replace x in the other equation with $\frac{-8 - y}{2}$, and a single equation in terms of y remains. This equation can be solved for a numerical value of y.

$$-4x + 2y = 16$$

$$-4\left(\frac{-8 - y}{2}\right) + 2y = 16$$

$$-2(-8 - y) + 2y = 16$$

$$16 + 2y + 2y = 16$$

$$16 + 4y = 16$$

$$4y = 0$$

$$y = 0$$

KAPLAN

19. D

Factor: $\dfrac{2x^2 + 5x - 3}{4x^2 - 1} = \dfrac{(x + 3)(2x - 1)}{(2x + 1)(2x - 1)}$.

Now cancel: $\dfrac{(x + 3)}{(2x + 1)}$.

Hard

20. E

Rearrange $x^2 - 9 < 0$ to get $x^2 < 9$. We're looking for all the values of x that would fit this inequality. We need to consider both positive and negative values of x. Remember that $3^2 = 9$ and also that $(-3)^2 = 9$.

If x is positive, and $x^2 < 9$, we can simply say that $x < 3$. But what if x is negative? x can take on only values whose square is less than 9. In other words, x cannot be less than or equal to -3. (Think of smaller numbers like -4 or -5; their squares are greater than 9.) So if x is negative, $x > -3$. x can also be 0. Therefore, $-3 < x < 3$.

If you had trouble solving algebraically, you could have tried each answer choice:

Choice (A): Say $x = -4$.

$(-4)^2 - 9 = 16 - 9 = 7$. No good.

Choice (B): Say $x = 4$.

$4^2 - 9 = 16 - 9 = 7$. No good.

Choice (C): Since 4 was too big, anything greater than 9 is too big. No good.

Choice (D): Combination of (A) and (B), which were both wrong. No good.

Clearly, choice (E) must be correct.

21. A

Factor the quadratic expression into a pair of binomials, using FOIL in reverse.

The product of the Last terms in the binomials $= rs = -15$.

The sum of the Outer and Inner terms $= rx + sx = -2x$, $r + s = -2$.

With a little trial and error it becomes clear that $r = -5$ and $s = 3$, or $r = 3$ and $s = -5$.

The problem asks for one possible value for $r - s$. Since you don't know which number is r and which is s, $r - s$ could be $(-5) - 3$, or $3 - (-5)$. $-5 - 3 = -8$, which is not among the answer choices. But $3 - (-5) = 3 + 5 = 8$, which is choice (A).

22. D

We must try to get rid of the denominator by factoring it out of the numerator. $n - 4\sqrt{n} + 4$ is a difficult expression to work with. It may be easier if we let $t = \sqrt{n}$. Keep in mind then that $t^2 = (\sqrt{n})(\sqrt{n}) = n$.

Then $n - 4\sqrt{n} + 4 = t^2 - 4t + 4$.

Using FOIL in reverse, $t^2 - 4t + 4 = (t - 2)(t - 2) = (\sqrt{n} - 2)(\sqrt{n} - 2)$.

So $\dfrac{n - 4\sqrt{n} + 4}{\sqrt{n} - 2} = \dfrac{(\sqrt{n} - 2)(\sqrt{n} - 2)}{(\sqrt{n} - 2)} = \sqrt{n} - 2$.

Or pick a number for n (a perfect square, such as 25, is a good choice) and try each answer choice. Whichever method you use, choice (D) is correct.

23. 9

Here's an example of a question that, though tough-looking at first glance, is easily manageable once you realize that it involves little more than straight substitution. Plug in -4 wherever you see x:

$$f(x) = |x^2 + 2x + 1|$$
$$f(-4) = |(-4)^2 + 2(-4) + 1|$$
$$f(-4) = |16 - 8 + 1|$$
$$f(-4) = 9$$

24. C

Know the difference between domain and range. The domain of a function is the set of values for which the function is defined. The range of a function is the set of outputs or results of the function. Theoretical problems such as this can be hard, but knowing what the question is asking for is half of the battle. You know that x cannot be zero because, if it were, the function would be undefined. This consideration eliminates all choices except (C) and (E). The value $x = \frac{1}{2}$ satisfies the function, so eliminate (E), since $\frac{1}{2}$ is not an integer. This leaves only (C).

25. C

First, plug in the first set of values ($f = 10$ and $r = 300$) to find k. Then use k and the new value of r, (which is 750), to find the new value of f.

$$10 = k(300)$$

$$\frac{10}{300} = \frac{1}{30} = k$$

$$f = \frac{1}{30}(750) = 25$$

26. 32

To answer the question you must find the value of m.

$$\ast\, m \,\ast = 4$$

$$\frac{(\sqrt{m})^3}{2} = 4$$

$$(\sqrt{m})^3 = 8$$

$$\sqrt{m} = 2$$

$$m = 4$$

So: $\ast\, 4m \,\ast = \ast\, 4(4) \,\ast = \ast\, 16 \,\ast$

$$= \frac{(\sqrt{16})^3}{2}$$

$$= \frac{4^3}{2}$$

$$= \frac{64}{2} = 32.$$

Chapter Twelve: **General Word Problems**

Words in English can have meanings and equivalent symbols in mathematical language. Word problems test your ability to translate plain English into math language. For example, if a word problem asks for "the sum of two numbers," it's really asking you to add the two numbers together, and "+" is the mathematical symbol. SAT test makers love to intersperse this type of question into the Math Section.

Although it's hard to outline the exact formula for solving a word problem, we can suggest some approaches to get you started. First, eliminate any extraneous information. You can do this by underlining the important information, such as the actual question being asked or the available constants. Some word problems can be solved most efficiently by representing the problem as an algebraic equation. For these types, try to identify the smallest unknown quantity and assign it a variable. Once you do that, you can start writing the other unknown quantities in terms of the smallest unknown. Next, write out the equation using the variables and constants. Finally, solve the equation for the unknown (the variable).

Don't let word problems intimidate you. They're not asking you anything you don't know; they're simply asking you in a different way. Take them one step at a time and you will succeed. For further reading on this subject:

64. Translating from English into Algebra

Chapter Twelve Practice Set
Answer Sheet

1. Ⓐ Ⓑ Ⓒ Ⓓ Ⓔ
2. Ⓐ Ⓑ Ⓒ Ⓓ Ⓔ
3. Ⓐ Ⓑ Ⓒ Ⓓ Ⓔ
4. Ⓐ Ⓑ Ⓒ Ⓓ Ⓔ
5. Ⓐ Ⓑ Ⓒ Ⓓ Ⓔ
6. Ⓐ Ⓑ Ⓒ Ⓓ Ⓔ
7. Ⓐ Ⓑ Ⓒ Ⓓ Ⓔ
8. Ⓐ Ⓑ Ⓒ Ⓓ Ⓔ
9. Grid-in below

10. Grid-in below
11. Ⓐ Ⓑ Ⓒ Ⓓ Ⓔ
12. Grid-in below
13. Grid-in below
14. Ⓐ Ⓑ Ⓒ Ⓓ Ⓔ
15. Ⓐ Ⓑ Ⓒ Ⓓ Ⓔ
16. Grid-in below
17. Grid-in below
18. Ⓐ Ⓑ Ⓒ Ⓓ Ⓔ

19. Ⓐ Ⓑ Ⓒ Ⓓ Ⓔ
20. Ⓐ Ⓑ Ⓒ Ⓓ Ⓔ
21. Ⓐ Ⓑ Ⓒ Ⓓ Ⓔ
22. Ⓐ Ⓑ Ⓒ Ⓓ Ⓔ
23. Ⓐ Ⓑ Ⓒ Ⓓ Ⓔ
24. Ⓐ Ⓑ Ⓒ Ⓓ Ⓔ
25. Ⓐ Ⓑ Ⓒ Ⓓ Ⓔ
26. Ⓐ Ⓑ Ⓒ Ⓓ Ⓔ
27. Ⓐ Ⓑ Ⓒ Ⓓ Ⓔ

28. Ⓐ Ⓑ Ⓒ Ⓓ Ⓔ
29. Ⓐ Ⓑ Ⓒ Ⓓ Ⓔ
30. Ⓐ Ⓑ Ⓒ Ⓓ Ⓔ
31. Grid-in below
32. Ⓐ Ⓑ Ⓒ Ⓓ Ⓔ
33. Ⓐ Ⓑ Ⓒ Ⓓ Ⓔ

9.

10.

12.

13.

16.

17.

31.

KAPLAN

PRACTICE SET

Basic

1. Before the market opens on Monday, a stock is priced at $25. If its price decreases $4 on Monday, increases $6 on Tuesday, and then decreases $2 on Wednesday, what is the final price of the stock on Wednesday?

   (A) $12
   (B) $21
   (C) $25
   (D) $29
   (E) $37

2. If three times x is equal to x decreased by 2, then x is

   (A) -2

   (B) -1

   (C) $-\dfrac{2}{3}$

   (D) 1

   (E) $\dfrac{3}{2}$

3. Greg's weekly salary is $70 less than Joan's, which is $50 more than Sue's. If Sue earns $280 per week, how much does Greg earn per week?

   (A) $160
   (B) $260
   (C) $280
   (D) $300
   (E) $400

4. If the sum of a, b, and c is twice the sum of a minus b and a minus c, then $a =$

   (A) $b + c$
   (B) $3b + 3c$
   (C) $3b - c$
   (D) $2b + 3c$
   (E) $-b - c$

5. During a certain week, a post office sold $280 worth of 14-cent stamps. How many of these stamps did they sell?

   (A) 20
   (B) 2,000
   (C) 3,900
   (D) 20,000
   (E) 39,200

6. Diane painted $\dfrac{1}{3}$ of her room with $2\dfrac{1}{2}$ cans of paint. How many more cans of paint will she need to finish painting her room?

   (A) 5

   (B) $7\dfrac{1}{2}$

   (C) 10

   (D) $12\dfrac{1}{2}$

   (E) 15

7. Liza took $5n$ photographs on a certain trip. If she gives n photographs to each of her 3 friends, how many photographs will she have left?

   (A) $2n$
   (B) $3n$
   (C) $4n - 3$
   (D) $4n$
   (E) $4n + 3$

8. Ed has $100 more than Robert. After Ed spends $20 on groceries, Ed has 5 times as much money as Robert. How much money does Robert have?

   (A) $20
   (B) $30
   (C) $40
   (D) $50
   (E) $120

9. The average of 5 numbers is 13. If the average of 4 of these numbers is 10, what is the fifth number?

10. An office has 27 employees. If there are 7 more women than men in the office, how many employees are women?

Medium

11. Between 1950 and 1960 the population of Country A increased by 3.5 million people. If the amount of increase between 1960 and 1970 was 1.75 million more than the increase from 1950 to 1960, what was the total amount of increase in population in Country A between 1950 and 1970?

    (A) 1.75 million
    (B) 3.5 million
    (C) 5.25 million
    (D) 7 million
    (E) 8.75 million

12. On a scaled map, a distance of 10 centimeters represents 5 kilometers. If a street is 750 meters long, what is its length on the map, in centimeters? (1 kilometer = 1,000 meters)

13. In a certain baseball league, each team plays 160 games. After playing half of their games, Team A has won 60 games and Team B has won 49 games. If Team A wins half of its remaining games, how many of its remaining games must Team B win to have the same number of wins as Team A at the end of the season?

14. A painter charges $12 an hour, while his son charges $6 an hour. If the father and his son worked the same amount of time together on a job, how many hours did each of them work if the combined charge for their labor was $108?

    (A) 6
    (B) 8
    (C) 9
    (D) 12
    (E) 18

15. A man has an estate worth $15 million that he will either divide equally among his 10 children or among his 10 children and 5 stepchildren. How much more will each of his children inherit if his 5 stepchildren are excluded?

    (A) $500,000
    (B) $1,000,000
    (C) $1,500,000
    (D) $2,500,000
    (E) $5,000,000

16. An hour-long test has 60 problems. If a student completes 30 problems in 20 minutes, how many seconds does he have on average for completing each of the remaining problems?

17. At a clothing company, each blouse requires 1 yard of material, 4 shirts require 2 yards of material, and 1 blouse and 2 dresses require 4 yards of material. How many yards of material are needed to make 1 blouse, 1 shirt, and 1 dress?

18. If the product of 3 and x is equal to 2 less than y, which of the following must be true?

    (A) $6x - y - 2 = 0$
    (B) $6x - 6 = 0$
    (C) $3x - y - 2 = 0$
    (D) $3x + y - 2 = 0$
    (E) $3x - y + 2 = 0$

19. If a man earns $200 for his first 40 hours of work in a week and is then paid $1\frac{1}{2}$ times his regular hourly rate for any additional hours, how many hours must he work to make $230 in a week?

    (A) 4
    (B) 5
    (C) 6
    (D) 44
    (E) 45

20. In a typical month, $\frac{1}{2}$ of the UFO sightings in a certain state are attributable to airplanes and $\frac{1}{3}$ of the remaining sightings are attributable to weather balloons. If there were 108 UFO sightings during one typical month, how many would be attributable to weather balloons?

    (A) 18
    (B) 24
    (C) 36
    (D) 54
    (E) 72

21. Ms. Smith drove a total of 700 miles on a business trip. If her car averaged 35 miles per gallon of gasoline and gasoline cost an average of $1.25 per gallon, how much did she spend on gasoline for this trip?

    (A) $17.50
    (B) $25.00
    (C) $35.00
    (D) $70.00
    (E) $250.00

22. Gheri is n years old. Carl is 6 years younger than Gheri and 2 years older than Jean. What is the sum of the ages of all 3?

    (A) $3n + 16$
    (B) $3n + 4$
    (C) $3n - 4$
    (D) $3n - 8$
    (E) $3n - 14$

23. During a drought the amount of water in a pond was reduced by a third. If the amount of water in the pond was 48,000 gallons immediately after the drought, how many thousands of gallons of water were lost during the drought?

    (A) 6,000
    (B) 12,000
    (C) 18,000
    (D) 24,000
    (E) 30,000

Hard

24. There is enough candy in a bag to give 12 pieces of candy to each of 20 children, with no candy left over. If 5 children do not want any candy, how many pieces of candy can be given to each of the others?

    (A) 12
    (B) 15
    (C) 16
    (D) 18
    (E) 20

25. Chris has twice as many baseball cards as Lee. If Chris gives Lee 10 of his baseball cards, he will have half as many as Lee. How many baseball cards do Chris and Lee have together?

    (A) 10
    (B) 20
    (C) 30
    (D) 40
    (E) 60

26. The total fare for 2 adults and 3 children on an excursion boat is $14. If each child's fare is one half of each adult's fare, what is the adult fare?

    (A) $2.00
    (B) $3.00
    (C) $3.50
    (D) $4.00
    (E) $4.50

KAPLAN

27. Doris spent $\frac{2}{3}$ of her savings on a used car, and she spent $\frac{1}{4}$ of her remaining savings on a new carpet. If the carpet cost her $250, how much were Doris's original savings?

   (A) $1,000
   (B) $1,200
   (C) $1,500
   (D) $2,000
   (E) $3,000

28. If John gives Allen $5 and Allen gives Frank $2 , the 3 boys will have the same amount of money. How much more money does John have than Allen?

   (A) $3
   (B) $5
   (C) $6
   (D) $7
   (E) $8

29. Ida owes her parents x dollars. Last month she paid $\frac{1}{6}$ of the amount owed. This month she paid them $\frac{1}{6}$ of the remaining amount plus $20.00. In terms of x, how much money does she still owe?

   (A) $\dfrac{x - 20}{6}$

   (B) $\dfrac{5}{6}x - 20$

   (C) $\dfrac{5x - 20}{6}$

   (D) $\dfrac{25}{36}x - 20$

   (E) $\dfrac{25x - 20}{36}$

30. John can shovel a certain driveway in 50 minutes. If Mary can shovel the same driveway in 20 minutes, how long will it take them, to the nearest minute, to shovel the driveway if they work together?

   (A) 12
   (B) 13
   (C) 14
   (D) 16
   (E) 18

31. In a group of 60 workers, the average (arithmetic mean) salary is $80 a day per worker. If some of the workers earn $75 a day and all the rest earn $100 a day, how many workers earn $75 a day?

32. A street vendor sells two types of newspapers, one for $.25 and the other for $.40. If she sold 100 newspapers for $28.00, how many newspapers did she sell at $.25?

   (A) 80
   (B) 60
   (C) 50
   (D) 40
   (E) 20

33. A grocer has c pounds of coffee that he wants to divide equally among s sacks. If n more sacks are to be used, then each sack would hold how many fewer pounds of coffee?

   (A) $\dfrac{c}{s + n}$

   (B) $\dfrac{c}{s + cn}$

   (C) $\dfrac{c}{s^2 + sn}$

   (D) $\dfrac{cn}{s + n}$

   (E) $\dfrac{cn}{s^2 + sn}$

ANSWERS AND EXPLANATIONS

Basic

1.   C

Translate directly into math. A price decrease makes the price smaller, so we subtract. A price increase makes the price greater, so we add. For the final price we get

$$\$25 - \$4 + \$6 - \$2 = \$25 + \$0 = \$25$$

So the final price is $25.

2.   B

Translate piece by piece: "three times x" $= 3x$, "x decreased by 2" $= x - 2$.

So $3x = x - 2$

Solve for x:

$$3x - x = -2$$
$$2x = -2$$
$$x = -1$$

3.   B

Sue makes $280. If Joan makes $50 more than this, then Joan must make $280 + $50, or $330. Greg makes $70 less than this amount, or $330 − $70, or $260.

4.   A

Translate piece by piece:

"the sum of a, b, and c" $= a + b + c$

"twice the sum of a minus b and a minus c" $=$

$2[(a - b) + (a - c)]$

So $a + b + c = 2[(a - b) + (a - c)]$

Solve for a:

$$a + b + c = 2a - 2b + 2a - 2c$$
$$a + b + c = 4a - 2b - 2c$$
$$b + c + 2b + 2c = 4a - a$$
$$3b + 3c = 3a$$
$$b + c = a$$

5.   B

To calculate the number of 14-cent stamps sold by the post office, divide the total amount of money spent on these stamps by the cost of each stamp. This means dividing $280 by 14¢. Since the units are not the same, we convert 14¢ to dollars to get $.14 , so that we are dividing dollars by dollars. We get $280 \div .14 = 2{,}000$. So 2,000, 14-cent stamps were sold.

6.   A

Diane has painted $\frac{1}{3}$ of her room with $2\frac{1}{2}$ cans of paint. To complete the remaining $\frac{2}{3}$ of her room, twice as much paint will be needed. So $2 \times 2\frac{1}{2} = 5$ more cans are needed.

7.   A

Liza starts with $5n$ photographs. If she gives n photos to each of her 3 friends, she gives away $3 \times n$, or $3n$, photos. She is left with $5n - 3n$, or $2n$, photos.

8.   A

Translate to get two equations. Let E be the amount Ed has and R be the amount Robert has.

"Ed has $100 more than Robert" becomes $E = R + 100$.

"Ed spends $20" means he'll end up with $20 less, or $E - 20$.

"5 times as much as Robert" becomes $5R$.

So $E - 20 = 5R$.

KAPLAN

Substitute $R + 100$ for E in the second equation and solve for R:

$$E - 20 = 5R$$
$$(R + 100) - 20 = 5R$$
$$R + 80 = 5R$$
$$80 = 4R$$
$$20 = R$$

So Robert has $20.

9. 25

Average $= \dfrac{\text{sum of the terms}}{\text{number of terms}}$, so $13 =$ the sum of the 5 numbers $\div 5$.

That means the sum is 5×13, or 65. If four of these numbers have an average of 10, their sum must be 4×10, or 40. The fifth number must make up the difference between 40 and 65, which is 25.

10. 17

What 2 numbers 7 apart add up to 27? With trial and error you should be able to find them pretty quickly: 10 and 17. So there must be 17 women working at the office.

Alternatively, set up two equations each with two unknowns. There are 27 employees at the office total, all either men or women, so m (the number of men) $+ w$ (the number of women) $= 27$. There are 7 more women than men, so: $m + 7 = w$, or $m = w - 7$.

Substitute $w - 7$ for m into the first equation:

$$(w - 7) + w = 27$$
$$2w - 7 = 27$$
$$2w = 34$$
$$w = 17$$

There are 17 women in the office. (In problems like these, check at the end to make sure you answered the right question. It would have been easy here to misread the question and solve for the number of men.)

Medium

11. E

In Country A, the amount of population increase between 1960 and 1970 was 1.75 million more than the amount of increase between 1950 and 1960, or 1.75 million more than 3.5 million. So the increase between 1960 and 1970 must have been $1.75 + 3.5$ million, or 5.25 million. The total growth in population over the 2 decades equals 3.5 million (the amount of growth between 1950 and 1960), plus 5.25 million (the amount of growth between 1960 and 1970), for a total increase of 8.75 million.

12. 1.5 or 3/2

Start by converting kilometers to meters. Since a meter is smaller than a kilometer, we must multiply. We're told that a length of 10 centimeters on the map represents 5 kilometers, or 5,000 meters; therefore, 1 centimeter must represent $\dfrac{1}{10}$ as much, or 500 meters. We want to know how many centimeters would represent 750 meters. We could set up a proportion here, but it's quicker to use common sense. We have a distance of $1\dfrac{1}{2}$ times 500 meters ($750 = 1\dfrac{1}{2} \times 500$), so we need a map distance of $1\dfrac{1}{2} \times 1$ centimeter, or 1.5 centimeters.

13. 51

Since the teams have played half their games, there are 80 games left. If Team A wins half its remaining games, that's another 40 games, for a total of $60 + 40$, or 100, games. Team B has won 49 games so far, so in order to tie Team A, it must win another $100 - 49$, or 51, games.

14. A

When the painter and his son work together, they charge the sum of their hourly rates, $12 + $6, or $18, per hour. Their bill equals the product of this combined rate and the number of hours they work. Therefore $108 must equal $18 per hour times the number of hours they worked. We need to divide $108 by $18 per hour to find the number of hours. $108 ÷ $18 = 6.

15. A

The amount each of the children stands to gain equals the difference between what he or she will make if the stepchildren are excluded and what he or she will make if they're included. If the stepchildren are excluded, the children will inherit $15 million divided by 10 (the number of children), or $1.5 million each. If the stepchildren are included, they'll inherit $15 million divided by 15 (the number of children and stepchildren combined) or $1 million each. The difference is $1.5 million − $1 million, or $500,000.

16. 80

The student has done 30 of the 60 problems, and has used up 20 of the 60 minutes. Therefore, he has 60 − 30, or 30 problems left, to be done in 60 − 20, or 40 minutes. We find his average time per problem by dividing the time by the number of problems.

$$\text{Time per problem} = \frac{40 \text{ minutes}}{30 \text{ problems}}$$

$$= \frac{4}{3} \text{ minutes per problem}$$

Each minute has 60 seconds. So we multiply by 60 to find the number of seconds.

$$\frac{4}{3} \text{ minutes} \times 60 \, \frac{\text{seconds}}{\text{minute}} = 80 \text{ seconds}$$

17. 3

We need to keep track of the amount of material that it takes to make each of the different items of clothing. Each blouse requires 1 yard of material. Four shirts require 2 yards of material; therefore, each shirt requires $\frac{2}{4}$, or $\frac{1}{2}$ yard. One blouse and 2 dresses require a total of 4 yards. One of these yards goes to the blouse, leaving 3 yards for the 2 dresses, so a single dress requires $\frac{3}{2}$, or $1\frac{1}{2}$, yards of material. Now let's find how much we need for the assortment we want: 1 blouse, 1 shirt, 1 dress. One blouse takes 1 yard. One shirt takes $\frac{1}{2}$ yard. And the dress takes $1\frac{1}{2}$ yards. So the amount of material needed is $1 + \frac{1}{2} + 1\frac{1}{2}$ yards, or 3 yards.

18. E

Translate into math, remembering that "2 less than y" means $y − 2$, not $2 − y$.

"The product of 3 and x" means $3x$. So we have the equation $3x = y − 2$.

Since this doesn't match any of the answer choices, we have to determine which of the answer choices corresponds to it. Since all the answer choices are equations in which the right side is zero, let's move all the terms in our equation to the left side. We get $3x − y + 2 = 0$, which is choice (E).

19. D

To learn the man's overtime rate of pay we have to figure out his regular rate of pay. Divide the amount of money made, $200, by the time it took to make it, 40 hours. $200 ÷ 40 hours = $5 per hour. That is his normal rate. The man is paid time and a half for overtime, so when working more than 40 hours, he makes $\frac{3}{2} \times 5 per hour = $7.50 per hour.

Now we can figure out how long it takes the man to make $230. It takes him 40 hours to make the first $200. The last $30 are made at the overtime rate. Since it takes the man 1 hour to make $7.50 at this rate, we can figure out the number of extra hours by dividing $30 by $7.50 per hour. $30 ÷ $7.50 per hour = 4 hours. The total time needed is 40 hours plus 4 hours, or 44 hours.

20. A

We need to find a fraction of a fraction. The total number of UFO sightings is 108. Of these, $\frac{1}{2}$ turn out to be airplanes: $\frac{1}{2} \times 108 = 54$. If $\frac{1}{2}$ are airplanes, $\frac{1}{2}$ are not, so 54 sightings remain that are not airplanes. Of these 54, $\frac{1}{3}$ are weather balloons. We multiply $\frac{1}{3} \times 54$ to find the number of weather balloons, which is 18.

21. B

If Ms. Smith's car averages 35 miles per gallon, then she can go 35 miles on 1 gallon. To go 700 miles, she will need 700 ÷ 35, or 20, gallons of gasoline. The average price of gasoline was $1.25 per gallon, so she spent 20 × $1.25, or $25, for the gasoline on her trip.

22. E

Gheri is n years old. Carl is 6 years younger than Gheri, or $n - 6$ years old. Jean is 2 years younger than Carl, or $n - 6 - 2 = n - 8$ years old. The sum of their ages is then $n + (n - 6) + (n - 8) = 3n - 14$ years.

This problem could also be solved by picking numbers. Let's say that Gheri is 20 years old (so $n = 20$). Carl is 6 years younger, or 14, and Jean is 2 years younger still, or 12. The sum of their ages is 20 + 14 + 12 = 46. Now we plug $n = 20$ into each answer choice and see which one, or ones, have a value of 46. A little quick math will show you that only choice (E) works.

23. D

$\frac{1}{3}$ of the original volume of water in the pond was lost during the drought. The amount of water that remains must be $\frac{2}{3}$ of the original amount, that is, twice as much as was lost. So the $\frac{1}{3}$ that was lost is equal to half of what was left. That is, the amount of water lost $= \frac{48,000}{2} =$ 24,000 gallons of water.

Or, set up an equation in which W represents how much water was originally in the pond:

$$W - \frac{1}{3}W = 48,000$$

$$\frac{2}{3}W = 48,000$$

$$W = 72,000$$

The amount lost was $\frac{1}{3}$ of the original amount, or $\frac{1}{3}$ of W, which is $\frac{1}{3}(72,000) = 24,000$.

Hard

24. C

Find the total number of pieces of candy in the bag, then divide by the number of children who will be sharing them. There's enough candy to give 12 pieces to each of 20 children, so there are 12 × 20, or 240, pieces of candy total. Five children do not want candy, so there remain 20 − 5, or 15, children to share the 240 pieces of candy. Each will get 240 ÷ 15, or 16, pieces of candy.

25. C

Let C represent the number of baseball cards Chris has, and L represent the number of baseball cards Lee has. Since Chris has twice as many baseball cards as Lee, we can write

$$C = 2L.$$

If Chris gives Lee 10 baseball cards, then he will have 10 fewer, or $C - 10$, and Lee will have 10 more, or $L + 10$. In this case Chris would end up with half as many as Lee, so

$$C - 10 = \frac{1}{2}(L + 10).$$

We have 2 equations with 2 variables. Solve for C and L. Substitute the first expression for C—that is, $C = 2L$—into the second equation and solve for L.

$$2L - 10 = \frac{1}{2}(L + 10)$$

$$4L - 20 = L + 10$$

$$3L = 30$$

$$L = 10$$

26. D

If each adult's fare is twice as much as each child's fare, then 2 adult fares cost as much as 4 child fares. This, added to the 3 children's fares, gives us a total of $4 + 3$, or 7, children's fares. This equals \$14. If 7 children's fares cost \$14, then the cost of each child's fare is $\frac{14}{7}$, or \$2. Adult fares cost twice as much, or \$4.

If you get stumped on a problem like this, you can try backsolving, plugging in each answer choice to see which one gives the correct total cost of \$14. (For an example of backsolving, see the next solution.)

27. E

The \$250 that Doris spent on the carpet is $\frac{1}{4}$ of the $\frac{1}{3}$ of Doris's savings that's left over after she buys the car, or $\frac{1}{4} \times \frac{1}{3} = \frac{1}{12}$ of her original savings. Therefore, her original savings must have been $12 \times \$250$ or \$3,000.

You can also work backward and try plugging in the answer choices on this one. We'll start with choice (C), because it is the middle value answer choice.

Choice (C): If Doris originally had \$1,500, then spent $\frac{2}{3}$ of that on the car, she was left with $\frac{1}{3} \times \$1,500$, or \$500. The amount spent on the carpet was $\frac{1}{4}$ of this, and $\frac{1}{4} \times \$500 = \$125$, not \$250. So this choice is too small, and we move to the next, larger choice. Choice (D): $\frac{1}{3} \times \$2,000$ is about \$667. And $\frac{1}{4}$ of that is somewhere between \$150 and \$200. Still too small.

So choice (E)—the only remaining choice that is larger—must be correct. You could check it out, although it's not necessary.

28. E

Let the amount of John's money $= J$ and let the amount of Allen's money $= A$. John gives \$5 to Allen so now he has $J - 5$ and Allen has $A + 5$. Allen gives \$2 to Frank so now he has \$2 less, or $A + 5 - 2 = A + 3$. They all have the same amount of money now, so

$$A + 3 = J - 5$$

or

$$A + 8 = J$$

Since Allen needs \$8 to have the same as John, John has \$8 more.

29. D

The best way to solve this problem is to pick a number for x. Choose a number that is divisible by 6: Let $x = 180$.

Last month she paid $\frac{1}{6} \times \$180$, or \$30. So she still owes $\$180 - \$30$, or \$150. This month she paid them $(\frac{1}{6} \times \$150) + \$20 = \$25 + \$20$, or \$45. So she still owes $\$150 - \$45$, or \$105. Now try each of the answer choices to eliminate any answer choice that does not equal 105

when $x = 180$.

Choice (A): $[180 - 20] \div 6 = 160 \div 6 = 26.67$. Discard.

Choice (B): $(5 \div 6)(180) - 20 = 150 - 20 = 130$. Discard.

Choice (C): $[(5)(180) - 20] \div 6 = 880 \div 6 = 146.67$. Discard.

Choice (D): $(25 \div 36)(180) - 20 = 125 - 20 = 105$. Possibly correct.

Choice (E): $[(25)(180) - 20] \div 36 = 4480 \div 36 = 124.44$. Discard.

Since choice (D) was only one that yielded 105 when $x = 180$, it is the correct answer.

30. C

John can shovel the whole driveway in 50 minutes, so each minute he does $\frac{1}{50}$ of the driveway. Mary can shovel the whole driveway in 20 minutes; in each minute, she does $\frac{1}{20}$ of the driveway. In one minute they do $\frac{1}{50} + \frac{1}{20} = \frac{2}{100} + \frac{5}{100} = \frac{7}{100}$.

If they do $\frac{7}{100}$ of the driveway in one minute, they do the entire driveway in $\frac{100}{7}$ minutes. (If you do $\frac{1}{2}$ of a job in 1 minute, you do the whole job in the reciprocal of $\frac{1}{2}$, or 2, minutes.) So all that remains is to round off $\frac{100}{7}$ to the nearest integer. Since $\frac{100}{7} = 14\frac{2}{7}$, $\frac{100}{7}$ is approximately 14. It takes about 14 minutes for both of them to shovel the driveway.

31. 48

If the average salary of the 60 workers is $80, the total amount received by the workers is $60 \times \$80$, or $4,800. This equals the total income from the $75 workers plus the total income from the $100 workers. Let x represent the number of $75 workers.

Since we know there are 60 workers altogether, and everyone earns either $75 or $100, then $60 - x$ must earn $100. We can set up an equation for the total amount received by the workers by multiplying the rate times the number of workers receiving that rate and adding:

$$75x + 100(60 - x) = 4,800$$

Solve this equation to find x, the number of workers earning $75.

$$75x + 6,000 - 100x = 4,800$$
$$-25x = -1,200$$
$$25x = 1,200$$
$$x = 48$$

There were 48 workers earning $75.

32. A

Call the number of 25-cent newspapers x, and the number of 40-cent newspapers y. Since she sold 100 newspapers in total, $x + y = 100$. Also, the total cost of these newspapers was $28.00, or 2,800 cents. So $25x + 40y = 2,800$. We want to find x, the number of 25-cent newspapers sold. From the first equation, $y = 100 - x$. Substitute this value for y into the second equation, and solve for x.

$$25x + 40y = 2,800$$
$$25x + 40(100 - x) = 2,800$$
$$25x + 4,000 - 40x = 2,800$$
$$25x - 40x = 2,800 - 4,000$$
$$-15x = -1,200$$
$$x = -1,200 \div (-15)$$
$$x = 80$$

So she sold 80 newspapers at 25 cents each.

33. E

Pick numbers for all 3 variables so you can easily determine the relationship among them:

Let $c = 20$ pounds of coffee.

Let $s = 4$ sacks.

Let $n = 6$ additional sacks.

Since the grocer originally wanted to divide c pounds of coffee into s sacks, there would have been $\frac{c}{s}$ pounds per sack, or 20 pounds of coffee ÷ 4 sacks = 5 pounds per sack. But now the coffee is to be divided equally among $s + n$ sacks, or 20 pounds of coffee ÷ (4 + 6) sacks = $\frac{20}{10}$, or 2 pounds per sack. Therefore, the difference between the original number of pounds per sack and the new number of pounds per sack is 5 − 2, or 3 pounds per sack. So now, try each of the answer choices to eliminate any choice that does not equal 3 when $c = 20$, $s = 4$, and $n = 6$:

Choice (A): $\frac{c}{s + n} = 20 ÷ [4 + 6] = 20 ÷ 10 = 2$. Discard.

Choice (B): $\frac{c}{s + cn} = 20 ÷ [4 + (20)(6)] = 20 ÷ 124 = 5 ÷ 31$. Discard.

Choice (C): $\frac{c}{s^2 + sn} = 20 ÷ [(4^2 + (4)(6)] = 20 ÷ 40 = 1 ÷ 2$. Discard.

Choice (D): $\frac{cn}{s + n} = (20)(6) ÷ [4 + 6] = 120 ÷ 10 = 12$. Discard.

Choice (E): $\frac{cn}{s^2 + sn} = (20)(6) ÷ [4^2 + (4)(6)] = 120 ÷ 40 = 3$. Correct.

Since (E) was the only one that yielded 3, it is the correct answer.

KAPLAN

Chapter Thirteen: **Logic Word Problems**

Logic word problems aren't necessarily any harder than average word problems. They're just logic-based and often involve some sort of *counting* or *probability* formula. A lot of people find this to be one of the most confusing question types on the math portion of the SAT. The confusion can result from the fact that the answers are often hard to predict, or estimate. Sometimes a table, organized list, or drawing will help. You might see something like this: Jacqui has four jackets, six blouses, three skirts, and two pairs of shoes. How many different outfits, consisting of a jacket, blouse, skirt, and a pair of shoes could Jacqui possibly put together? You're being asked how many different outfits Jacqui could make by mixing and matching the clothes she has. The way to solve this problem is to *count the elements*, or items, in each outfit that Jacqui could make and then add them all up. An even easier way to solve this is to multiply all the elements (4 × 6 × 3 × 2) and get 144. Jacqui has 144 possible outfits to choose from.

Probability questions are a type of logic word problem you might encounter on the SAT. They ask for the odds or likelihood of a certain thing happening. That certain thing is referred to as an *event*, and in any event, there are a limited number of possible outcomes. This set of all possible outcomes is often referred to as the *sample space*.

Probability solutions can be expressed as fractions or decimals between zero and one. An event that is very likely to happen will be closer to one, while an unlikely event will have a solution closer to zero. For further reading:

42. Counting the Possibilities

43. Probability

Chapter Thirteen Practice Set
Answer Sheet

1. Ⓐ Ⓑ Ⓒ Ⓓ Ⓔ
2. Ⓐ Ⓑ Ⓒ Ⓓ Ⓔ
3. Grid-in below
4. Ⓐ Ⓑ Ⓒ Ⓓ Ⓔ
5. Ⓐ Ⓑ Ⓒ Ⓓ Ⓔ
6. Ⓐ Ⓑ Ⓒ Ⓓ Ⓔ
7. Ⓐ Ⓑ Ⓒ Ⓓ Ⓔ
8. Ⓐ Ⓑ Ⓒ Ⓓ Ⓔ
9. Grid-in below

10. Ⓐ Ⓑ Ⓒ Ⓓ Ⓔ
11. Ⓐ Ⓑ Ⓒ Ⓓ Ⓔ
12. Ⓐ Ⓑ Ⓒ Ⓓ Ⓔ
13. Ⓐ Ⓑ Ⓒ Ⓓ Ⓔ
14. Ⓐ Ⓑ Ⓒ Ⓓ Ⓔ
15. Ⓐ Ⓑ Ⓒ Ⓓ Ⓔ
16. Ⓐ Ⓑ Ⓒ Ⓓ Ⓔ
17. Ⓐ Ⓑ Ⓒ Ⓓ Ⓔ
18. Ⓐ Ⓑ Ⓒ Ⓓ Ⓔ

19. Grid-in below
20. Ⓐ Ⓑ Ⓒ Ⓓ Ⓔ
21. Ⓐ Ⓑ Ⓒ Ⓓ Ⓔ
22. Grid-in below
23. Grid-in below
24. Ⓐ Ⓑ Ⓒ Ⓓ Ⓔ
25. Grid-in below

3.

9.

19.

22.

23.

25.

PRACTICE SET

Basic

1. Team *X* and Team *Y* have a tug of war. From their starting positions Team *X* pulls Team *Y* forward 3 meters, and Team *X* is then pulled forward 5 meters. Team *Y* then pulls Team *X* forward 2 meters. If the first team to be pulled forward 10 meters loses, how many more meters must Team *Y* pull Team *X* forward to win?

    (A)   0
    (B)   4
    (C)   6
    (D)   8
    (E)   14

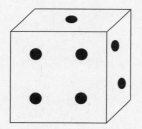

2. On the face of a regular die, the dots are arranged in such a way that the total number of dots on any 2 opposite faces is 7. If the figure above shows a regular die, what is the total number of dots on the faces that are not shown?

    (A)   7
    (B)   9
    (C)   12
    (D)   13
    (E)   14

3. Out of 40 sandwiches, 19 are turkey, 9 are bologna, and the rest are tuna fish. If one sandwich is randomly picked, what is the probability of picking a tuna fish sandwich?

4. Achmed finds that by wearing different combinations of the jackets, shirts, and pairs of trousers that he owns, he can make up 90 different outfits. If he owns 5 jackets and 3 pairs of trousers, how many shirts does he own?

    (A)   3
    (B)   6
    (C)   12
    (D)   18
    (E)   30

9	8	6	3

5. The figure above shows an example of a 4-digit identification code used by a certain bank for its customers. If the digits in the code must appear in descending numerical order and no digit can be used more than once, what is the difference between the largest and the smallest possible codes?

    (A)   6,666
    (B)   5,555
    (C)   5,432
    (D)   4,444
    (E)   1,110

6. Bill purchased an item and received no change. Before the purchase, he had only a $5 bill, two $10 bills, and a $20 dollar bill. How many distinct possibilities were there for the total amount of his purchase?

    (A)   3
    (B)   4
    (C)   6
    (D)   9
    (E)   10

7. A box contains 5 right-handed gloves and 6 left-handed gloves. If Sabina randomly removes 1 glove from the box, how many times must she remove a glove in order to be certain to get a right-handed glove?

(A) 5

(B) 6

(C) 7

(D) 10

(E) 11

Medium

8. A vault holds only 8-ounce tablets of gold and 5-ounce tablets of silver. If there are 130 ounces of gold and silver total, what is the greatest amount of gold that can be in the vault, in ounces?

(A) 40

(B) 80

(C) 120

(D) 128

(E) 130

9. Five light bulbs that are either on or off are lined up in a row. A certain code uses different combinations of lights turned on to represent different words. If exactly 2 lights must be turned on to represent a word, how many different words can be formed using the 5 light bulbs?

10. Robert purchased $2,000 worth of U.S. savings bonds. If bonds are sold in $50 or $100 denominations only, which of the following CANNOT be the number of U.S. savings bonds that Robert purchased?

(A) 20

(B) 27

(C) 30

(D) 40

(E) 50

11. At a parade, balloons are given out in the order of blue, red, red, yellow, yellow, yellow, blue, red, red, yellow, yellow, yellow, etcetera. If this pattern continues, how many red balloons will have been given out when a total of 70 balloons have been distributed?

(A) 18

(B) 22

(C) 24

(D) 26

(E) 35

12. Twelve index cards, numbered 3 through 14, are placed in an empty box. If one card is randomly drawn from the box, what is the probability that a prime number will be on the card?

(A) $\frac{1}{4}$

(B) $\frac{1}{3}$

(C) $\frac{5}{12}$

(D) $\frac{1}{2}$

(E) $\frac{5}{7}$

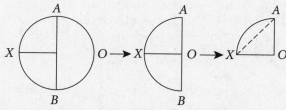

13. In the figure above, a circular sheet of paper is folded along diameter *AB*, and then along radius *OX*. If the folded paper is then cut along dotted line *AX* and unfolded, which of the following could result?

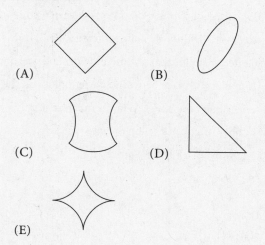

(A)

(B)

(C)

(D)

(E)

14. A class of 40 students is to be divided into smaller groups. If each group is to contain 3, 4, or 5 people, what is the largest number of groups possible?

(A) 8
(B) 10
(C) 12
(D) 13
(E) 14

$$A = \{0, 1, -3, 6, -8\}$$
$$B = \{-1, 2, -4, 7\}$$

15. If *a* is a number that is randomly selected from set *A*, and *b* is a number that is randomly selected from set *B*, what is the probability that $ab < 0$?

(A) $\frac{1}{4}$

(B) $\frac{1}{3}$

(C) $\frac{2}{5}$

(D) $\frac{4}{9}$

(E) $\frac{1}{2}$

16. A vending machine dispenses gumballs in a regularly repeating cycle of 10 different colors. If a quarter buys 3 gumballs, what is the minimum amount of money that must be spent before 3 gumballs of the same color are dispensed?

(A) $1.00
(B) $1.75
(C) $2.00
(D) $2.25
(E) $2.50

Hard

17. During a season in a certain basketball league, every team plays every other team in the league 10 times. If there are 10 teams in the league, how many games are played in the league in one season?

(A)   45
(B)   90
(C)   450
(D)   900
(E)   1,000

KAPLAN

18. Henry and Eleanor are waiting in line for a movie. If Henry is fourth in line, and there are n people ahead of Eleanor, where $n > 4$, how many people are between Henry and Eleanor?

    (A) $n - 5$
    (B) $n - 4$
    (C) $n - 3$
    (D) $n + 3$
    (E) $n + 4$

19. If 3 coins are tossed simultaneously, what is the probability of getting exactly 2 tails?

20. The largest number in a series of consecutive even integers is w. If the number of integers is p, what is the smallest number in terms of w and p ?

    (A) $w - 2p$

    (B) $w - p + 1$

    (C) $w - 2(p - 1)$

    (D) $p - 6 + w$

    (E) $w - \dfrac{p}{2}$

21. A picket fence is composed of x pickets, each of which is $\dfrac{1}{2}$ inch wide. If there are 6 inches of space between each pair of pickets, which of the following represents the length of the fence, in feet?
    (1 foot = 12 inches.)

    (A) $\dfrac{13}{2}x$

    (B) $\dfrac{13}{2}x - 6$

    (C) $\dfrac{13}{24}x$

    (D) $\dfrac{13x + 1}{24}$

    (E) $\dfrac{13x - 12}{24}$

22. There are 7 people on committee A and 8 people on committee B. If 3 people serve on both committees, how many people serve on only 1 of the committees?

23. At a certain factory $\dfrac{5}{8}$ of the workers are married and $\dfrac{3}{4}$ are at least 40 years old. If $\dfrac{1}{4}$ of the married workers are younger than 40, what fraction of the workers who are at least 40 are not married?

24. Poplar trees are planted on both sides of a straight street for a length of $\dfrac{3}{8}$ of a kilometer. Each tree is planted in a plot that is 1 meter wide, and there are 16 meters of space between adjacent plots on the same side of the street. What is the maximum number of poplars lining the street?
    (1 kilometer = 1,000 meters.)

    (A) 36
    (B) 40
    (C) 42
    (D) 44
    (E) 46

25. 5 friends won a total of 3 tickets to a concert. How many different combinations of 3 of the friends using the tickets are possible?

ANSWERS AND EXPLANATIONS

Basic

1.   C

Find out how much Team X has moved so far. Team X pulled Team Y forward 3 meters, so X moved backward 3 meters. Then Team X was pulled forward 5 meters and then a further 2 meters. In total, then, Team X has moved forward $(-3) + 5 + 2 = 4$ meters. Team X must be pulled forward a further 6 meters to be pulled 10 meters forward.

2.   E

A die has 6 faces, and the number of dots on opposite faces sum to 7. Since we can see the faces corresponding to 1, 2, and 4 dots in the picture, the ones we cannot see must contain 6, 5, and 3 dots respectively. Since $6 + 5 + 3 = 14$, there are 14 dots hidden from view.

3.   3/10, or .3

First find the number of tuna fish sandwiches. Out of the 40 sandwiches, 19 are turkey and 9 are bologna, so the remaining $40 - 19 - 9$, or 12, are tuna fish. So the probability of picking out a tuna fish sandwich is 12 out of 40, or $\frac{12}{40}$, or $\frac{3}{10}$.

4.   B

Achmed owns 3 pairs of trousers and 5 jackets. For every pair of trousers, he can wear 5 different jackets, giving 5 different combinations for each pair of trousers, or $3 \times 5 = 15$ different combinations of trousers and jackets. With each of these combinations he can wear any of his different shirts. The different combinations of shirts, jackets, and trousers is (number of shirts) $\times$ 15. We are told this equals 90, so number of shirts $= \frac{90}{15} = 6$.

5.   A

We need the difference between the largest and smallest possible codes. A digit cannot be repeated, and the digits must appear in descending numerical order. The largest such code will have the largest digit, 9, in the thousands place, followed by the next largest digits, 8, 7, and 6, in the next three places, so 9,876 is the largest possible number. For the smallest, start with the smallest digit, 0, and put it in the ones place. Working up from there—we end up with 3,210 as the smallest possible code. The difference between the largest and smallest codes is $9,876 - 3,210 = 6,666$.

6.   D

Bill had a $5 bill, two $10 bills, and a $20 bill, for a total of $45. Since he didn't receive any change after purchasing an item, he must have paid exactly the amount of the purchase. He didn't have to spend all his money, though, so the cost wasn't necessarily $45. We know that all of Bill's bills are in amounts that are divisible by 5, so the purchase price must also be divisible by 5. The smallest denomination that Bill has is a $5 bill. So we can start with $5, and then count up all the possible distinct combinations of these bills. These are $5 ($5 bill), $10 ($10 bill), $15 ($5 + $10 bills), $20 ($20 bill), $25 ($5 + $20 bills), $30 ($10 + $20 bills), $35 ($5 + $10 + $20 bills), $40 ($10 + $10 + $20 bills), and $45 (all 4 bills). So, in fact, all prices that are multiples of 5 between $5 and $45 are possible; there are 9 in all.

7.   C

Sabina cannot be certain that she will pick a right-handed glove until all of the left-handed gloves have been removed. Suppose she's not having much luck and she keeps picking left-handed gloves. After she's picked all 6 left-handed gloves, the seventh glove that she picks must be right-handed. So she must pick out 7 gloves in order to be certain she'll have a right-handed glove.

Medium

8.   C

The vault has a total of 130 ounces of gold and silver. Not all of the 130 ounces can be gold, since 130 is not a multiple of 8. There must be some silver in there as well. The largest multiple of 8 less than 130 is 16×8 or 128, but this can't be the amount of gold either, since this leaves only 130 − 128, or 2 ounces for the silver, and each silver tablet weighs 5 ounces. The next smallest multiple of 8 is 15 × 8 or 120. That leaves us with 130 − 120, or 10 ounces of silver, and since 2 × 5 = 10, this amount works. There are 15 tablets of gold, for a total of 120 ounces, and 2 tablets of silver, for a total of 10 ounces. So 120 ounces is the greatest possible amount of gold.

9. 10

In a combinations problem, the key is to count the possibilities in an organized way. Let's call the 5 light bulbs *A, B, C, D,* and *E.* If bulb *A* is turned on, we can also turn on *B,* or *C,* or *D,* or *E.* That's 4 pairs. Now we count starting with bulb *B,* but we have to skip *A,* because we already counted the *A-B* combination. So we have *B* and *C, B* and *D,* and *B* and *E*—3 more combinations. Next, we have *C* and *D,* and *C* and *E.* Finally we have *D* and *E.* This adds up to 10 possible pairs of lights turned on at the same time.

10. E

This is best solved intuitively. The maximum number of bonds that can be bought is when all the bonds are in $50 denominations. Since Robert bought $2,000 worth of bonds, the maximum number of bonds he could buy is $\frac{2,000}{50} = 40$ bonds. Answer choice (E) is 50, which is too much. If he bought any $100 bonds he would spend even more money. So it is impossible to buy $2,000 worth of bonds by purchasing fifty $100 or $50 bonds.

11. C

This balloon distribution is an unending series of cycles. Each cycle is 1 blue, 2 red, and 3 yellow, so each cycle contains 6 balloons, 2 of which are red. In 70 balloons, there are $\frac{70}{6} = 11\frac{4}{6}$ cycles; that is, 11 complete cycles and then the first 4 balloons in the next cycle. Since each cycle has 2 red balloons, you will have distributed 2 × 11, or 22, red balloons by the 66th. After the 66th balloon, you go

through the beginning of a new cycle, so the 67th balloon is blue, the 68th and 69th red, and the 70th yellow. This adds 2 more red balloons, for a total of 24 in the first 70.

12. C

Since probability equals the number of desired events divided by the number of possible events, we need to find out how many of the cards have prime numbers on them: 4, 6, 8, 9, 10, 12, and 14 are all divisible by smaller numbers, so they're not prime. That leaves 3, 5, 7, 11, and 13 as the primes from 3 to 14, inclusive. So 5 of the 12 cards have prime numbers on them. That means 5 of the 12 possible outcomes fit the description, so the probability is $\frac{5}{12}$, answer choice (C).

13. A

Label a point *Y* directly across the circle from point *X* to keep track of what's happening to the circle as we fold it.

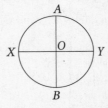

The first fold, along diameter *AB,* brings *Y* right on top of *X.*

The second fold, along radius *OX*, brings *B* right on top of *A*.

With the first fold, we have two semicircular pieces of paper, one on top of the other, folded along *AB*. If we were to cut the line *AX* after the first fold, we would also cut the top piece from *A* to *Y*. With the second fold, there are 4 quarter-circles. Cutting through the top piece from *A* to *X*, we would also cut through the second piece from *A* to *Y*, the third piece from *B* to *Y*, and the fourth piece from *B* to *X*. This would leave a square with the 4 corners *A*, *X*, *B*, and *Y* and the center *O* after the paper was unfolded:

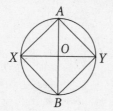

14. D

We will get the maximum number of groups by making each group as small as possible. Each group must have at least 3 people in it, so divide 40 by 3 to find the number of 3-person groups:

$$\frac{40}{3} = 13 \text{ with a remainder of } 1.$$

So we have 13 groups with 1 person left over. Since each group must have at least 3 people, we must throw the extra lonely student in with one of the other groups. So we have 12 groups with 3 students each, and 1 group with 4 students, for a maximum total of 13 groups.

15. C

First of all, how many pairs can come from the two sets? Each of the 5 numbers in set *A* can be paired with 4 different numbers from set *B*. So there are 4 × 5, or 20, possible pairs. Now in order for *ab* to be less than 0, or negative, 1 of the variables must be positive and the other

negative. So we need to find the number of possible pairs of numbers that would include 1 positive number and 1 negative number.

Consider the possible pairs. First of all, any number paired off with 0 from set *A* will have a product of 0. Since we need pairs with a product less than 0, these 4 pairs are out. Of the 4 pairs with 1 from set *A*, two will be negative: 1 × (−1) and 1 × (−4). Likewise, two of the pairs possible with −3 will be negative: (−3) × 2 and (−3) × 7, and the same is true for 6 and −8. So the number of pairs with a negative product is 2 + 2 + 2 + 2, or 8.

The probability of getting a pair of numbers with a negative product is therefore 8 out of 20, or $\frac{8}{20}$, which can be reduced to $\frac{2}{5}$.

16. B

Since the vending machine dispenses gumballs in a regular cycle of 10 colors, there are exactly 9 other gumballs dispensed between each pair of gumballs of the same color. For example, gumballs 1 and 11 must be the same color, as must gumballs 2 and 12, 42 and 52, etcetera. To get 3 gumballs all of the same color, you get the first gumball, then 9 of another color before another the same color as the first, then nine of another color before the third of the same color as the first. That's a total of 1 + 9 + 1 + 9 + 1 = 21 gumballs to get three matching ones.

Since each quarter buys 3 gumballs, and you need 21 gumballs in all, you have to spend $\frac{21}{3} = 7$ quarters to get three matching gumballs. 7 × $0.25 = $1.75.

Hard
17. C

In our 10-team league, each team plays the other 9 teams 10 times each. 9 × 10 = 90, so each team plays 90 games. Since there are 10 different teams, and 10 × 90 = 900, a total of 900 games are played by the 10 teams. But this counts each game twice, since it counts when

Team *A* plays Team *B* as one game and when Team *B* plays Team *A* as another game. But they're the same game. So, we must halve the total to take into account the fact that 2 teams play each game: $\frac{900}{2} = 450$. So 450 games are played in total.

18. B

Method I: Common sense.

There are *n* people ahead of Eleanor in line. One of them is Henry. Three more of them are in front of Henry (since Henry is fourth in line). So that makes 4 people who are not behind Henry. All the rest, or *n* − 4, are behind Henry and in front of Eleanor, so *n* − 4 is our answer.

Method II: Picking numbers.

Say Eleanor is 6th in line. Henry is 4th in line, so there is 1 person between them, the person 5th in line. There are *n* people ahead of Eleanor, and since Eleanor is 6th, *n* = 5. Substitute this in the answer choices and see which separates Henry and Eleanor by 1.

Choice (A): *n* − 5 = 5 − 5 = 0. Discard.

Choice (B): *n* − 4 = 5 − 4 = 1. Hold onto.

Choice (C): *n* − 3 = 5 − 3 = 2. Discard.

Choice (D): *n* + 3 = 5 + 3 = 8. Discard.

Choice (E): *n* + 4 = 5 + 4 = 9. Discard.

Only answer choice (B) gives a separation of 1; this must be the correct answer.

19. 3/8, or .375

To solve this one we must determine how many different ways the 3 coins could land, and then count the number of possibilities that have exactly 2 coins tails-up. It's easiest to do this systematically on paper, using "H" for "Heads" and "T" for "Tails."

H-H-H	T-H-H
H-H-T	T-H-T
H-T-H	T-T-H
H-T-T	T-T-T

Be sure to find every combination. There are 8 possible outcomes when the 3 coins are thrown. Only 3 of them have exactly 2 tails showing. (Remember: The combination with 3 tails up doesn't fit the description.) So the probability of getting exactly two tails is 3 out of 8, or $\frac{3}{8}$.

20. C

Since we are dealing with a series of consecutive even numbers, each term is 2 more than the previous term. Let's work backward from *w*. If there were 2 numbers in the series, the first number would be the even number just before *w*, or *w* − 2. If there were 3 numbers, the first would be *w* − 2 × 2, or *w* − 4. If there were 4 terms, the first would be *w* − 2 × 3, or *w* − 6. To find the first term in the series, we must subtract 2 from *w* once for each term in the series, with the exception of *w* itself. If there are *p* terms in the series (including *w* itself), we must subtract 2 × (*p* − 1) from *w* to get the smallest term. Therefore, the smallest term is *w* − 2(*p* − 1).

Alternatively, we could pick numbers. Say *w* = 6, and *p* = 3. Then we have the series 2, 4, 6. The smallest number is 2. Plug our values for *p* and *w* into the answer choices and eliminate any choice that does not give us an answer of 2.

Choice (A): *w* − 2*p* = 6 − 6 = 0. Discard.

Choice (B): *w* − *p* + 1 = 6 − 3 + 1 = 4. Discard.

Choice (C): *w* − 2(*p* − 1) = 6 − 2(2) = 2. Hold.

Choice (D): *p* − 6 + *w* = 3 − 6 + 6 = 3. Discard.

Choice (E): $w - \frac{p}{2} = 6 - \frac{3}{2} = \frac{9}{2}$. Discard.

Since answer choice (C) is the only one that works, it must be the right answer.

21. E

The picket fence contains x pickets, each of $\frac{1}{2}$ inch width.

The total width of the pickets in the fence is $\frac{1}{2} \times (x)$ or $\frac{x}{2}$

inches. There are 12 inches in a foot, so the width of the

pickets in inches represents $\frac{x}{24}$ feet. (Divide to get the

larger unit.) Now we must find the total width between

the pickets. Are there x spaces between the x pickets? No.

Let's look at a simple example. Suppose there are 3 pick-

ets in the fence:

PICKETS

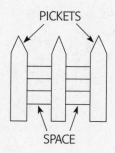

SPACE

Then there are 3 posts, but only 2 spaces between them.

In general, if there are x pickets in a straight fence, there

are $(x - 1)$ spaces between the pickets. Since each space

is 6 inches wide, the total width of the spaces is

$6(x - 1)$ inches, or $\frac{6(x - 1)}{12}$ feet.

Therefore, the total length of the fence in feet is

Pickets + spaces $= \frac{x}{24} + \frac{6(x - 1)}{12} = \frac{x}{24} + \frac{12(x - 1)}{24}$

$= \frac{13x - 12}{24}$

22. 9

Of the 7 people on committee A, 3 of them are also on
committee B, leaving $7 - 3$, or 4 people who are only on
committee A. Similarly, there are 8 people on committee
B; 3 of them are on both committees, leaving $8 - 3$, or 5
people only on committee B. There are 4 people only on
A, and 5 people only on B, making $4 + 5$ or 9 people on
only one committee.

23. 3/8, or .375

To avoid working with lots of fractions, pick a number for
the number of workers in the factory, one that is divisible
by all the denominators in the given ratios. Let's take 32 as
the total number of workers in the factory. There are 4 different groups of workers; make a chart to illustrate:

	Under 40	40+	Totals
Married	5	15	20
Unmarried		9	
Totals		24	32

The 4 groups of workers are (1) married and under 40,

(2) married and 40 or older, (3) unmarried and under

40, and (4) unmarried and 40 or older. The chart also

includes numbers for totals, so let's start by filling in as

many spaces as we can. The grand total of workers is

32. We're told $\frac{5}{8}$ are married so $\frac{5}{8} \times 32$, or 20, workers

are married. Put 20 in the "total married" slot. We're also

told that $\frac{3}{4}$ of the workers are at least 40, so put $\frac{3}{4} \times 32$,

or 24 in the "40+" slot. Now, we're told that $\frac{1}{4}$ of the

married workers are under 40. That means $\frac{1}{4} \times 20$, or

5, workers are married and under 40, so put a 5 in that

space. Since there are 20 total who are married and 5 of

KAPLAN

them are under 40, 15 must be 40 or older, so put a 15 in that space. Since the total number of workers 40 or older is 24, and the number of those who are married is 15, there must be 9 who are not married and 40 or older (24 − 15 = 9). The fraction of workers 40 or older who are not married is $\frac{9}{24}$, or $\frac{3}{8}$.

24. E

Each plot contains one poplar, and each plot is 1 meter in width. There are 16 meters between every two adjacent plots. Starting at the first poplar, there is 1 meter for the plot, plus 16 meters of space before the next plot, for a total of 17 meters. The second plot then takes up 1 meter, plus 16 meters of space between that plot and the third plot, or 17 more meters. So we need 17 meters for each plot and the space before the next plot. The street is $\frac{3}{8}$ kilometer long. We change this to meters by multiplying $\frac{3}{8}$ by 1,000—the number of meters in a kilometer. The street is 375 meters long. Each plot and the space before the next plot take up 17 meters, so we divide 17 into 375 to find the number of plots and spaces we can fit in: $\frac{375}{17}$ gives us 22 with 1 left over. This is the number of plots followed by a space. But there is no need for a space after the last plot—there is a space only between pairs of plots;

since there's no plot after the last one, there's no need to have a space there. So 374 meters contain 22 plots and the spaces between them, and then there is 1 more plot in the last meter of space, for a total of 23 poplars on each side. Since there are poplars on both sides of the street, we can fit 46 poplars in all.

25. 10

Use the combination formula: $\frac{n!}{k!(n-k)!}$, where n is the number of things in the group and k is the number of things in the subgroup. In this case, you have a group of 5 from which you must identify the number of permissible subgroups of 3, so:

$$\frac{5!}{3!2!} = \frac{5 \times 4 \times 3 \times 2 \times 1}{3 \times 2 \times 1 \times 2 \times 1} = \frac{5 \times 4}{2 \times 1} = 10.$$

Chapter Fourteen: **Lines and Angles**

Many of the basic geometry questions you'll see on the SAT have to do with lines and angles. An *angle* is the intersection of two rays that have the same end point or *vertex*. A *line* is a two-dimensional figure that has no endpoints. In other words, in geometric terms, a line goes on in both directions forever. There are several important kinds of lines to remember, like *parallel lines*, which are two lines that are always the same distance from one another and never intersect. *Perpendicular lines* are lines that intersect at a point and specifically form a 90 degree angle. Two lines that intersect at any other angle are just called *intersecting lines*. A *transversal* is a line that intersects two other lines. A *line segment* is just a part of a line with two endpoints. A *ray* is similar to a line, but instead of continuing on forever in both directions without any endpoints, it has one endpoint and goes on forever in one direction.

Acute, obtuse, straight, and right angles are all classified according to their degree measure. An *acute* angle is an angle that has a measure between 0 and 90 degrees. An *obtuse* angle is an angle that has a measure between 90 and 180 degrees. A *straight* angle is an angle that measures 180 degrees. A *right* angle is an angle that measures exactly 90 degrees.

There are several special pairs of angles. *Supplementary angles*, for instance, are two angles whose degree measure adds up to 180 degrees. *Complementary angles* are two angles whose degree measure adds up to 90 degrees. Two angles that are adjacent, and supplementary, and also have a non-shared side are known as a *linear pair*. Usually this pair of angles is formed by two intersecting lines. If you have two congruent angles that share a vertex and whose sides form two pairs of opposite rays, you have *vertical angles*.

Lines and angles are the subject of some of the more basic SAT geometry questions, and you'll need to understand the basics to tackle the more complicated stuff. This might sound like a lot, but you can handle it. For further reading:

76. Intersecting Lines
77. Parallel Lines and Transversals

Chapter Fourteen Practice Set
Answer Sheet

1. Ⓐ Ⓑ Ⓒ Ⓓ Ⓔ   9. Grid-in below
2. Ⓐ Ⓑ Ⓒ Ⓓ Ⓔ   10. Ⓐ Ⓑ Ⓒ Ⓓ Ⓔ
3. Ⓐ Ⓑ Ⓒ Ⓓ Ⓔ   11. Ⓐ Ⓑ Ⓒ Ⓓ Ⓔ
4. Ⓐ Ⓑ Ⓒ Ⓓ Ⓔ   12. Grid-in below
5. Ⓐ Ⓑ Ⓒ Ⓓ Ⓔ   13. Ⓐ Ⓑ Ⓒ Ⓓ Ⓔ
6. Grid-in below   14. Ⓐ Ⓑ Ⓒ Ⓓ Ⓔ
7. Ⓐ Ⓑ Ⓒ Ⓓ Ⓔ   15. Grid-in below
8. Grid-in below   16. Grid-in below

PRACTICE SET

Basic

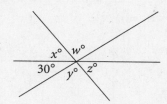

1. In the figure above, $w + x + y + z =$

   (A) 330
   (B) 300
   (C) 270
   (D) 240
   (E) 210

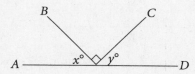

2. In the figure above, what is the value of $x + y$?

   (A) 30
   (B) 60
   (C) 90
   (D) 110
   (E) It cannot be determined from the information given.

3. If Y is the midpoint of line segment XZ, then which of the following is true?

   (A) $XY < YZ$

   (B) $YZ < XY$

   (C) $XZ < YZ$

   (D) $\frac{1}{2}XZ = 2XY$

   (E) $2YZ = XZ$

Medium

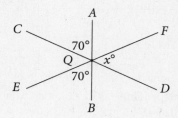

Note: Figure not drawn to scale.

4. In the figure above, $\overline{AB}$, $\overline{CD}$, and $\overline{EF}$ all intersect at point Q. What is the value of x?

   (A) 30
   (B) 40
   (C) 50
   (D) 60
   (E) 70

5. In $\overline{PS}$ above, $PQ = 3$, $RS = 4$, and $PS = 10$. What is the distance from S to the midpoint of $\overline{QR}$?

   (A) 4.5
   (B) 5.5
   (C) 6
   (D) 6.5
   (E) 7

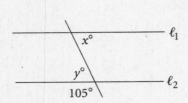

6. In the figure above, if $\ell_1 \parallel \ell_2$, then what is the value of $x + y$?

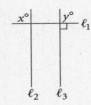

7. In the figure above, if $x = y$, which of the following MUST be true?

    I. $\ell_2 \parallel \ell_3$

    II. $\ell_1 \perp \ell_2$

    III. Any line that intersects ℓ_1 also intersects ℓ_2.

    (A) I only

    (B) II only

    (C) III only

    (D) I and II only

    (E) I, II, and III

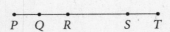

8. In the figure above, Q is the midpoint of $\overline{PR}$ and R is the midpoint of $\overline{PS}$. If $PT = 16$ and $QR = 3$, what is the length of ST?

9. What is the measure, in degrees, of the smaller of 2 angles that together form a straight line if the ratio of the measure of the larger angle to the smaller angle is 7 to 2?

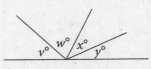

Note: Figure not drawn to scale.

10. In the figure above, $v = 2w$, $w = 2x$, and $x = \dfrac{y}{3}$. What is the value of y?

    (A) 18

    (B) 36

    (C) 45

    (D) 54

    (E) 60

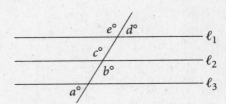

11. In the figure above, $\ell_1 \parallel \ell_2$ and $\ell_2 \parallel \ell_3$. What is the value of $a + b + c + d + e$?

    (A) 180

    (B) 270

    (C) 360

    (D) 450

    (E) It cannot be determined from the information given.

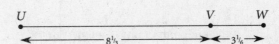

12. In the figure above, if X (not shown) is the midpoint of $\overline{UV}$, and if Y (not shown) is the midpoint of $\overline{VW}$, what is the length of $\overline{XY}$?

Hard

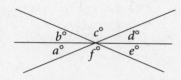

13. Which of the following must be true of the angles marked in the figure above?

    I. $a + b = d + e$

    II. $b + e = c + f$

    III. $a + c + e = b + d + f$

(A) I only

(B) I and II only

(C) I and III only

(D) II and III only

(E) I, II, and III

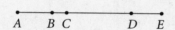

14. In the diagram above, $AD = BE = 6$ and $CD = 3(BC)$. If $AE = 8$, then $BC =$

(A) 6

(B) 4

(C) 3

(D) 2

(E) 1

15. In the figure above, the ratio of $\overline{AB}$ to $\overline{BC}$ is 5 to 3. If $AC = 1$, what is the distance from A to the point (not shown) that is $\dfrac{1}{3}$ of the distance from B to C.

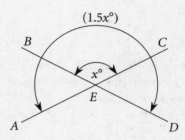

16. In the figure above, what is the degree measure of $\angle AEB$?

KAPLAN

ANSWERS AND EXPLANATIONS

Basic

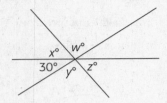

1. B

In the diagram, the unmarked angle and the 30° angle are vertical angles; therefore, the unmarked angle must also measure 30°. The sum of the measures of the angles around a point is 360°, so we can set up the following equation:

$$30 + x + w + 30 + z + y = 360$$

Rearranging the terms on the left side of the equation gives:

$$w + x + y + z + 60 = 360$$
$$w + x + y + z = 360 - 60 = 300$$

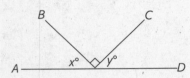

2. C

There's no way to find either x or y alone, but their sum is a different story. Since AD is a straight line, the angle marked $x°$, the angle marked $y°$, and the right angle together make up a straight angle, which measures 180°. So:

$$x + y + 90 = 180$$
$$x + y = 180 - 90 = 90$$

3. E

Draw line segment XZ with Y as its midpoint:

Since Y is the midpoint of XZ, $XY = YZ$. Therefore, choices (A) and (B) are false and can be eliminated. Choice (C) is false because the length of the whole segment cannot

be less than a part of the segment. Choice (D) is false because $2XY = XZ$. So choice (E) is correct because twice the length of half of the segment equals the whole segment.

4. B

Angle x is vertical, and therefore equal, to angle CQE. All the angles on one side of a straight line add up to 180 degrees, so $70 + 70 + m\angle CQE = 180$, so $m\angle CQE = 40$ degrees, and $x = 40$.

5. B

$$QR = PS - (PQ + RS)$$
$$QR = 10 - (3 + 4) = 10 - 7 = 3$$
$$\frac{QR}{2} = 1.5$$
$$\frac{QR}{2} + RS = 1.5 + 4 = 5.5$$

6. 150

The angles represented by $y°$ and 105° are supplementary because they form a straight line. Therefore, $y + 105 = 180$, and $y = 75$. Since $\ell_1 \parallel \ell_2$, angles y and x have equal measures because they are alternate interior angles. Therefore, $x = 75$.

So $x + y = 75 + 75$, or 150.

Medium

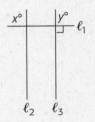

7. D

From the diagram, we see that the angle marked $y°$ is supplementary to a right angle. This means that y must be $180 - 90$, or 90. We are told that x equals y, so x must also be 90. This means that both ℓ_2 and ℓ_3 are perpendicular to ℓ_1; therefore, they must be parallel to each other. This means that, statements I and II are true. But statement III is not necessarily true. For instance, ℓ_3 intersects ℓ_1, but never meets ℓ_2.

8.   4

If $QR = 3$, $PQ = 3$. Then $PR = 6$, which means that RS is also 6 and that PS is therefore 12. If $PT = 16$ and $PS = 12$, ST must be $16 - 12 = 4$.

9.   40

If the angles together form a straight line, their sum is 180°. If the ratio of the larger to the smaller is 7 to 2, then 9—the sum of the parts of the ratio—relates to 180 in the same way that the parts themselves do. $\frac{180}{9} = 20$, so the larger angle is $7 \times 20 = 140$ and the smaller angle is $2 \times 20 = 40$.

10.   D

The sum $v + w + x + y$ must equal 180 since the angles with these measures together form a straight line. Since the question asks for the value of y, define all variables in terms of y. If $w = 2x$ and $x = \frac{y}{3}$, then $w = \frac{2y}{3}$. Similarly, $v = 2w$, so $v = 2\left(\frac{2y}{3}\right)$ or $\frac{4y}{3}$. Substitute the angles in terms of y into the equation:

$$v + w + x + y = 180$$

$$\frac{4y}{3} + \frac{2y}{3} + \frac{y}{3} + y = 180$$

$$\frac{7y}{3} + y = 180$$

$$\frac{10y}{3} = 180$$

$$y = \frac{3}{10} \times 180 = 3 \times 18 = 54.$$

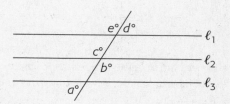

11. E

We're given that ℓ_1, ℓ_2, and ℓ_3 are all parallel to one another. Remember, when parallel lines are cut by a transversal, all acute angles formed by the transversal are equal, all obtuse angles are equal, and any acute angle is supplementary to any obtuse angle. We can get 2 pairs of supplementary angles from the 5 marked angles:

$$\underbrace{a + b}_{180} + \underbrace{c + d}_{180} + e$$

We're left with $360 + e$. Since we don't know the value of e, we cannot find the sum. So choice (E) is correct.

12. $\frac{23}{4}$, or 5.75

If X and Y are the midpoints of $\overline{UV}$ and $\overline{VW}$, respectively, then the length of XY equals half the length of the whole line segment UW.

$$UW = 8\frac{1}{3} + 3\frac{1}{6} = 8\frac{2}{6} + 3\frac{1}{6} \quad 11\frac{1}{2}, \text{ or } \frac{23}{2}.$$

So the length of $XY = \frac{1}{2} \times \frac{23}{2} = \frac{23}{4}$, or 5.75 in decimal form.

Hard

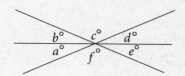

13. C

We have three pairs of vertical angles around the point of intersection: a and d, b and e, and c and f. Therefore, $a = d$, $b = e$, and $c = f$. Let's look at the three statements one at a time.

KAPLAN

I: $a + b = d + e$. Since $a = d$ and $b = e$, this is true. Eliminate choice (D).

II: $b + e = c + f$. We know that $b = e$ and $c = f$, but we don't how the pairs relate to each other. Statement II does not have to be true. Eliminate choices (B) and (E).

III: $a + c + e = b + d + f$. This is true, since $a = d$, $c = f$, and $b = e$. That is, we can match each angle on one side of the equation with a different angle on the other side. Statement III must be true.

Statements I and III must be true. So choice (C) is correct.

14. E

Since AE is a line segment, all the lengths are additive, so $AE = AD + DE$. We're told that $AD = 6$ and $AE = 8$. So $DE = AE - AD = 8 - 6 = 2$. We're also told that $BE = 6$. So $BD = BE - DE = 6 - 2 = 4$. We have the length of BD, but still need the length of BC. Since $CD = 3(BC)$, the situation looks like this:

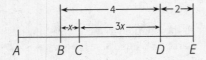

Here x stands for the length of BC. Since $BD = 4$, we can write:

$$x + 3x = 4$$
$$4x = 4$$
$$x = 1$$

So $BC = 1$, answer choice (E).

15. $\frac{3}{4}$ or .75

Begin by converting a part to part ratio to a part to whole ratio. If $\overline{AB}$ to $\overline{BC}$ is 5 to 3, then $\overline{AB}$ is $\frac{5}{8}$ of $\overline{AC}$ and $\overline{BC}$ is $\frac{3}{8}$ of $\overline{BC}$. So a point "that is $\frac{1}{3}$ of the distance from B to C" is $\frac{1}{3} \times \frac{3}{8} = \frac{1}{8}$. Having determined that AB is $\frac{5}{8}$, now add $\frac{5}{8}$ to $\frac{1}{8}$ to get $\frac{6}{8} = \frac{3}{4} = .75$.

16. 36

The angle measuring $(1.5x)°$ is made up of $\angle AEB$, $\angle BEC$, and $\angle CED$. That is, $m\angle AEB + m\angle BEC + m\angle CED = (1.5x)°$. We can rearrange this to get an expression for $m\angle AEB$, the angle we want. We get:

$$m\angle AEB = 1.5x° - m\angle BEC - m\angle CED$$

Since $m\angle BEC = x°$, substitute $x°$ for $m\angle BEC$:

$$m\angle AEB = 1.5x° - x° - m\angle CED$$
$$= 0.5x° - m\angle CED$$

Also, $\angle AEB$ and $\angle CED$ are vertical angles, so $m\angle AEB = m\angle CED$. Let's put this into our equation:

$$m\angle AEB = 0.5x° - m\angle AEB$$
$$2(m\angle AEB) = 0.5x°$$
$$m\angle AEB = 0.25x°$$

Now we need to find out what x is to get a value for $m\angle AEB$. Since $\angle AED$ and $\angle BEC$ are also vertical angles, $m\angle AED = m\angle BEC$, or $m\angle AED = x°$. Marking this in on our diagram, we see that the sum of all the angles around point E is $1.5x° + x° = 2.5x°$, which equals $360°$.

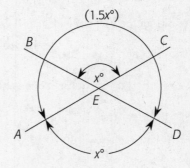

Therefore $2.5x = 360$, or $x = 144$.

Since the measure of $\angle AEB$ is $.25x°$, we get
$$m\angle AEB = .25(144°) = 36°.$$

Chapter Fifteen: **Triangles**

Triangles appear on the SAT as often as all of the other geometric figures combined! They are an SAT favorite, to be sure. The good news is that a triangle is the simplest *polygon* (many-sided figure) there is. It has three sides and three angles. The degree measure of the angles in any triangle—no matter how it's shaped or how big it is—will always add up to 180 degrees.

Triangles are generally classified in two ways—by side and by angle. Let's look at the classification of triangles by sides. There are three types of side classifications: *scalene, isosceles*, and *equilateral*. A scalene triangle has three sides of all different lengths. An isosceles triangle has two sides of equal length, often referred to as *legs*. Because of the equal sides in an isosceles triangle, the angles sitting opposite the equal sides also have to be equal. Finally, an equilateral triangle has three sides of equal length. Naturally, all of the angles have to be equal as well, and these triangles can sometimes be referred to as *equiangular*.

Now let's classify triangles by angles. When a triangle has three angles that are all individually less than 90 degrees, it's called an *acute triangle*. If you come across a triangle with one angle that is greater than 90 degrees, you have an *obtuse triangle*. So if you are given a triangle that has one angle that measures exactly 90 degrees, based on your knowledge of lines and angles, what kind of triangle do you think it is? If you're thinking *right triangle* you're correct. Now this next part might sound a little tricky, but bear with us. Triangles are classified by both side and angles, and therefore fall into two categories. For example a triangle that has a 90 degree angle and three sides of different length is a *right scalene triangle*.

The last thing that you need to know about triangles is the category we call *special triangles*. These triangles are special because each one conforms to a specific set of rules or characteristics. This category includes the 3-4-5 triangle, 5-12-13 triangle, 30-60-90 triangle, and 45-45-90 triangle. For further reading:

78. Interior and Exterior Angles of a Triangle

79. Similar Triangles

80. Area of a Triangle

81. Triangle Inequality Theorem

82. Isosceles and Equilateral Triangles

83. Pythagorean Theorem

84. The 3-4-5 Triangle

85. The 5-12-13 Triangle

86. The 30-60-90 Triangle

87. The 45-45-90 Triangle

Chapter Fifteen Practice Set
Answer Sheet

1. Grid-in below
2. Ⓐ Ⓑ Ⓒ Ⓓ Ⓔ
3. Ⓐ Ⓑ Ⓒ Ⓓ Ⓔ
4. Ⓐ Ⓑ Ⓒ Ⓓ Ⓔ
5. Ⓐ Ⓑ Ⓒ Ⓓ Ⓔ
6. Ⓐ Ⓑ Ⓒ Ⓓ Ⓔ
7. Ⓐ Ⓑ Ⓒ Ⓓ Ⓔ
8. Ⓐ Ⓑ Ⓒ Ⓓ Ⓔ
9. Ⓐ Ⓑ Ⓒ Ⓓ Ⓔ

10. Ⓐ Ⓑ Ⓒ Ⓓ Ⓔ
11. Grid-in below
12. Grid-in below
13. Ⓐ Ⓑ Ⓒ Ⓓ Ⓔ
14. Ⓐ Ⓑ Ⓒ Ⓓ Ⓔ
15. Grid-in below
16. Ⓐ Ⓑ Ⓒ Ⓓ Ⓔ
17. Grid-in below
18. Ⓐ Ⓑ Ⓒ Ⓓ Ⓔ

19. Ⓐ Ⓑ Ⓒ Ⓓ Ⓔ
20. Ⓐ Ⓑ Ⓒ Ⓓ Ⓔ
21. Ⓐ Ⓑ Ⓒ Ⓓ Ⓔ
22. Ⓐ Ⓑ Ⓒ Ⓓ Ⓔ
23. Grid-in below
24. Ⓐ Ⓑ Ⓒ Ⓓ Ⓔ
25. Grid-in below
26. Grid-in below
27. Grid-in below

28. Ⓐ Ⓑ Ⓒ Ⓓ Ⓔ
29. Ⓐ Ⓑ Ⓒ Ⓓ Ⓔ
30. Ⓐ Ⓑ Ⓒ Ⓓ Ⓔ
31. Ⓐ Ⓑ Ⓒ Ⓓ Ⓔ
32. Ⓐ Ⓑ Ⓒ Ⓓ Ⓔ
33. Ⓐ Ⓑ Ⓒ Ⓓ Ⓔ

34. Grid-in below

1.  11. 12. 15. 17.

23. 25. 26. 27. 34.

KAPLAN

PRACTICE SET

Basic

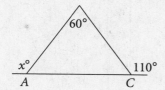

1. In the figure above, $x =$

2. In the figure above, $x = 2z$ and $y = 3z$. What is the value of z?

   (A) 24
   (B) 30
   (C) 36
   (D) 54
   (E) 60

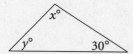

3. In the figure above, what is x in terms of y?

   (A) $150 - y$
   (B) $150 + y$
   (C) $80 + y$
   (D) $30 + y$
   (E) $30 - y$

4. The angles of a triangle are in the ratio of 2:3:4. What is the degree measure of the largest angle?

   (A) 40
   (B) 80
   (C) 90
   (D) 120
   (E) 150

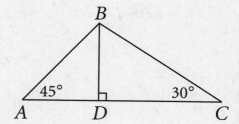

5. In the figure above, if $AB = 2$, what is the length of BC?

   (A) $\sqrt{2}$
   (B) 2
   (C) $2\sqrt{2}$
   (D) 3
   (E) $\sqrt{6}$

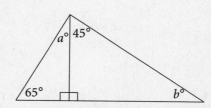

Note: Figure not drawn to scale.

6. In the figure above, what is the value of $a + b$?

   (A) 45
   (B) 70
   (C) 90
   (D) 145
   (E) 170

KAPLAN

7. If two sides of a triangle are 8 and 5, each of the following could be the measure of the third side EXCEPT

   (A) 4
   (B) 5
   (C) 8
   (D) 12
   (E) 13

8. If the area of a right triangle is 15, what is its perimeter?

   (A) 11
   (B) 15
   (C) 16
   (D) 17
   (E) The answer cannot be determined from the information provided.

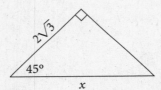

9. In the figure above, what is the measure of x ?

   (A) $2\sqrt{3}$
   (B) $2\sqrt{6}$
   (C) 6
   (D) $6\sqrt{2}$
   (E) 8

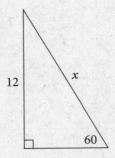

10. In the figure above, what is the measure of x?

    (A) $6\sqrt{2}$
    (B) 12
    (C) $8\sqrt{2}$
    (D) $8\sqrt{3}$
    (E) 14

11. If the perimeter of isosceles triangle ABC is 20 and the length of side AC is 8, what is one possible value for the length of side BC ?

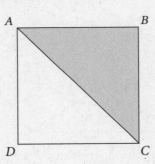

12. In square ABCD shown above, if AC = 5, what is the area of the shaded region?

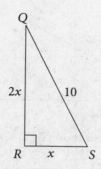

13. In the figure above, what is the area of right $\triangle QRS$?

(A) $4\sqrt{5}$

(B) 10

(C) $8\sqrt{5}$

(D) 20

(E) 40

Medium

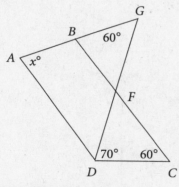

14. In the figure above, if $AD \parallel BC$, then $x =$

(A) 20

(B) 30

(C) 50

(D) 60

(E) 70

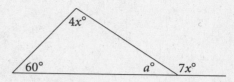

Note: Figure not drawn to scale.

15. What is the value of a in the figure above?

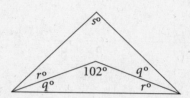

Note: Figure not drawn to scale.

16. In the figure above, what is the value of s?

(A) 12

(B) 24

(C) 78

(D) 102

(E) 156

17. A circle and a triangle lie in a plane. What is the maximum number of points at which the circle and the triangle could intersect?

18. If the 3 interior angles of a triangle are x degrees, $x - 4$ degrees and $2x$ degrees, which of the following must be true:

   I.   The triangle is right.

   II. $3x - 5 = 133$

   III.   If the measure of the smallest angle is increased by 48 degrees, the resulting angle would be right.

(A) I only

(B) II only

(C) III only

(D) II and III only

(E) None of the above

KAPLAN

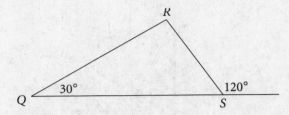

Note: Figure not drawn to scale.

19. In the figure above, what is the measure of ∠BED?

(A) 40°

(B) 55°

(C) 65°

(D) 80°

(E) It cannot be determined from the information given.

20. What is the length of the hypotenuse of an isosceles right triangle with an area of 32?

(A) 4

(B) $4\sqrt{2}$

(C) 8

(D) $8\sqrt{2}$

(E) $\sqrt{3}$

21. In $\triangle QRS$ shown above, if $QS = 6$, $RS =$

(A) 12

(B) $6\sqrt{3}$

(C) 6

(D) $3\sqrt{3}$

(E) 3

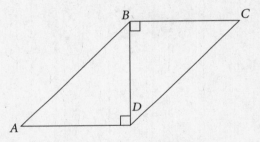

Note: Figure not drawn to scale.

22. If $AD = 2CD$ and $BD = BC = 6$, what is the length of AB?

(A) $6\sqrt{2}$

(B) 9

(C) 12

(D) $12\sqrt{2}$

(E) 18

KAPLAN

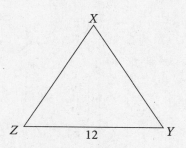

23. If $\angle XYZ \cong \angle XZY$ and the area of $\triangle XYZ$ is 48, what is the perimeter of the figure above?

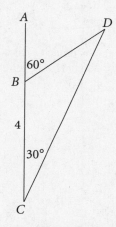

24. In the figure above, if $\angle DBA$ has measure 60°, $\angle DCB$ has measure 30°, and $BC = 4$, what is the length of BD?

    (A) $\sqrt{2}$

    (B) 4

    (C) $4\sqrt{2}$

    (D) $4\sqrt{3}$

    (E) 8

25. What is the area of an isosceles right triangle with a hypotenuse of 2?

Hard

26. The length of each side of a certain triangle is an even number. If no two of the sides have the same length, what is the smallest perimeter the triangle could have?

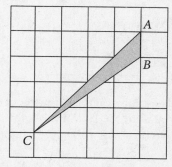

27. The figure above consists of 36 squares, each with a side of 1. What is the area of $\triangle ABC$?

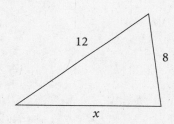

28. Based on the figure above, if x is an integer, what is the probability that x is even?

    (A) $\dfrac{1}{5}$

    (B) $\dfrac{2}{5}$

    (C) $\dfrac{7}{15}$

    (D) $\dfrac{1}{20}$

    (E) $\dfrac{2}{25}$

KAPLAN

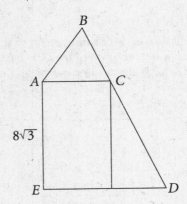

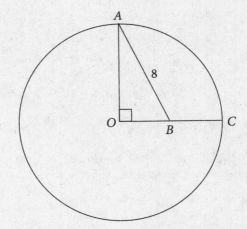

29. In the figure above, if the perimeter of equilateral $\triangle ABC$ is 24, and $AC \parallel ED$, what is the perimeter of $ABDE$?

    (A) $12(3 + \sqrt{3})$

    (B) $8(6 + \sqrt{3})$

    (C) $4(17 + 7\sqrt{3})$

    (D) $72\sqrt{3}$

    (E) $8(3 + 11\sqrt{3})$

31. In the figure above, circle O has a circumference of 12π. If $AB = 8$, what is the length of BC?

    (A) $2\sqrt{7}$

    (B) $2(3 - \sqrt{7})$

    (C) $2(6 - \sqrt{7})$

    (D) $4\sqrt{5}$

    (E) $2(3 - 2\sqrt{5})$

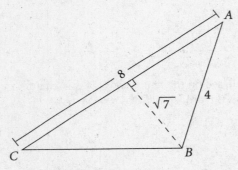

Note: Figure not drawn to scale.

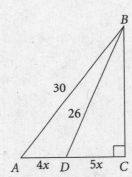

30. In the above figure, what is the length of BC?

    (A) $4\sqrt{2}$

    (B) $4\sqrt{3}$

    (C) $4\sqrt{5}$

    (D) $\sqrt{74}$

    (E) $4\sqrt{7}$

32. What is the length of BC in the figure above?

    (A) 10

    (B) 16

    (C) 18

    (D) 20

    (E) 24

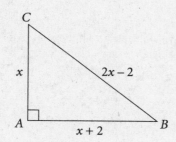

33. In right triangle ABC above, $x =$

    (A) 6
    (B) 8
    (C) $6\sqrt{2}$
    (D) 10
    (E) 13

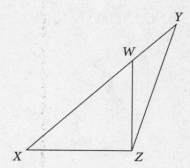

Note: Figure not drawn to scale.

34. In the figure above, the ratio of the area of $\triangle WXZ$ to the area of $\triangle WYZ$ is 7:2. If $XY = 21$, what is the length of segment WY?

KAPLAN

ANSWERS AND EXPLANATIONS

Basic

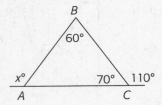

1. 130

The angle with measure $x°$ is an exterior angle of the triangle; therefore it must equal the sum of the 2 remote interior angles: $\angle ABC$ and $\angle BCA$. $\angle ABC$ has a measure of 60°. Since $\angle BCA$ is supplementary to the angle marked 110°, its measure must be 180° − 110°, or 70°. Therefore, $x = 60 + 70$, or 130.

2. C

Since the angle marked $x°$ and the angle marked $y°$ together form a straight angle, their measures must sum to 180°.

Substitute in $2z$ for x and $3z$ for y, and solve for z.

$$x + y = 180$$
$$2z + 3z = 180$$
$$5z = 180$$
$$z = \frac{1}{5} \times 180 = 36$$
$$z = 36$$

3. A

Once again, we are dealing with the sum of the interior angles in a triangle. We can write:

$$x + y + 30 = 180$$
$$x + y = 180 - 30$$
$$x + y = 150$$

Subtracting y from each side, we find that

$$x = 150 - y.$$

4. B

The measures of the three interior angles are in the ratio of 2:3:4, and they must add up to 180 degrees. So the 3 angles must have degree measures that are $2x$, $3x$, and $4x$. Find x:

$$2x + 3x + 4x = 180$$
$$9x = 180$$
$$x = 20$$

The largest angle has measure $4x$, or $4(20)$, which is 80.

5. C

$\triangle ABD$ has one angle of 90 degrees and another of 45 degrees. Therefore, it is an isosceles right triangle, with sides in the ratio $1:1:\sqrt{2}$. Since the hypotenuse is 2, the length of the legs must be $\frac{2}{\sqrt{2}} = \sqrt{2}$. $\triangle BCD$ has an angle of 30 degrees and another of 90 degrees. Therefore it is a 30-60-90 right triangle, with sides in the ratio $1:\sqrt{3}:2$. Since BD, the shorter leg, has a length of $\sqrt{2}$, the length of the hypotenuse must be twice this, or $2\sqrt{2}$.

6. B

You are given 2 right triangles, so off the bat you already know the measure of one of the angles in each triangle. You're also given the measure of an additional angle in each triangle. Armed with the knowledge that the sum of all the angles in any triangle will always be 180 degrees, all you have to do is subtract the sum of the given angles in each separate triangle from 180 to get a and b, and then add a and b. It should look like this:

$$180 - (65 + 90) = 25$$

$$180 - (45 + 90) = 45$$

$$45 + 25 = 70$$

or

$$65 + (a + 45) + b = 180$$

$$110 + a + b = 180$$

$$a + b = 70.$$

7.   E

Any side of a triangle must be greater than the difference and less than the sum of the other 2 sides. So the third side of this triangle must be greater than $8 - 5 = 3$, and less than $8 + 5 = 13$.

8.   E

Area of a triangle $= \left(\frac{1}{2}\right)bh$, so $15 = \left(\frac{1}{2}\right)bh$. From this, we can say that $bh = 30$—but that's all that can be said. Because b and h could have an infinite number of values, the question cannot be answered.

9.   B

In a 45-45-90 right triangle, the legs are equal, and the hypotenuse is the measure of a leg, multiplied by $\sqrt{2}$, so $x = 2\sqrt{3} \times \sqrt{2} = 2\sqrt{6}$.

10. D

Use the rules of 30-60-90 right triangles to solve for x. The side opposite 30 degrees is always half the hypotenuse; the side opposite 60 degrees is always whatever the side opposite 30 is , with $\sqrt{3}$ attached. Here the side opposite 30 is $\frac{x}{2}$, and the side opposite 60 is $\frac{x\sqrt{3}}{2}$:

$$\frac{x\sqrt{3}}{2} = 12$$

$$x\sqrt{3} = 24$$

$$x = \frac{24}{\sqrt{3}}$$

$$x = \frac{24}{\sqrt{3}} \times \frac{\sqrt{3}}{\sqrt{3}} = \frac{24\sqrt{3}}{3} = 8\sqrt{3}$$

11. 4, 6 or 8,

There are 3 possible ways to draw isosceles triangle ABC with a perimeter of 20 and AC with a length of 8:

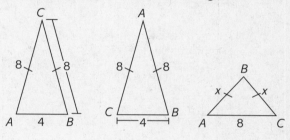

In the first case, AC and BC are the 2 equal sides in the isosceles triangle. Therefore, the length of BC is 8.

In the second case, AC and AB are the 2 equal sides. Therefore, the length of BC is $20 - 8 - 8$, or 4.

In the third case, BC and AB are the 2 equal sides. Let x represent the length of BC and AB. You know that the perimeter is 20, so $AC + BC + AB = 20$, or $8 + x + x = 20$. Solving for x, you find that $x = 6$. Therefore, the length of BC in this case is 6.

You're asked to find only one possible value for BC, so you can give 4, 6, or 8 and still be correct.

12. 25/4, or 6.25

Since *ABCD* is a square, diagonal *AC* divides it into two isosceles right triangles, one of which is shaded $\triangle ABC$. In an isosceles or 45-45-90 right triangle, the hypotenuse is equal to the length of a leg times $\sqrt{2}$. So leg $\times \sqrt{2} = AC$

$$\text{leg} \times \sqrt{2} = 5$$

$$\text{leg} = \frac{5}{\sqrt{2}}$$

The area of a triangle is $\frac{1}{2}$(base × height):

$$\text{area} = \left(\frac{1}{2} \frac{5}{\sqrt{2}} \times \frac{5}{\sqrt{2}}\right)$$

$$= \frac{1}{2}\left(\frac{25}{\sqrt{2} \times \sqrt{2}}\right)$$

$$= \frac{1}{2} \times \frac{25}{2}$$

$$= \frac{25}{4}$$

13. D

The area of a triangle is $\frac{1}{2}$(base × height). Since *QRS* is a right triangle, use the Pythagorean theorem—the sum of the squares of the 2 legs equals the square of the hypotenuse—to solve for each of these lengths:

$$x^2 + (2x)^2 = 10^2$$

$$x^2 + 4x^2 = 100$$

$$5x^2 = 100$$

$$x^2 = 20$$

$$x = \sqrt{20} = \sqrt{4} \times \sqrt{5} = 2\sqrt{5}$$

So the base is $2\sqrt{5}$ and the height is

$$2 \times 2\sqrt{5} = 4\sqrt{5}.$$

$$\text{Area} = \frac{1}{2}(2\sqrt{5})(4\sqrt{5})$$

$$= \frac{1}{2}(2 \times 4)(\sqrt{5} \times \sqrt{5})$$

$$= \frac{1}{2} \times 8 \times 5$$

$$= 20$$

Medium

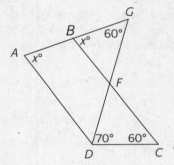

14. E

Since *BC* is parallel to *AD*, $\angle GBF$ must have the same degree measure as *x* (two parallel lines cut by transversal *AG*). Finding *x*, then, is the same as finding the measure of $\angle GBF$.

Let's look at $\triangle BFG$ and $\triangle DCF$. The 2 interior angles of these 2 triangles at point *F* must have the same degree measure, since they are a pair of vertical angles. In addition, each triangle has a 60 degree angle. Since we have 2 triangles with 2 pairs of equal angles, the third pair of angles must be equal, too, because the sum of all 3 angles in any triangle is 180 degrees. The third angle in $\triangle DCF$ has measure 70 degrees; therefore, $\angle GBF = x° = 70°$.

15. 40

The exterior angle of a triangle equals the sum of the 2 remote interior angles, so $7x = 4x + 60$, or $3x = 60$, or $x = 20$. The angle marked *a*° and that marked $7x°$ are supplementary, so $a + 7x = 180$, or $a + 7(20) = 180$, or $a = 40$.

Alternatively, you may have seen that the angle marked $a°$ and that marked $7x°$ were supplementary, which means that $a = 180 - 7x$. Since the sum of the interior angles of a triangle is 180°, $60 + 4x + (180 - 7x) = 180$. That is $4x - 7x = 180 - 60 - 180$, or $-3x = -60$, or $x = 20$. If $x = 20$, and $a = 180 - 7x$, then $a = 180 - 7(20) = 40$.

16. B

In smaller triangle, $q + r + 102 = 180$. Therefore, $q + r = 78$. The 2 lower angles of the quadrilateral are also $q + r$, and thus also equal to 78. The angles of the larger triangle can be related as $78 + 78 + s = 180$, so $s = 24$.

17. 6

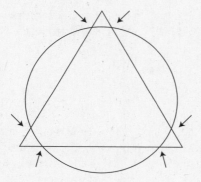

18. D

Because the angles in a triangle sum to 180 degrees, $x + (x - 4) + 2x = 180$. So $4x - 4 = 180$ and $4x = 184$, so $x = 46$. The 3 angles are $x = 46$ degrees, $x - 4 = 46 - 4 = 42$ degrees, and $2x = 2(46) = 92$ degrees. The greatest angle in the triangle is 92 degrees, so I is false and (A) can be eliminated. $3x - 5 = 3(46) - 5 = 138 - 5 = 133$, so II is true, and we can eliminate (C) and (E). $42 + 48 = 90$, so III is true.

19. B

Find x first. The sum of the angles of quadrilateral $DBCF$ is 360 degrees. Therefore, $2x + 75 + 85 + 2x = 360$, or $4x = 200$, so $x = 50$. In $\triangle DBE$, $x° + 75° + m\angle BED = 180°$, $50° + 75° + m\angle BED = 180°$, or $m\angle BED = 55°$.

20. D

The area of a right triangle is $\frac{1}{2}(\text{leg}_1 \times \text{leg}_2)$. Since an isosceles right triangle has legs of the same length, this equals $\frac{1}{2}(\text{leg})^2$. So $\frac{1}{2}(\text{leg})^2 = 32$, $(\text{leg})^2 = 64$, and leg $= \sqrt{64} = 8$. Therefore, the triangle has legs of length 8.

In an isosceles right triangle, the ratio of either leg to the hypotenuse is $1:\sqrt{2}$, so here the hypotenuse must be $8\sqrt{2}$ in length.

21. E

$\angle QSR$ is 60 degrees because it is supplementary to the exterior 120 degree angle. Therefore, $\angle QRS$ is 90 degrees because the sum of the measures of the angles of a triangle equals 180. So $\triangle QRS$ is a 30-60-90 right triangle, with side lengths in a ratio of $1:\sqrt{3}:2$. Since QS is 6, and it is the side opposite the 90 degree angle (i.e., it is the hypotenuse), it is twice the length of RS, the side opposite the 30 degree angle. Therefore, $RS = 3$.

22. E

Since $BD = BC$, $\triangle BCD$ is an isosceles right triangle. So the legs and the hypotenuse are in the ratio $1:1:\sqrt{2}$. Since the legs have length 6, CD has length $6\sqrt{2}$. Since $AD = 2CD$, $AD = 12\sqrt{2}$. By the Pythagorean theorem:

$$AB^2 = BD^2 + AD^2$$
$$= 6^2 + (12\sqrt{2})^2$$
$$= 36 + 288$$
$$= 324$$

So $AB = \sqrt{324} = 18$.

23. 32

Since $\angle XYZ \cong \angle XZY$, the sides opposite those angles are equal. Thus $XY = XZ$, so $\triangle XYZ$ is isosceles. To find the missing side lengths, you can divide $\triangle XYZ$ into 2 congruent right triangles:

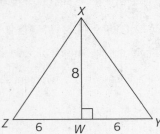

Let YZ be the base of $\triangle XYZ$. The altitude (height) is the

perpendicular line drawn from X to YZ. Since the area of a

triangle equals $\frac{1}{2} \times$ base $\times$ height, $\frac{1}{2} \times 12 \times XW = 48$, or

$XW = 8$. Now the altitude divides the base of $\triangle XYZ$ in half.

So $WY = 6$. $\triangle XWY$ is a special right triangle: Its sides are in

the ratio 6:8:10 (a multiple of 3:4:5). Therefore,

$XY = 10$, so $XZ = 10$ as well. So the perimeter of

$\triangle XYZ = 10 + 10 + 12 = 32$.

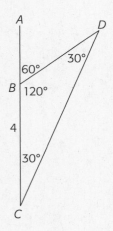

24. B

If $\angle DBA$ has a measure of 60 degrees, $\angle CBD$, which is supplementary to it, must have a measure of $180 - 60$, or 120 degrees.

$\angle BCD$ has a measure of 30 degrees; that leaves $180 - (120 + 30)$, or 30 degrees for the remaining interior angle: BDC.

Since $\angle BCD$ has the same measure as $\angle BDC$, $\triangle BCD$ is an isosceles triangle, and the sides opposite the equal angles will have equal lengths. Therefore, BD must have the same length as BC, 4.

25. 1

If an isosceles right triangle, the legs are equal, and the hypotenuse is the product of $\sqrt{2}$ and the measure of a leg. If 2 is the hypotenuse, each leg must be $\sqrt{2}$, because $\sqrt{2} \times \sqrt{2} = 2$. The area of a triangle is half the product of its base and height. In the case of an isosceles right triangle, base and height are equal and can simply be called x.

So the area is $\frac{x^2}{2} = \frac{(\sqrt{2}^2)}{2} = \frac{2}{2} = 1$.

Hard

26. 18

Let's try some numbers for the sides of the triangle. Keep in mind that the sum of any 2 sides of a triangle is always greater than the third side. Since we want to know the *smallest* perimeter possible, let's start with the smallest possible numbers. How about 2, 4, and 6? These are the 3 smallest distinct positive even numbers (we can't have negative lengths), but we can't make a triangle out of them, since the largest number is *not* less than the sum of the 2 smaller ones. The next 2 smallest combinations (2, 4, 8; and 2, 6, 8) can be crossed off for the same reason. Now try 4, 6, and 8: $4 + 6 > 8$; $6 + 8 > 4$; $4 + 8 > 6$. So the smallest possible perimeter is $4 + 6 + 8$, or 18.

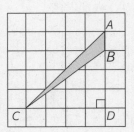

27. 2

(Note that we've added point D for clarity.) The area of a

triangle is $\frac{1}{2} \times$ base $\times$ height. If we treat AB as the base of

$\triangle ABC$, then the triangle's height is CD. Each square has side 1, so we can count the squares. $AB = 1$ and $CD = 4$, so the area is $\frac{1}{2} \times 1 \times 4 = 2$.

28. C

This question pulls together two topics that don't often cross paths: probability and the Triangle Inequality Theorem. The latter requires that in any triangle, the measure of any side be less than the sum of, but greater than the difference between, the 2 other sides. So x must be less than 20 and greater than 4. Given that x is an integer, you're left with these possibilities: 5, 6, 7, 8, 9, 10, 11, 12, 13, 14, 15, 16, 17, 18, 19. Probability is the number of desired outcomes over the number of possible outcomes. The possible outcomes in this situation are those 15 numbers just identified; the desired outcomes are the 7 integers in that set. So the probability that x is even is $\frac{7}{15}$.

29. B

Since $\triangle ABC$ is equilateral, its sides are the same length. So the length of any one side is $\frac{1}{3}$ of the perimeter. So $AC = AB = BC = \frac{24}{3} = 8$. Label the diagram accordingly. Draw a line from C perpendicular to DE at point F as shown:

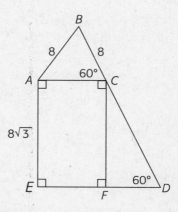

This forms rectangle $ACFE$. Side CF has the same length as opposite side AE, so it also equals $8\sqrt{3}$. Since AC and ED are parallel, $\angle FDC$ has the same measure as $\angle ACB$—that is, 60 degrees. You should recognize that $\triangle CDF$ is a 30-60-90 triangle with side lengths in a ratio of $1:\sqrt{3}:2$. So $FD = 8$ and $CD = 16$. So the perimeter of $ABDE = 8 + 24 + 16 + 8\sqrt{3}$, or $48 + 8\sqrt{3}$, or $8(6 + \sqrt{3})$.

30. A

If you turn the diagram around so that side AC is horizontal, it is easier to notice that the perpendicular dotted-line segment from point B divides $\triangle ABC$ into 2 right triangles. Label the point where this perpendicular line meets AC point D. BC is the hypotenuse of right $\triangle BDC$, and its leg BD is labeled as $\sqrt{7}$; if you knew the length of its other leg DC, you could use the Pythagorean theorem to find the length of BC. The other right triangle, ADB, shares leg BD, and its hypotenuse AB is of the length 4; use the Pythagorean theorem to find the length of its other leg AD:

$$(\sqrt{7})^2 + AD^2 = 4^2$$
$$7 + AD^2 = 16$$
$$AD^2 = 9$$
$$AD = 3$$

Since $AC = AD + DC$, $8 = 3 + DC$, so $DC = 5$. Now you can use the Pythagorean theorem to find BC :

$$(\sqrt{7})^2 + 5^2 = BC^2$$
$$7 + 25 = BC^2$$
$$32 = BC^2$$
$$\sqrt{32} = BC$$
$$\sqrt{16} \times \sqrt{2} = BC$$
$$4\sqrt{2} = BC$$

31. B

If the circumference of the circle O is 12π its radius is 6. (Remember, circumference = $2\pi r$.) Radius OC is made up of OB and BC, so the length of $BC = 6 - OB$. Since OB is a leg of right $\triangle AOB$, use the Pythagorean theorem to find its length. OA is a radius of the circle, so it must also be 6, and you are told that AB is 8, so:

$$6^2 + OB^2 = 8^2$$
$$36 + OB^2 = 64$$
$$OB^2 = 28$$
$$OB = \sqrt{28} = \sqrt{4} \times \sqrt{7} = 2\sqrt{7}$$

So $BC = 6 - 2\sqrt{7} = 2(3 - \sqrt{7})$

32. E

You can find the length of BC from the Pythagorean theorem, if you know the length of either AC or DC.

From the Pythagorean theorem: $AB^2 = AC^2 + BC^2$ and $BD^2 = DC^2 + BC^2$

So $BC^2 = AB^2 - AC^2$ and $BC^2 = BD^2 - DC^2$

So $AB^2 - AC^2 = BD^2 - DC^2$
$$30^2 - (9x)^2 = 26^2 - (5x)^2$$
$$900 - 81x^2 = 676 - 25x^2$$
$$900 - 676 = 81x^2 - 25x^2$$
$$224 = 56x^2$$
$$4 = x^2$$
$$2 = x$$

So $DC = 5 \times 2 = 10$ and $AC = 9 \times 2 = 18$.

You might recognize $\triangle ABC$ as a 3-4-5 right triangle, or $\triangle BCD$ as a 5-12-13 right triangle and so be able to calculate immediately that $BC = 24$. If not, use the Pythagorean theorem:

$$BC^2 = BD^2 - DC^2$$
$$= 26^2 - 10^2$$
$$= 576$$
$$BC = \sqrt{576} = 24$$

33. A

Using the Pythagorean theorem, we know that $BC^2 = AB^2 + AC^2$.

$$(2x - 2)^2 = (x + 2)^2 + x^2$$

Expand using FOIL:

$$4x^2 - 8x + 4 = 2x^2 + 4x + 4$$
$$4x^2 - 8x - 2x^2 - 4x = 4 - 4$$
$$2x^2 - 12x = 0$$

Factor out $2x$:

$$2x\,(x - 6) = 0$$

So $x = 0$ or $x = 6$. But $CA = x$, and CA is a length and therefore cannot be equal to zero. So $x = 6$.

34. 14/3 or 4.66 or 4.67

If you regard WX as the base of $\triangle WXZ$ and WY as the base of $\triangle WYZ$, you will notice that both triangles share the same altitude. We don't know its value, but since it is the same in each triangle, the ratio of the base WX of $\triangle WXZ$ to the base WY of $\triangle WYZ$ is 7:2. So the ratio of WX to WY is 7:2. Since these 2 segments make up XY, which has a length of 21:

$$7x + 2x = 21$$
$$9x = 21$$
$$x = \frac{7}{3}$$

$$WY = 2x = \frac{14}{3}.$$

Chapter Sixteen: **Quadrilaterals and Other Polygons**

As you know, a polygon is a many-sided figure. *Quadrilaterals* are polygons that specifically have four sides. Like any other polygon, quadrilaterals have special characteristics. The sum of the degree measure of the individual angles in any quadrilateral, for instance, will always add up to 360 degrees. Quadrilaterals are the second most common shape in geometry, as they include everything from *squares* to *trapezoids*.

A *parallelogram* is a particularly special kind of quadrilateral; it always has two opposite sides that are parallel to one another and of equal measure. It has other special characteristics as well; its diagonal will always create two congruent triangles.

It's not very often that you'll come across a polygon with more than four sides on the SAT, but it does happen. You won't have to know what to call it or how to apply an innovative use for it, but you might have to find the sum of the measure of the angles. There is a formula for this: In order to find the sum (S) of the measure of the angles, you need to subtract 2 from the number of sides (n) and multiply that answer by 180 degrees. The equation looks like this: $S = (n - 2)180°$. So if you have a 12-sided figure, the equation would be $S = (12 - 2)180°$. That reduces to $S = (10)180°$ or $1,800°$. For further reading:

88. Characteristics of a Rectangle

89. Characteristics of a Parallelogram

90. Characteristics of a Square

91. Interior Angles of a Polygon

Chapter Sixteen Practice Set
Answer Sheet

1. Ⓐ Ⓑ Ⓒ Ⓓ Ⓔ
2. Grid-in below
3. Ⓐ Ⓑ Ⓒ Ⓓ Ⓔ
4. Ⓐ Ⓑ Ⓒ Ⓓ Ⓔ
5. Ⓐ Ⓑ Ⓒ Ⓓ Ⓔ
6. Ⓐ Ⓑ Ⓒ Ⓓ Ⓔ
7. Grid-in below
8. Ⓐ Ⓑ Ⓒ Ⓓ Ⓔ
9. Grid-in below
10. Ⓐ Ⓑ Ⓒ Ⓓ Ⓔ

11. Ⓐ Ⓑ Ⓒ Ⓓ Ⓔ
12. Ⓐ Ⓑ Ⓒ Ⓓ Ⓔ
13. Ⓐ Ⓑ Ⓒ Ⓓ Ⓔ
14. Grid-in below
15. Ⓐ Ⓑ Ⓒ Ⓓ Ⓔ
16. Ⓐ Ⓑ Ⓒ Ⓓ Ⓔ
17. Ⓐ Ⓑ Ⓒ Ⓓ Ⓔ
18. Ⓐ Ⓑ Ⓒ Ⓓ Ⓔ
19. Ⓐ Ⓑ Ⓒ Ⓓ Ⓔ
20. Ⓐ Ⓑ Ⓒ Ⓓ Ⓔ

2.

7.

9.

14.

PRACTICE SET

Basic

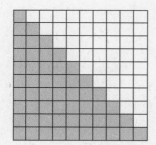

1. If each of the small squares in the figure above has area 1, what is the area of the shaded region?

   (A) 50
   (B) 55
   (C) 59
   (D) 60
   (E) 61

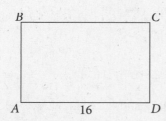

2. In the figure above, if the perimeter of rectangle *ABCD* is 56, and if the length of *AD* = 16, what is the area of *ABCD*?

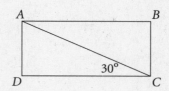

3. In the diagram above, *AD* = 4. What is the measure of $\overline{CD}$?

   (A) 4
   (B) 4.5
   (C) $4\sqrt{2}$
   (D) $4\sqrt{3}$
   (E) 8

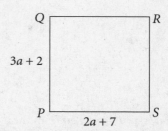

4. In the figure above, if *PQRS* is a square, what is the value of *a* ?

   (A) $\dfrac{9}{5}$

   (B) $\dfrac{9}{2}$

   (C) 5

   (D) 7

   (E) 9

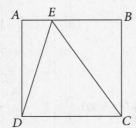

5. What is the ratio of the area of $\triangle DEC$ to the area of square $ABCD$ in the figure above?

(A) $\dfrac{1}{4}$

(B) $\dfrac{1}{3}$

(C) $\dfrac{1}{2}$

(D) $\dfrac{2}{1}$

(E) It cannot be determined from the information given.

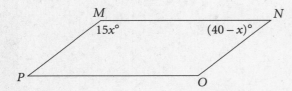

6. In the figure above, $MNOP$ is a parallelogram. What is the value of x?

(A) 20

(B) 10

(C) 5

(D) $\dfrac{25}{7}$

(E) $\dfrac{5}{2}$

7. The area of a certain rectangle is 36. If the ratio of the length of the rectangle to the width of the rectangle is 4 to 1, what is the perimeter of the rectangle?

Medium

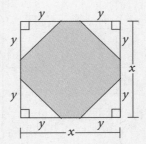

8. In the figure above, what is the area of the shaded region?

(A) $x^2 - y^2$

(B) $x^2 - 2y^2$

(C) $x^2 - 4y^2$

(D) $(x - y)(x - y)$

(E) $(x - 2y)(x - 2y)$

9. If the length of rectangle A is $\dfrac{1}{2}$ the length of rectangle B, and the width of rectangle A is $\dfrac{1}{2}$ the width of rectangle B, what is the ratio of the area of rectangle A to the area of rectangle B?

10. In quadrilateral $DEFG$, the degree measures of its 4 angles are in the ratio of 2:3:5:6. What is the difference in the degree measures between the largest and smallest angles?

(A) 135

(B) 112.5

(C) 90

(D) 67.5

(E) 45

11. What is the area of a regular hexagon with a perimeter of 6?

    (A) $\dfrac{3\sqrt{3}}{2}$

    (B) $\dfrac{3\sqrt{2}}{2}$

    (C) $\dfrac{2\sqrt{6}}{3}$

    (D) $\dfrac{3\sqrt{3}}{4}$

    (E) $\dfrac{\sqrt{3}}{4}$

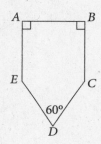 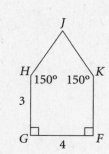

12. In the figure above, polygon *ABCDE* is congruent to polygon *FGHJK*. What is the area of polygon *ABCDE*?

    (A) 12
    (B) 16
    (C) $9 + 4\sqrt{3}$
    (D) $12 + 2\sqrt{3}$
    (E) $12 + 4\sqrt{3}$

13. In quadrilateral *ABCD*, $\angle A + \angle B + \angle C = 2(\angle D)$. What is the degree measure of $\angle D$?

    (A) 90
    (B) 120
    (C) 135
    (D) 270
    (E) It cannot be determined from the information given.

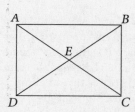

14. In the figure above, *ABCD* is a rectangle. If the area of $\triangle AEB$ is 8, what is the area of $\triangle ACD$?

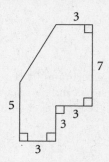

Note: Figure not drawn to scale.

15. What is the area of the above figure?

    (A) 18.5
    (B) 35.0
    (C) 42.0
    (D) 43.5
    (E) 60.5

Hard

16. The perimeter of a rectangle is $6w$. If one side has length $\dfrac{w}{2}$, what is the area of the rectangle?

    (A) $\dfrac{w^2}{4}$

    (B) $\dfrac{5w^2}{4}$

    (C) $\dfrac{5w^2}{2}$

    (D) $\dfrac{11w^2}{4}$

    (E) $\dfrac{11w^2}{2}$

KAPLAN

17. The length of each side of square *A* is increased by 100 percent to make square *B*. The length of each side of square *B* is then increased by 50 percent to make square *C*. By what percent is the area of square *C* greater than the sum of the areas of squares *A* and *B*?

    (A) 75%

    (B) 80%

    (C) 100%

    (D) 150%

    (E) 180%

18. What is the greatest number of rectangles with integer side lengths and perimeter 10 that can be cut from a piece of paper with width 24 and length 60?

    (A) 144

    (B) 180

    (C) 240

    (D) 360

    (E) 480

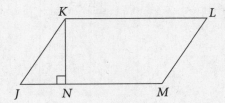

19. In the figure above, if the area of parallelogram *JKLM* is n, and if the length of *KN* is $n + \dfrac{1}{n}$, then the length of *JM* is

    (A) $\dfrac{1}{n}$

    (B) $\dfrac{1}{n+1}$

    (C) $n + 1$

    (D) $\dfrac{n^2}{n+1}$

    (E) $\dfrac{n^2}{n^2+1}$

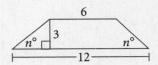

20. What is the perimeter of the trapezoid shown above?

    (A) 21

    (B) 24

    (C) $24 + \sqrt{2}$

    (D) $18 + 6\sqrt{2}$

    (E) $24\sqrt{2}$

ANSWERS AND EXPLANATIONS

Basic

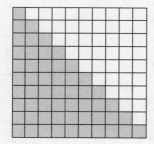

1.   B

The fastest way to get the total area is to count the number of shaded small squares in each row (there's a pattern here: each row has one more shaded square than the row above it), and add. This gives a total of $1 + 2 + 3 + 4 + 5 + 6 + 7 + 8 + 9 + 10$, or 55 shaded squares.

2.   192

To find the area of $ABCD$, you need to know the width and the length. The perimeter of a rectangle $= 2(l + w)$. Let AD be the length. Since you know the length and perimeter, plug in those values into the formula and solve for w, the width:

$$56 = 2(16 + w)$$
$$56 = 32 + 2w$$
$$24 = 2w$$
$$12 = w$$

Since the area of a rectangle $= l \times w$, the area of $ABCD = 16 \times 12$, or 192.

3.   D

The easiest way to solve this problem is to remember that 30-60-90 triangles have sides in the ratio $x : x\sqrt{3} : 2x$, where $2x$ is the length of the hypotenuse. $\overline{AD}$ is the shortest side of ADC, so $4 = x$. $\overline{CD}$ is the middle side, not the hypotenuse, so its length is $x\sqrt{3} = 4\sqrt{3}$.

4.   C

Since the lengths of each side of a square are the same, $PQ = PS$. Therefore:

$$3a + 2 = 2a + 7$$
$$a = 5$$

So choice (C) is correct.

5.   C

The height of $\triangle DEC$ is the perpendicular distance from point E to base DC, and that's the same as the length of side AD or side BC of the square. The base of $\triangle DEC$ is also a side of the square, so the area of $\triangle DEC$ must equal $\frac{1}{2}$ the length of a side of the square times the length of a side of the square. Or, calling the length of a side s, the area of $\triangle DEC$ is $\frac{1}{2}s^2$, while the area of the square is just s^2. Since the triangle has half the area of the square, the ratio is 1:2, or $\frac{1}{2}$.

6.   B

In a parallelogram, opposite angles are equal. Therefore $\angle P = (40 - x)°$ and $\angle O = 15x°$. The interior angles of any quadrilateral add up to 360°, so:

$$15x + 15x + 40 - x + 40 - x = 360$$
$$28x = 280$$
$$x = 10$$

7.   30

Call the length l and the width w. Then $lw = 36$ and $l = 4w$. Now simply substitute: $(4w)(w) = 36$. If $4w^2 = 36$, $w^2 = 9$ and $w = 3$. The length of the rectangle is therefore 12, so the perimeter is $2(l + w) = 2(12 + 3) = 30$.

Medium

8. B

The area of the shaded region is equal to the total area minus the unshaded region. The total area of the figure equals length × width = $x \times x = x^2$.

The unshaded region is made up of 4 right isosceles triangles with base and height equal to y.

Since area of a triangle = $\frac{1}{2}$ × base × height, the area of the 4 unshaded triangles = $4\left(\frac{1}{2}\right)(y)(y)$, or $2y^2$. Therefore,

the area of the shaded region equals $x^2 - 2y^2$, and choice

(B) is correct.

9. 1/4, or .25

Watch out for the trap: The ratio of areas is *not* the same as the ratio of lengths. We can pick numbers for the length and width of rectangle A. Let's pick 4 for the length and 2 for the width. The area of rectangle A is then 4 × 2, or 8. The length of rectangle B is twice the length of rectangle A : 2 × 4 = 8. The width of rectangle B is twice the width of rectangle A : 2 × 2 = 4. So the area of rectangle B is 8 × 4, or 32. Therefore, the ratio of the area of rectangle A to the area of rectangle B is $\frac{8}{32}$, or $\frac{1}{4}$.

As a general rule for similar polygons, the ratio of areas is equal to the square of the ratio of lengths.

10. C

The sum of the degree measures of the angles of a quadrilateral is 360. Since the angles of quadrilateral *DEFG* are in a ratio of 2:3:5:6, you can set up an equation in which x represents part of the ratio:

$$2x + 3x + 5x + 6x = 360$$
$$16x = 360$$
$$x = 22.5$$

Now find the difference in the degree measures of the largest and smallest angles:

$$6x - 2x = 4x = 4(22.5) = 90$$

So answer choice (C) is correct.

11. A

A regular hexagon is composed of 6 equilateral triangles. In this case, each triangle has a side measure of 1, because the hexagon contains 6 equal sides—it's a regular hexagon—whose perimeter is 6. So if you figure out the area of one equilateral triangle with sides measuring 1, and then multiply that area by 6, you'll have your answer. Begin with a picture, including an altitude—that is, the height of the triangle.

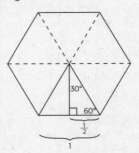

Notice the introduction of the altitude creates 2 congruent 30-60-90 triangles. Look at either one. If the side opposite 30° is $\frac{1}{2}$, the side opposite 60° is $\frac{\sqrt{3}}{2}$. So the area of the entire triangle above is $\left(\frac{1}{2}\right)(b)(h) = \left(\frac{1}{2}\right)(1)\left(\frac{\sqrt{3}}{2}\right) = \frac{\sqrt{3}}{4}$.

The area of a hexagon containing six such triangles is

$$6\left(\frac{\sqrt{3}}{4}\right) = \frac{3\sqrt{3}}{2}.$$

12. E

The first step is to combine the information in the 2 polygons into 1, since they are congruent and therefore identical. Then, you can divide the polygon into 2 parts, a rectangle and a triangle, find the area of each, and add them together. Again, combine information and divide into 2 parts:

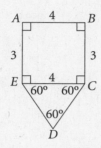

Area of rectangle:

$$4(3) = 12$$

Area of triangle:

To find the height, draw a line from D to the midpoint of $\overline{EC}$. This will divide the equilateral triangle into 2 congruent 30-60-90 right triangles with a hypotenuse of 4 and a short leg of 2. The height will be $2\sqrt{3}$. Therefore, the area of the equilateral triangle is $\frac{1}{2}(4)(2\sqrt{3}) = 4\sqrt{3}$. Then the total area of polygon is $12 + 4\sqrt{3}$.

13. B

Since the sum of the interior angles of a quadrilateral is $360°$, $A + B + C + D = 360$. At the same time, $A + B + C = 2D$. So we can substitute for $A + B + C$ in our first equation, to get:

$$2D + D = 360$$

$$3D = 360$$

$$D = 120$$

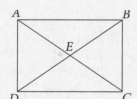

14. 16

The bases of $\triangle AEB$ and $\triangle ACD$ both have the same length, since $AB = CD$. We just need to find the relationship between their respective heights. AC and BD intersect at the center of the rectangle, which is point E. Therefore, the

perpendicular distance from E to side AB is half the distance from side CD to side AB. This means that the height of $\triangle AEB$ is half the height of $\triangle ACD$. So the area of $\triangle ACD$ is twice the area of $\triangle AEB$: $2 \times 8 = 16$.

Hard

15. D

This strange-looking figure can be viewed as three more familiar figures put together. It is made up of two rectangles and a triangle. You can find the area of the entire figure by adding the area of the triangle to the area of the two rectangles. Add some dotted lines so you can see this more clearly:

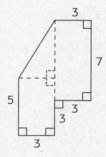

The area of the rectangle on the left is $5 \times 3 = 15$, and the area of the rectangle on the right is $7 \times 3 = 21$. To find the area of the triangle, you need to know its height and the length of its base. The length of the base of the triangle is the same as the width of the rectangle on the left, 3. The height of the triangle is a little harder to find. First, notice that the small segment of dotted line that makes up the right side of the rectangle on the left is $5 - 3 = 2$ units long. The entire dotted line is 7 units long, so the portion that represents the height of the triangle is $7 - 2 = 5$ units long. So the area of the triangle is $\frac{1}{2} \times 3 \times 5$, which is equal to 7.5. The total area of the figure, then, is $15 + 21 + 7.5 = 43.5$.

16. B

The sum of all 4 sides is $6w$. The 2 short sides add up to $\dfrac{w}{2} + \dfrac{w}{2}$, or w. This leaves $6w - w$, or $5w$, for the *sum* of the other 2 sides. *Each* long side is $\dfrac{1}{2}(5w)$, or $\dfrac{5}{2}w$.

So, Area $= \left(\dfrac{w}{2}\right)\left(\dfrac{5w}{2}\right) = \dfrac{5w^2}{4}$.

17. B

The best way to solve this problem is to pick a value for the length of a side of square A. We want our numbers to be easy to work with, so let's pick 10 for the length of each side of square A. The length of each side of square B is 100 percent greater, or twice as great as a side of square A. So the length of a side of square B is 2×10, or 20. The length of each side of square C is 50 percent greater, or $1\dfrac{1}{2}$ times as great as a side of square B. So the length of a side of square C is $1\dfrac{1}{2} \times 20$, or 30. The area of square A is 10^2, or 100. The area of square B is 20^2, or 400. The sum of the areas of squares A and B is $100 + 400$, or 500. The area of square C is 30^2, or 900. The area of square C is greater than the sum of the areas of squares A and B by or 400 $(900 - 500)$. By what percent is the area of square C greater than the sum of the areas of squares A and B? $\dfrac{400}{500} \times 100\%$, or 80%.

18. D

First, if a rectangle has perimeter 10, what could its dimensions be? Perimeter $= 2l + 2w$, or $2(l + w)$. The perimeter is 10, so $2(l + w) = 10$, or $l + w = 5$. Since l and w must be integers, there are 2 possibilities: $l = 4$ and $w = 1$ ($4 + 1 = 5$), or $l = 3$ and $w = 2$ ($3 + 2 = 5$). Let's consider each possibility separately.

If $l = 4$, how many of these rectangles fit along the length of the larger rectangle? The length of the larger rectangle is 60; $60 \div 4 = 15$, so 15 smaller rectangles fit, if they are lined up with their longer sides against the longer side of the large rectangle. The width of the smaller rectangles is 1, and the width of the large rectangle is 24. $24 \div 1 = 24$, so 24 small rectangles fit against the width of the large rectangle. The total number of small rectangles that fit inside the large rectangle is the number along the length times the number along the width, which is $15 \times 24 = 360$.

In the second case, $l = 3$ and $w = 2$. $60 \div 3 = 20$, so 20 small rectangles fit along the length; $24 \div 2 = 12$, so 12 small rectangles fit along the width. Therefore the total number of small rectangles is 20×12, or 240. We're asked for the greatest number, which we got from the first case: 360.

19. E

The area of a parallelogram $=$ base $\times$ height. You're given that the area of $JKLM = n$, and the length of the height $KN = n + \dfrac{1}{n}$. So plug these variables into the formula and solve for the length of JM:

$$n = \left(n + \dfrac{1}{n}\right) \times (JM)$$

Find a common denominator for n and $\dfrac{1}{n}$:

$$n = \left(\dfrac{n^2}{n} + \dfrac{1}{n}\right) \times (JM)$$

$$n = \left(\dfrac{n^2 + 1}{n}\right) \times (JM)$$

Solve for *JM* by multiplying both sides by the reciprocal of

$\frac{n^2 + 1}{n}$:

$$\left(\frac{n}{n^2 + 1}\right) \times n = \left(\frac{n}{n^2 + 1}\right) \times \left(\frac{n^2 + 1}{n}\right) \times (JM)$$

$$\frac{n^2}{n^2 + 1} = JM$$

Therefore, choice (E) is correct.

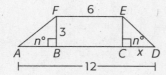

20. D

We've labeled points *A*, *B*, *C*, *D*, *E*, and *F* in the diagram above for clarity. If we drop a perpendicular line segment from point *E* to point *C* on side *AD*, our figure is divided into 2 right triangles and a rectangle in the middle. *BC* is opposite *EF* in rectangle *BCEF*, so *BC* must also be 6. The trapezoid is an isosceles trapezoid because the base angles are congruent. Because of this fact, △*ABF* and △*CDE* are both the same shape and size, so *AB* is the same length as *CD*. If we call this length *x*, we can set up an equation:

$$AB + BC + CD = 12$$
$$x + 6 + x = 12$$
$$2x = 6$$
$$x = 3$$

At this point, we have lengths for *FE*, *AB*, *BC*, and *CD* as follows:

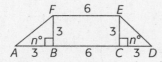

We still need the length of *AF* and the length of *DE* to get the perimeter.

Notice that △*ABF* and △*CDE* are both right isosceles triangles. Since the lengths of the sides of an isosceles right triangle are in a ratio of $1:1:\sqrt{2}$, the length of *AF* and *DE* is $3 \times \sqrt{2}$, or $3\sqrt{2}$. (If you didn't recognize this, you could have used the Pythagorean theorem to find the lengths of *AF* and *DE*.)

Adding together the lengths of the four sides gives us $6 + 12 + 3\sqrt{2} + 3\sqrt{2}$, or $18 + 6\sqrt{2}$.

Chapter Seventeen: **Circles**

The definition of a circle makes this shape sound a lot more complicated than it really is. In a circle, all points lie equidistant from a central point. If you draw several lines from the center of a circle out to its edge, they'll be the same length no matter where they're drawn.

There are a few basic things you need to know about circles for the SAT. One is the term *circumference*. That's the distance around the circle. The *diameter* is another; its measure is the longest distance from one side of the circle to the other, essentially a segment whose endpoints are on the circle, and that passes through the center of the circle. The formula for finding the circumference is π × diameter. By the way—although π is a non-repeating decimal, the standard abbreviation is 3.14.

An *arc* is a curved segment that is a piece of the circumference. A *chord* is a line segment whose endpoints are both on the circle. A *radius* is a segment that originates in the center and whose other endpoint is on the circle. You have to use a radius to find the area of a circle: Square the given radius and multiply it by π. The formula looks like this: πr^2, or 3.14 × (radius)^2. Finally, you'll need to understand the term *sector*. Think of a sector as a piece of pie, or a wedge of the circle. For more information about circles:

92. Circumference of a Circle

93. Length of an Arc

94. Area of a Circle

95. Area of a Sector

96. Tangency

Chapter Seventeen Practice Set
Answer Sheet

1. Ⓐ Ⓑ Ⓒ Ⓓ Ⓔ   9. Ⓐ Ⓑ Ⓒ Ⓓ Ⓔ
2. Ⓐ Ⓑ Ⓒ Ⓓ Ⓔ   10. Ⓐ Ⓑ Ⓒ Ⓓ Ⓔ
3. Ⓐ Ⓑ Ⓒ Ⓓ Ⓔ   11. Ⓐ Ⓑ Ⓒ Ⓓ Ⓔ
4. Ⓐ Ⓑ Ⓒ Ⓓ Ⓔ   12. Ⓐ Ⓑ Ⓒ Ⓓ Ⓔ
5. Grid-in below   13. Ⓐ Ⓑ Ⓒ Ⓓ Ⓔ
6. Ⓐ Ⓑ Ⓒ Ⓓ Ⓔ   14. Ⓐ Ⓑ Ⓒ Ⓓ Ⓔ
7. Ⓐ Ⓑ Ⓒ Ⓓ Ⓔ   15. Ⓐ Ⓑ Ⓒ Ⓓ Ⓔ
8. Ⓐ Ⓑ Ⓒ Ⓓ Ⓔ

5.

	/	/	
•	•	•	•
0	0	0	0
1	1	1	1
2	2	2	2
3	3	3	3
4	4	4	4
5	5	5	5
6	6	6	6
7	7	7	7
8	8	8	8
9	9	9	9

PRACTICE SET

Basic

1. If the area of a circle is 64π, then the circumference of the circle is

   (A) 8π
   (B) 16π
   (C) 32π
   (D) 64π
   (E) 128π

2. If d is the diameter of a circle, then πd^2 represents

   (A) the area of the circle
   (B) half the area of the circle
   (C) twice the area of the circle
   (D) one-fourth the area of the circle
   (E) four times the area of the circle

3. If the minute hand of a clock moves 45 degrees, how many minutes of time have passed?

   (A) 6
   (B) 7.5
   (C) 15
   (D) 30
   (E) 36.5

4. If the circumference of a circle is 1, what is the radius of the circle?

   (A) $\dfrac{1}{2\pi}$

   (B) $\dfrac{1}{\pi}$

   (C) $\dfrac{1}{2}$

   (D) $\dfrac{\pi}{2}$

   (E) π

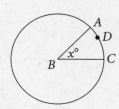

Note: Figure not drawn to scale.

5. In the figure above, the ratio of the circumference of circle B to the length of arc ADC is 8:1. What is the value of x?

Medium

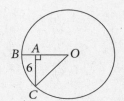

Note: Figure not drawn to scale.

6. In the figure above, if the area of the circle with center O is 100π and CA has a length of 6, what is the length of AB?

   (A) 2
   (B) 3
   (C) 4
   (D) 5
   (E) 6

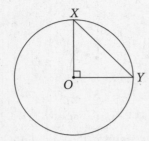

7. In the figure above, O is the center of the circle. If the area of triangle XOY is 25, what is the area of the circle?

    (A) 25π

    (B) $25\pi\sqrt{2}$

    (C) 50π

    (D) $50\pi\sqrt{3}$

    (E) 625π

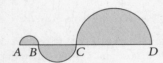

Note: Figure not drawn to scale.

8. Each of the 3 shaded regions above is a semicircle. If $AB = 4$, $CD = 2BC$, and $BC = 2AB$, then the area of the entire shaded figure is

    (A) 28π

    (B) 42π

    (C) 84π

    (D) 96π

    (E) 168π

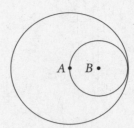

9. In the diagram above, if the circle with center A has an area of 72π, what is the area of the circle with center B?

    (A) 18π

    (B) 24π

    (C) 30π

    (D) 36π

    (E) 48π

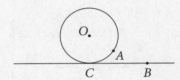

10. In the figure above, O is the center of the circle with radius x (not shown). If $\overline{CB}$ is tangent to the circle at C and $CB = 2x$, what is the measure of $\overline{AB}$?

    (A) $x\sqrt{5} - x$

    (B) $x\sqrt{5}$

    (C) 5

    (D) $5x - x$

    (E) $5x$

Hard

11. If the diameter of a circle increases by 50 percent, by what percent will the area of the circle increase?

    (A) 25%

    (B) 50%

    (C) 100%

    (D) 125%

    (E) 225%

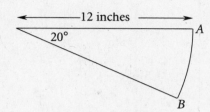

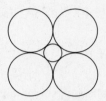

12. The figure above shows the path traced by the hand of a scale as it moves from *A* to *B*. What is the area, in square inches, of the region passed over by the scale's hand?

    (A) 2π

    (B) 8π

    (C) 12π

    (D) 16π

    (E) 144π

14. The total area of the four equal circles in the figure above is 36π, and the circles are all tangent to one another. What is the diameter of the small circle?

    (A) $6\sqrt{2}$

    (B) $6 + \sqrt{2}$

    (C) $3\sqrt{2} - 3$

    (D) $6\sqrt{2} - 6$

    (E) $6\sqrt{2} + 6$

13. If an arc with a length of 12π is $\dfrac{3}{4}$ of the circumference of a circle, what is the shortest distance between the endpoints of the arc?

    (A) 4

    (B) $4\sqrt{2}$

    (C) 8

    (D) $8\sqrt{2}$

    (E) 16

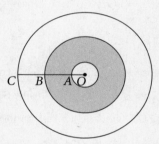

15. The diagram above shows three circles, all of which share a common origin *O*. If the lengths of $\overline{AB}$ and $\overline{BC}$ are both equal to the diameter of the smallest circle, what is the probability that a randomly selected point within the diagram will fall within the shaded region?

    (A) $\dfrac{8}{25}$

    (B) $\dfrac{9}{25}$

    (C) $\dfrac{1}{9}$

    (D) $\dfrac{5}{8}$

    (E) $\dfrac{8}{9}$

ANSWERS AND EXPLANATIONS

Basic

1. B

We need to find the radius in order to get the circumference. The area is 64π, so use the area formula to get the radius:

$$\text{Area} = \pi r^2 = 64\pi$$
$$r^2 = 64$$
$$r = 8$$

The circumference, which is $2\pi r$, is $2\pi(8)$, or 16π.

2. E

The diameter of a circle is twice the radius, or $d = 2r$. Therefore, $\pi d^2 = \pi(2r)^2 = 4\pi r^2$, which is four times the area of the circle.

3. B

The minute hand of a clock traces out a complete circle every hour. That is, it moves 360° every 60 minutes. Since 45° is $\frac{1}{8}$ of 360°, the time it takes to move 45° will be $\frac{1}{8}$ of 60 minutes, that is, 7.5 minutes.

4. A

$C = \pi d = 2\pi r = 1$. If $2\pi r = 1$, then $r = \dfrac{1}{2\pi}$

5. 45

We need to use the following ratio.

$$\frac{\text{length of arc}}{\text{circumference}} = \frac{\text{measure of arc's central angle}}{360°}$$

The measure of the arc's central angle is x degrees, and the length of the arc is $\frac{1}{8}$ of the circumference:

$$\frac{1}{8} = \frac{x}{360}$$
$$x = 45$$

Medium

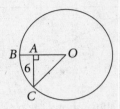

6. A

Since we know the area of circle O, we can find the radius of the circle. And if we find the length of OA, then AB is just the difference between OB and OA.

Since the area of the circle is 100π, the radius must be $\sqrt{100}$ or 10. Radius OC, line segment CA, and line segment OA together form a right triangle, so we can use the Pythagorean theorem to find the length of OA. But notice that 10 is twice 5 and 6 is twice 3, so right triangle ACO has sides whose lengths are in a 3-4-5 ratio.

OA must have a length of twice 4, or 8. AB is the segment of radius OB that's not a part of OA; its length equals the length of OB minus the length of OA, or $10 - 8 = 2$.

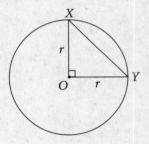

7. C

Each leg of right triangle XOY is also a radius of circle O. If we call the radius r, then the area of $\triangle XOY$ is $\left(\frac{1}{2}\right)(r)(r)$, or $\frac{r^2}{2}$. At the same time, the area of circle O is πr^2. So, we can use the area of $\triangle XOY$ to find r^2, and then multiply r^2 by π to get the area of the circle.

$$\text{Area of } \triangle XOY = \frac{r^2}{2} = 25$$

$$r^2 = 50$$

$$\text{Area of circle } O = \pi r^2 = \pi(50) = 50\pi$$

Note: It is unnecessary (and extra work) to find the actual value of r, since the value of r^2 is sufficient to find the area.

8. B

Since you're given the diameter of the smallest semicircle ($AB = 4$), you should begin with this semicircle. The radius of semicircle AB is $\frac{4}{2}$, or 2. The area of a semicircle is half the area of the circle, or $\frac{1}{2}\pi r^2$. So the area of semicircle AB is $\frac{1}{2}\pi(2)^2$, or 2π. $BC = 2AB$, so $BC = 2(4)$, or 8.

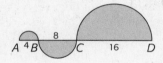

The radius of semicircle BC is 4, so the area of semicircle BC is $\frac{1}{2}\pi(4)^2$, or 8π. $CD = 2BC$, so $CD = 2(8)$, or 16. The radius of semicircle CD is 8, so the area of semicircle CD is $\frac{1}{2}\pi(8)^2$, or 32π. Adding the three areas together gives $2\pi + 8\pi + 32\pi$, or 42π.

9. A

If you draw a radius of the larger circle from A to the point on the circumference where the 2 circles touch, you can see that the diameter of the smaller circle is equal to the radius of the larger circle. That is, the radius of circle B is half the radius of the circle A. Find the radius of the larger circle:

$$\pi r^2 = 72\pi$$

$$r^2 = 72$$

$$r = \sqrt{72} = 6\sqrt{2}$$

So the radius of the smaller circle is half this, or $3\sqrt{2}$. Its area $= \pi(3\sqrt{2})^2 = 18\pi$.

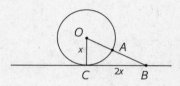

10. A

$OC = x$, and you're given that $CB = 2x$, so use the Pythagorean theorem to solve for OB:

$$x^2 + (2x)^2 = (OB)^2$$

$$x^2 + 4x^2 = (OB)^2$$

$$5x^2 = (OB)^2$$

$$x\sqrt{5} = OB$$

OA is a radius of the circle and is therefore equal to x, so $AB = OB - OA = x\sqrt{5} - x$

Hard

11. D

The fastest method is to pick a value for the diameter of the circle. Let's suppose that the diameter is 4. Then the radius is $\frac{4}{2}$, or 2, which means that the area is $\pi(2)^2$, or 4π. Increasing the diameter by 50 percent means adding on half of its original length: $4 + (50\% \text{ of } 4) = 4 + 2 = 6$. So the new radius is $\frac{6}{2}$, or 3, which means that the area of the circle is now $\pi(3)^2$, or 9π. The percent increase is the amount of increase, over the original area, times 100%. That's $\frac{9\pi - 4\pi}{4\pi} \times 100\% = \frac{5\pi}{4\pi} \times 100\%$, or 125%.

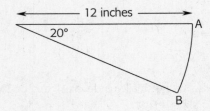

12. B

If the hand turned all the way around, it would trace out a full circle. In the question, the hand moves 20°, which is $\frac{20}{360}$, or $\frac{1}{18}$ of a full circle. So the area it covers is $\frac{1}{18}$ of the area of a circle with radius 12:

Area $= \frac{1}{18}\pi(12)^2 = \frac{144}{18}\pi = 8\pi$

13. D

Call the endpoints of the arc A and B and the center of the circle C. Major arc AB represents $\frac{3}{4}$ of 360 degrees, or 270 degrees. Therefore, minor arc AB is $360° - 270°$, or 90°. Since AC and CB are both radii of the circle, $\triangle ABC$ must be an isosceles right triangle:

You can find the distance between A and B if you know the radius of the circle. Major arc AB, which takes up $\frac{3}{4}$ of the circumference, has a length of 12π, so the entire circumference is 16π. The circumference of any circle is 2π times the radius, so a circle with circumference 16π must have radius 8. The ratio of a leg to the hypotenuse in an isosceles right triangle is $1:\sqrt{2}$. The length of AB is $\sqrt{2}$ times the length of a leg, or $8\sqrt{2}$.

14. D

Connect the centers of the circles O, P, and Q as shown. Each leg in this right triangle consists of 2 radii. The hypotenuse consists of 2 radii plus the diameter of the small circle.

You can find the radii of the large circles from the given information. Since the total area of the 4 large circles is 36π, each large circle has area 9π. Since the area of a circle is πr^2, we know that the radii of the large circles all have length 3.

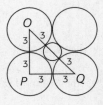

Therefore, each leg in the isosceles right triangle OPQ is 6. The hypotenuse then has length $6\sqrt{2}$. (The hypotenuse of an isosceles right triangle is always $\sqrt{2}$ times a leg.) The hypotenuse is equal to 2 radii plus the diameter of the small circle, so $6\sqrt{2} = 2(3) +$ diameter, or diameter $= 6\sqrt{2} - 6$.

15. A

The probability that a randomly selected point will fall within the shaded area is equal to the ratio of the area that is shaded to the area of the entire figure. The area of the entire figure is equal to the area of the largest circle, and the area of the shaded area is equal to the area of the second circle minus the area of the smallest circle. To make the calculations easier, you can assume that the radius of the smallest circle equals 1, so its diameter is 2. Then the radius of the second circle is 3 and the radius of the largest circle is 5. Then the shaded area is $\pi(3^2) - \pi(1^2) = 9\pi - \pi = 8\pi$. The total area of the figure is $\pi(5^2) = 25\pi$. The probability is $\frac{8\pi}{25\pi} = \frac{8}{25}$.

Chapter Eighteen: **Multiple Figures**

Some SAT questions combine different geometric figures. These types of questions require the use of multiple formulas and multiple concepts. As long as you feel confident about your knowledge of circles, triangles, polygons, lines, and angles, the questions should be a breeze. Just remember not to get overwhelmed or bogged down in extraneous information. Break the problems down into their separate parts. Think about what information you need to solve, and then, one at a time, apply the concepts you already know.

Chapter Eighteen Practice Set
Answer Sheet

1. Ⓐ Ⓑ Ⓒ Ⓓ Ⓔ   5. Grid-in below

2. Ⓐ Ⓑ Ⓒ Ⓓ Ⓔ   6. Ⓐ Ⓑ Ⓒ Ⓓ Ⓔ

3. Ⓐ Ⓑ Ⓒ Ⓓ Ⓔ   7. Ⓐ Ⓑ Ⓒ Ⓓ Ⓔ

4. Ⓐ Ⓑ Ⓒ Ⓓ Ⓔ   8. Ⓐ Ⓑ Ⓒ Ⓓ Ⓔ

5.

	/	/	
.	.	.	.
	0	0	0
1	1	1	1
2	2	2	2
3	3	3	3
4	4	4	4
5	5	5	5
6	6	6	6
7	7	7	7
8	8	8	8
9	9	9	9

PRACTICE SET

Basic

1. A triangle of height 5 and base 4 has an area exactly $\frac{1}{3}$ that of a rectangle with height 5. What is the width of the rectangle?

    (A) 4
    (B) 5
    (C) 6
    (D) 8
    (E) 10

Medium

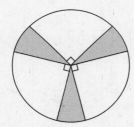

2. In the circle above, 3 right angles have vertices at the center of the circle. If the radius of the circle is 8, what is the combined area of the shaded regions?

    (A) 8π
    (B) 9π
    (C) 12π
    (D) 13π
    (E) 16π

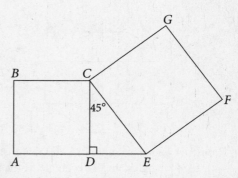

3. In the figure above, *ABCD* and *CEFG* are squares. If the area of *CEFG* is 36, what is the area of *ABCD*?

    (A) 6
    (B) 6√2
    (C) 9
    (D) 18
    (E) 24

4. A triangle and a circle have equal areas. If the base of the triangle and the diameter of the circle each have length 5, what is the height of the triangle?

    (A) $\frac{5}{2}$

    (B) $\frac{5}{2}\pi$

    (C) 5π

    (D) 10π

    (E) It cannot be determined from the information given.

KAPLAN

Hard

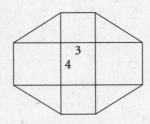

5. The figure above is composed of 9 regions: 4 squares, 4 triangles, and 1 rectangle. If the rectangle has length 4 and width 3, what is the perimeter of the entire figure?

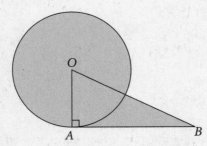

Note: Figure not drawn to scale.

6. In the figure above, if radius *OA* is 8 and the area of right triangle *OAB* is 32, what is the area of the shaded region?

(A) $64\pi + 32$

(B) $60\pi + 32$

(C) $56\pi + 32$

(D) $32\pi + 32$

(E) $16\pi + 32$

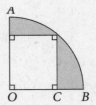

7. In the figure above, *AB* is an arc of a circle with center *O*. If the length of arc *AB* is 5π and the length of *CB* is 4, what is the sum of the areas of the shaded regions?

(A) $25\pi - 60$

(B) $25\pi - 48$

(C) $25\pi - 36$

(D) $100\pi - 48$

(E) $100\pi - 36$

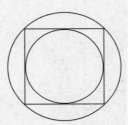

8. In the figure above, the smaller circle is inscribed in the square and the square is inscribed in the larger circle. If the length of each side of the square is *s*, what is the ratio of the area of the larger circle to the area of the smaller circle?

(A) $2\sqrt{2}$

(B) 2

(C) $\sqrt{2}$

(D) $2s$

(E) $s\sqrt{2}$

ANSWERS AND EXPLANATIONS

Basic

1.   C

Let's call the width of the rectangle w. The area of the

rectangle, then, is w times 5, its height. The area of the

triangle is $\frac{1}{2}$ times the base times the height, or

$\frac{1}{2} \times 4 \times 5 = 10$. The area of the triangle is $\frac{1}{3}$ the area of

the rectangle, so we know that $\frac{1}{3} \times w \times 5 = 10$. Multiply

both sides of this equation by 3 to get $5w = 30$, so $w = 6$.

Medium

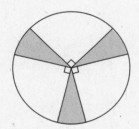

2.   E

The 3 right angles define 3 sectors of the circle, each with

a central angle of 90°. Together, the 3 sectors account for

$\frac{270°}{360°}$, or $\frac{3}{4}$ of the area of the circle, leaving $\frac{1}{4}$ of the cir-

cle for the shaded regions. So the total area of the shaded

regions $= \frac{1}{4} \times \pi(8)^2$, or 16π.

3.   D

Notice that both squares share a side with right triangle
CDE. Since square *CEFG* has an area of 36, *CE* has a
length of $\sqrt{36}$, or 6. Since right triangle *CDE* has a 45
degree angle, *CDE* must be an isosceles right triangle.
Therefore, *CD* and *DE* are the same length. Let's call that
length x.

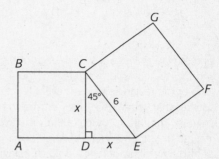

Remember, we're looking for the area of square *ABCD*,
which will be x^2. Using the Pythagorean theorem on
$\triangle CDE$, we get:

$$(\text{leg})^2 + (\text{leg})^2 = (\text{hypotenuse})^2$$
$$x^2 + x^2 = 6^2$$
$$2x^2 = 36$$
$$x^2 = 18$$

So the area is 18. (There's no need to find x.)

4.   B

The diameter of the circle is 5, so the radius is $\frac{5}{2}$ and the

area is $\pi\left(\frac{5}{2}\right)^2$ or $\frac{25}{4}\pi$. This is equal to the area of the

triangle. Since the base of the triangle is 5, we can solve

for the height:

$$\left(\frac{1}{2}\right)(5)(h) = \frac{25}{4}\pi$$
$$5h = \frac{50}{4}\pi$$
$$h = \frac{50}{20}\pi$$
$$h = \frac{5}{2}\pi$$

Hard

5. 34

The central rectangle shares a side with each of the 4 squares, and the 4 squares form the legs of the 4 right triangles. Two of the rectangle's sides have a length of 4, so the 2 squares that share these sides must also have sides of length 4. The other 2 sides of the rectangle have a length of 3, so the other 2 squares, which share these sides, must also have sides of length 3. Each triangle shares a side with a small square and a side with a large square, so the legs of each triangle have lengths of 3 and 4, respectively.

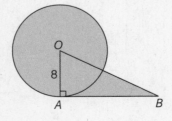

Since the legs are of length 3 and 4, the hypotenuse of each triangle must have a length of 5. (This is the familiar 3-4-5 right triangle.) The perimeter is the sum of the hypotenuses of the triangles and a side from each square:

$$\text{Perimeter} = 4(5) + 2(4) + 2(3)$$
$$= 20 + 8 + 6$$
$$= 34$$

6. C

The total area of the shaded region equals (the area of the circle) + (the area of the right triangle) − (the area of overlap). The area of circle O is $\pi(8)^2$, or 64π. The area of right triangle OAB is 32. So we just need to find the area of overlap, the area of right triangle OAB inside circle O, which forms a sector of the circle. Let's see what we can find out about $\angle AOB$, the central angle of the sector.

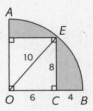

The area of right triangle OAB is 32, and its height is the radius of circle O. So $\frac{1}{2}(8)(AB) = 32$, or $AB = 8$. Since $AB = OA$, $\triangle OAB$ is an isosceles right triangle. Therefore, $\angle AOB$ has a measure of 45°. So the area of the sector is $\frac{45}{360}(64\pi)$, or 8π. Now we can get the total area of the shaded region:

$$64\pi + 32 - 8\pi = 56\pi + 32$$

7. B

The total area of the shaded regions equals the area of the quarter circle minus the area of the rectangle. Since the length of arc AB (a quarter of the circumference of circle O) is 5π, the whole circumference equals $4 \times 5\pi$, or 20π. Thus, the radius OE has length 10. (We've added point E in the diagram for clarity.) Since OB also equals 10, $OC = 10 - 4$, or 6. This tells us that $\triangle OEC$ is a 6-8-10 right triangle and $EC = 8$.

Now we know the dimensions of the rectangle, so we can find its area: area $= \ell \times w = 8 \times 6 = 48$. And the area of the quarter circle equals $\frac{1}{4}\pi(10)^2$ or 25π. Finally, we can get the total area of the shaded regions:

$$\text{Area of shaded regions} = \frac{1}{4} \times \pi \times (10)^2 - 48$$
$$= 25\pi - 48$$

8.   B

The length of each side of the square is given as s.

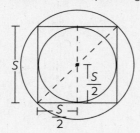

A side of the square has the same length as the diameter of the smaller circle. (You can see this more clearly if you draw the vertical diameter in the smaller circle. The diameter you draw will connect the upper and lower tangent points where the smaller circle and square intersect.)

This means that the radius of the smaller circle is $\frac{s}{2}$, so its area is $\left(\frac{s}{2}\right)^2\pi$, or $\frac{s^2}{4}\pi$. Now draw a diagonal of the square, and you'll see that it's the diameter of the larger circle. The diagonal breaks up the square into 2 isosceles right triangles, where each leg has length s, as we see in the diagram. So the diagonal must have length $s\sqrt{2}$. Therefore, the radius of the larger circle is $\frac{s\sqrt{2}}{2}$, so its area is $\left(\frac{s\sqrt{2}}{2}\right)^2\pi$, or $\frac{2s^2}{4}\pi$, or $\frac{s^2}{2}\pi$. This is twice the area of the smaller circle.

KAPLAN

Chapter Nineteen: **Coordinate Geometry**

The most basic element of coordinate geometry is the *coordinate plane* or *coordinate system*. The plane contains two perpendicular number lines, the *x-axis* (horizontal) and the *y-axis* (vertical). The two axes intersect at a point called the *origin*, which is represented as (0, 0). Any point on the coordinate plane can be represented by an *ordered pair* of numbers, a set of two numbers in the specific order of *x, y*. This ordered pair represents the point's position on the coordinate plane. It's like giving the point an address, so you can always find it. The first number is the horizontal distance from the origin, and the second number is the vertical distance from the origin. This coordinate plane can be used to graph and solve equations, graph lines, line segments, rays, angles, and other geometric figures.

There are also certain formulas you'll need to know when solving coordinate geometry problems. You might be asked to find the distance between two points. This is not purely a counting problem. Think of this in terms of the point's "address." The question isn't asking how many blocks up and over, but rather, how far the distance is, as the crow flies, or straight from one point to the other. You would need to use the *distance formula* in this case, which is $d = \sqrt{(x_2 - x_1)^2 + (y_2 - y_1)^2}$. You might also be asked about things such as the *slope* or *intercept*. Here are some topics for further reading:

72. Finding the Distance Between Two Points
73. Using Two Points to Find the Slope
74. Using an Equation to Find the Slope
75. Using an Equation to Find an Intercept
100. Finding the Midpoint

Chapter Nineteen Practice Set
Answer Sheet

1. Ⓐ Ⓑ Ⓒ Ⓓ Ⓔ
2. Ⓐ Ⓑ Ⓒ Ⓓ Ⓔ
3. Ⓐ Ⓑ Ⓒ Ⓓ Ⓔ
4. Ⓐ Ⓑ Ⓒ Ⓓ Ⓔ
5. Ⓐ Ⓑ Ⓒ Ⓓ Ⓔ
6. Grid-in below
7. Ⓐ Ⓑ Ⓒ Ⓓ Ⓔ
8. Ⓐ Ⓑ Ⓒ Ⓓ Ⓔ

9. Ⓐ Ⓑ Ⓒ Ⓓ Ⓔ
10. Ⓐ Ⓑ Ⓒ Ⓓ Ⓔ
11. Grid-in below
12. Ⓐ Ⓑ Ⓒ Ⓓ Ⓔ
13. Ⓐ Ⓑ Ⓒ Ⓓ Ⓔ
14. Grid-in below
15. Grid-in below
16. Ⓐ Ⓑ Ⓒ Ⓓ Ⓔ

6.

11.

14.

15.

PRACTICE SET

Basic

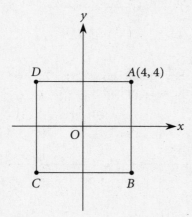

1. In the figure above, *ABCD* is a square centered at the origin. If the coordinates of vertex *A* are (4, 4), what are the coordinates of vertex *C* ?

   (A) $(-4\sqrt{2}, -4\sqrt{2})$
   (B) $(-4\sqrt{2}, -4)$
   (C) $(-4, -4)$
   (D) $(-4, 4)$
   (E) $(4, -4)$

2. If point *A* has coordinates (1, 2) and point *B* has coordinates (9, 8), what is the distance between points *A* and *B*?

   (A) 10
   (B) 9
   (C) 8
   (D) 7
   (E) 6

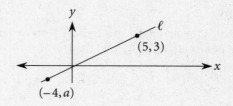

3. In the above figure, if the slope of line , is $\frac{4}{9}$, what is the value of *a* ?

   (A) −3
   (B) −2
   (C) −1
   (D) 1
   (E) 2

4. Points *P* and *Q* lie on the same line and have coordinates (1, 3) and (5, 8), respectively. Which of the following points lies on the same line as points *P* and *Q* ?

   (A) (−4, −5)
   (B) (−3, −2)
   (C) (−2, −3)
   (D) (−1, −4)
   (E) (0, −1)

5. If point *P* is at (4, 5) and point *Q* is at (2, 9), what is the midpoint of *PQ*?

   (A) (2, 5)
   (B) (2, 7)
   (C) (3, 7)
   (D) (3, 9)
   (E) (4, 9)

6. What is the slope of the line in the coordinate plane containing the points (3, 8) and (9, 10)?

KAPLAN

Medium

7. What is the perimeter of a triangle with vertices at the points $(1, 4)$, $(1, 7)$, and $(4, 4)$?

   (A) $3 + \sqrt{2}$

   (B) $3\sqrt{2}$

   (C) 6

   (D) $6 + 3\sqrt{2}$

   (E) $9 + 3\sqrt{2}$

8. If the slope of a line containing the points $(3, a)$ and $(b, 3)$ is 2, what is a in terms of b?

   (A) $\dfrac{b-3}{2}$

   (B) $2b - 3$

   (C) $\dfrac{2b-3}{2}$

   (D) $9 - 2b$

   (E) $\dfrac{9-b}{2}$

9. If the coordinates of point X are $(5, 12)$ and the coordinates of point Y are $(0, -2)$, what is the length of $\overline{XY}$?

   (A) $3\sqrt{15}$

   (B) 12

   (C) 14

   (D) $10\sqrt{2}$

   (E) $\sqrt{221}$

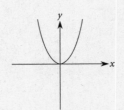

10. If the above graph shows $f(x) = 7x^2$, which of the following is a graph of $f(x) = 7x^2 + 1$

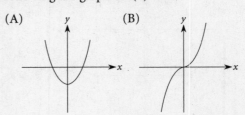

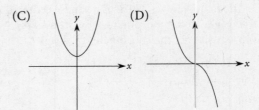

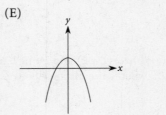

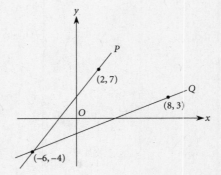

11. In the figure above, what is the positive difference between the slopes of lines P and Q?

Hard

12. If lines p and q are parallel to each other, which of the following statements must be true?

    I.   The slope of p is positive.
    II. The slope of q is the reciprocal of the slope of p.
    III. The slopes of p and q are equal.

    (A) I only
    (B) II only
    (C) III only
    (D) I and II
    (E) I and III

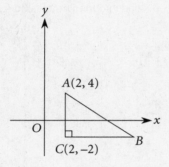

13. In the rectangular coordinate system above, if the area of right triangle ABC is 24, what are the coordinates of point B?

    (A) $(10, -2)$
    (B) $(10, 2)$
    (C) $(2, 6)$
    (D) $(8, -2)$
    (E) It cannot be determined from the information given.

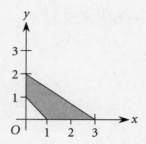

14. In the figure above, what is the area of the shaded region?

15. If the slope of a line is $-\dfrac{5}{3}$ and a point on the line is $(3, 5)$, what is the y-intercept?

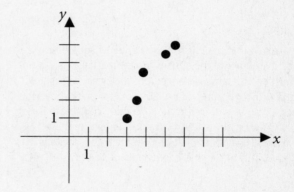

16. Which of the lines described by the following equations best fits these points?

    (A) $y = .3x - 3$
    (B) $y = .7x + 2$
    (C) $y = 1.3x - 3$
    (D) $y = 1.4x + 5$
    (E) $y = 4x - 3$

KAPLAN

ANSWERS AND EXPLANATIONS

Basic

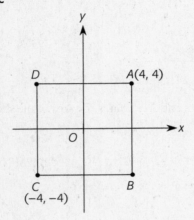

1. C

We are told that the origin is the center of square *ABCD*. Since the center of the square bisects the diagonals, point *C* must be the same distance from the origin as point *A*, and directly opposite point *A*. Since *A* is 4 units above the *x*-axis, *C* will be 4 units below it, so the *y*-coordinate is negative. Likewise, since *A* is 4 units to the right of the *y*-axis, *C* will be 4 units to the left of it, so the *x*-coordinate is also negative. This makes the coordinates of point *C* (−4, −4).

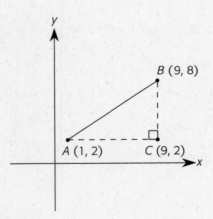

2. A

Draw a diagram. Plotting the points shows that *AB* isn't parallel to one of the axes, so, to find its length, treat it as the hypotenuse of a right triangle. Draw a line from point *A* parallel to the *x*-axis and draw a line from point *B* parallel

to the *y*-axis. The point where they meet, *C*, has coordinates (9, 2). Since $\triangle ABC$ is a right triangle, $AB^2 = AC^2 + BC^2$. Since AC is parallel to the *x*-axis, its length is determined by the difference between the *x*-coordinates of its endpoints: $9 - 1 = 8$. Since *BC* is parallel to the *y*-axis, its length is determined by the difference between the *y*-coordinates of its endpoints: $8 - 2 = 6$. You should recognize this as a 6-8-10 right triangle, making the hypotenuse $AB = 10$. If not, you can use the Pythagorean theorem to solve for *AB*: $AB^2 = AC^2 + BC^2$, $AB^2 = 8^2 + 6^2$, $AB^2 = 64 + 36$, $AB^2 = 100$, $AB = 10$.

3. C

Since the slope of a line = (difference of the *y*-coordinates) ÷ (difference of the *x*-coordinates), you can plug the given coordinates and slope into the formula and solve for *a* :

$$\text{Slope} = \frac{\text{change in } y}{\text{change in } x}$$

$$\frac{4}{9} = \frac{3 - a}{5 - (-4)}$$

$$\frac{4}{9} = \frac{3 - a}{9}$$

$$4 = 3 - a$$

$$a = -1$$

4. B

Since the slope remains the same between any two points on a given line, the slope between the correct answer and *P* or *Q* will be the same as the slope between *P* and *Q*. First find the slope of the line:

$$\text{Slope} = \frac{\text{change in } y}{\text{change in } x}$$

$$= \frac{8 - 3}{5 - 1}$$

$$= \frac{5}{4}$$

Now see which answer choice also gives a slope of $\frac{5}{4}$:

Choice (A): $\frac{8 - (-5)}{5 - (-4)} = \frac{13}{9}$. Eliminate.

Choice (B): $\frac{8 - (-2)}{5 - (-3)} = \frac{10}{8} = \frac{5}{4}$.

So choice (B) is correct because the line between it and point Q has a slope of $\frac{5}{4}$. At this point on the actual test you would move on to the next question. However, we'll go through the remaining choices to prove that they're false.

Choice (C): $\frac{8 - (-3)}{5 - (-2)} = \frac{11}{7}$. Eliminate.

Choice (D): $\frac{8 - (-4)}{5 - (-1)} = \frac{12}{6}$. Eliminate.

Choice (E): $\frac{8 - (-1)}{5 - (-0)} = \frac{9}{5}$. Eliminate.

5. C

The midpoint of a line segment whose ends are at points (x_1, y_1) and (x_2, y_2) is the point $\left(\frac{x_1 + x_2}{2}, \frac{y_1 + y_2}{2} \right)$. So

$$\frac{4 + 2}{2} = \frac{6}{2} = 3$$

$$\frac{5 + 9}{2} = \frac{14}{2} = 7$$

The midpoint is (3, 7).

6. 1/3 or .333

The slope of a line equals the rise over the run, which you can determine by finding the difference between the y-coordinates of the two points and dividing that by the difference between the x-coordinates of the two points. So the slope of the line containing points (3, 8) and (9, 10) equals $\frac{10 - 8}{9 - 3} = \frac{2}{6} = \frac{1}{3}$.

Medium

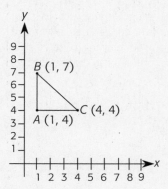

7. D

Start by plotting the points and labeling them. Let A be (1, 4), B be (1, 7), and C be (4, 4). Notice that we have a triangle with side AB parallel to the y-axis, AC parallel to the x-axis, and BC as the third side. Since the x- and y-axes are perpendicular, AB and AC must be perpendicular, so we have a right triangle with BC as the hypotenuse. We need to find the length of the sides. The length of AB is the distance from (1, 4) to (1, 7). Since the x-coordinates are the same, the horizontal distance between the points is 0, so all we need is the vertical distance. This is the difference of the y-coordinates: $7 - 4 = 3$. Similarly, the distance from A to C is just the horizontal distance: $4 - 1 = 3$. So far we have a right triangle with two legs of length 3. Since the legs are equal, it must be an isosceles right triangle, and the hypotenuse must be $\sqrt{2} \times$ one of the legs, or $3\sqrt{2}$. Now we can find the perimeter.

$$\text{Perimeter} = AB + AC + BC$$
$$= 3 + 3 + 3\sqrt{2}$$
$$= 6 + 3\sqrt{2}$$

8. D

Since slope $= \frac{\text{change in } y}{\text{change in } x}$, plug the given coordinates and slope into the formula and solve for a in terms of b:

$$2 = \frac{3 - a}{b - 3}$$
$$2(b - 3) = 3 - a$$
$$2b - 6 = 3 - a$$
$$2b - 9 = -a$$
$$9 - 2b = a$$

9. E

Remember that there's almost always more than one good way to approach a question. Here, you could draw a diagram and figure the answer out geometrically, make an educated guess based on your drawing, or solve algebraically, using the distance formula. The distance between points (x_1, y_1) and (x_2, y_2) is

$$\sqrt{(x_2 - x_1)^2 + (y_2 + y_1)^2}$$

$$\sqrt{(0 - 5)^2 + (-2 - 12)^2}$$

$$\sqrt{25 + 196} = \sqrt{221}$$

10. C

Plug in 0 for x:

$$f(x) = 7x^2 + 1$$
$$y = 7(0)^2 + 1$$
$$y = 1$$

This eliminates (A), (B), and (D). Now plug in 1 for x:

$$f(x) = 7x^2 + 1$$
$$y = 7(1)^2 + 1$$
$$y = 8$$

This eliminates (E), leaving (C).

11. 7/8 or .875

First, you need to find the slopes of lines P and Q, respectively:

$$\text{Slope} = \frac{\text{change in } y}{\text{change in } x}$$

$$\text{Slope of line } P = \frac{7 - (-4)}{2 - (-6)} = \frac{11}{8}$$

$$\text{Slope of line } Q = \frac{3 - (-4)}{8 - (-6)} = \frac{7}{14} = \frac{1}{2}$$

So the positive difference between the slopes is

$$\frac{11}{8} - \frac{1}{2} = \frac{11}{8} - \frac{4}{8} = \frac{7}{8}, \text{ or .875 expressed as a decimal.}$$

Hard

12. C

Go through each of the statements to see which one(s) must be true:

Statement I is not necessarily true. All you're given is that lines p and q are parallel. You're not given the coordinates

of any points on line p. So you can't determine the actual slope of line p. Parallel lines have equal slopes. So statement II is only true if the line p has a slope of 1 or −1, i.e., it is not always true. Since the lines are parallel, statement III is true. Therefore, choice (C) is correct.

13. A

Notice that point B is on the base of the right triangle. So we need the length of the base to determine the coordinates of point B. We can quickly get the height of the triangle, since we're given the coordinates of points A and C. The height is the difference in their y-coordinates: $4 - (-2) = 4 + 2 = 6$. We're given that the area of right triangle ABC is 24, so we can use the area formula to find the length of the base:

$$\text{Area} = \frac{1}{2}b \times h$$

$$24 = \frac{1}{2}b(6)$$

$$\frac{24 \times 2}{6} = b$$

$$8 = b$$

Since BC has a length of 8, point B must be 8 units directly to the right of point C, so add 8 to the x-coordinate of C to get the x-coordinate of B: $2 + 8 = 10$. Points B and C are at the same height, so their y-coordinates are the same. So point B has coordinates $(10, -2)$. You could have eliminated choices (B) and (C) immediately, since point B lies below the x-axis and must therefore have a negative y-coordinate.

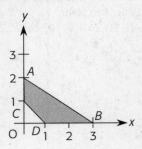

14. 5/2 or 2.5

To get the area of the shaded region, we can subtract the area of right triangle COD from the area of right triangle AOB. (We've labeled these points in the diagram for clarity.) OB lies along the x-axis, so its length is just the difference in x-coordinates between O and B : $3 - 0 = 3$.

Similarly, the length of *OD* is 1 − 0, or 1. *OA* lies along the *y*-axis, so its length is just the difference in y-coordinates between *O* and *A*: 2 − 0 = 2. Similarly, the length of *OC* is 1 − 0, or 1. Now we can get the respective areas of the triangles:

$$\text{Area of } \triangle AOB = \frac{1}{2}(3)(2) = 3$$

$$\text{Area of } \triangle COD = \frac{1}{2}(1)(1) = \frac{1}{2}$$

Now we take the difference in areas:

$$3 - \frac{1}{2} = 2\frac{1}{2} = \frac{5}{2}$$

15. 10

The *y*-intercept of a line is the *y*-coordinate of the point where the line intersects the *y*-axis. Therefore, the *x*-coordinate of the *y*-intercept must be 0. Since you're given the slope of the line and the coordinates of another point on the line, you can plug the given information into the slope formula and solve for the *y*-intercept:

$$\text{Slope} = \frac{\text{change in } y}{\text{change in } x}$$

$$-\left(\frac{5}{3}\right) = \frac{5 - y}{3 - 0}$$

$$-\left(\frac{5}{3}\right) = \frac{5 - y}{3}$$

$$-5 = 5 - y$$

$$-10 = -y$$

$$10 = y$$

You could also have found the *y*-intercept if you used the slope-intercept equation of a line: $y = mx + b$ (where *m* is the slope and *b* is the *y* intercept).

Plug in the coordinates of the given point for *x* and *y*, and plug in $-\left(\frac{5}{3}\right)$ for the slope:

$$5 = -\left(\frac{5}{3}\right)(3) + b$$

$$5 = -5 + b$$

$$10 = b$$

16. C

See what information you can glean from the graph. What should the slope of the line be? Where would the *y*-intercept be? Because the position of the dots on the graph increases along the *y*-axis slightly faster than it increases along the *x*-axis, the slope of the graph must be slightly greater than 1. Although it is difficult to locate the *y*-intercept precisely, it must certainly be negative. Each of these pieces of information allows you to rule out some of the possible answers, leaving only one, $y = 1.3x − 3$.

Choice (A) has a slope that is too small (too flat). Choice (B) has a *y*-intercept too large. Choice (C) is a good fit. Choice (D) has a *y*-intercept too large. Choice (E) has a slope that is too large (too steep).

Chapter Twenty: **Solids**

Although questions about solids are pretty rare on the SAT, you should be completely prepared for anything. One category of solids you might be asked about is the platonic solids. This category includes the cube (hexahedron) and the pyramid (tetrahedron). Some other kinds of solids you might see are spheres, cones, and cylinders.

The main difference between geometry that deals with solids and geometry that deals with plane figures (such as polygons) is that geometric solids are three-dimensional objects. Three-dimensional objects have properties like *surface area* (the sum of the areas of each plane surface of the solid), and *volume* (the measure of the space occupied by the solid, as an example, how much liquid it could hold). For further reading on solids:

97. Surface Area of a Rectangular Solid
98. Volume of a Rectangular Solid
99. Volume of a Cylinder

Chapter Twenty Practice Set
Answer Sheet

1. Grid-in below
2. Grid-in below
3. (A) (B) (C) (D) (E)
4. Grid-in below
5. (A) (B) (C) (D) (E)

6. (A) (B) (C) (D) (E)
7. (A) (B) (C) (D) (E)
8. (A) (B) (C) (D) (E)
9. (A) (B) (C) (D) (E)
10. Grid-in below

PRACTICE SET

Basic

1. If a right cylinder with a radius of 2 has a volume of 100π, what is the height of the cylinder?

2. A cube and a rectangular solid are equal in volume. If the lengths of the edges of the rectangular solid are 4, 8, and 16, what is the length of an edge of the cube?

3. What is the maximum number of rectangular blocks, each measuring 3 inches by 8 inches by 12 inches, that can fit inside a rectangular box with dimensions 27 inches by 60 inches by 64 inches?

   (A) 72
   (B) 144
   (C) 288
   (D) 360
   (E) 540

4. What is the maximum number of boxes with dimensions 2 inches by 3 inches by 4 inches that could fit in a cube-shaped box with a volume of 1 cubic foot?

5. What is the volume of a cube with a surface area of 96?

   (A) 8
   (B) 16
   (C) 27
   (D) 48
   (E) 64

Medium

6. A cylinder has a volume of 72π cubic inches and a height of 8 inches. If the height is increased by 4 inches, what will be the new volume of the cylinder, in cubic inches?

   (A) 576π
   (B) 9π
   (C) 108π
   (D) 328π
   (E) 76π

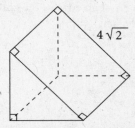

7. If the solid above is half of a cube, then the volume of the solid is

   (A) 16
   (B) 32
   (C) 42
   (D) 64
   (E) 64√2

8. Milk is poured from a full rectangular container with dimensions 4 inches by 9 inches by 10 inches into a cylindrical container with a diameter of 6 inches. Assuming the milk does not overflow the container, how many inches high will the milk reach?

   (A) $\frac{60}{\pi}$

   (B) 24

   (C) $\frac{40}{\pi}$

   (D) 10

   (E) 3π

KAPLAN

Hard

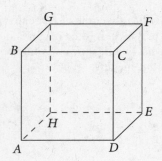

9. If the length of an edge in the cube above is 3, what is the length of *AF* ?

    (A) $2\sqrt{3}$

    (B) $3\sqrt{2}$

    (C) $3\sqrt{3}$

    (D) 6

    (E) 9

10. A rectangular block with a volume of 250 cubic inches was sliced into 2 cubes of equal volume. How much greater, in square inches, is the combined surface area of the 2 cubes than the original surface area of the rectangular block?

ANSWERS AND EXPLANATIONS

Basic

1. 25

Think of a right cylinder as a circle with height. The volume of a right cylinder is $\pi r^2 h$. Given a volume of 100π, you can determine the height by solving

$$100\pi = \pi r^2 h$$
$$100\pi = \pi(2)^2 h$$
$$100\pi = 4\pi h$$
$$h = \frac{100\pi}{4\pi} = 25$$

2. 8

We can determine the volume of the rectangular solid since we're given all its dimensions: 4, 8, and 16. The volume of a rectangular solid is equal to $l \times w \times h$. So the volume of this solid is $16 \times 8 \times 4$, and this must equal the volume of the cube as well. The volume of a cube is the length of an edge cubed, so we can set up an equation to solve for e:

$$e^3 = 16 \times 8 \times 4.$$

To avoid the multiplication, let's break the 16 down into 2×8:

$$e^3 = 2 \times 8 \times 8 \times 4$$

We can now combine 2×4 to get another 8:

$$e^3 = 8 \times 8 \times 8$$
$$e = 8$$

The length of an edge of the cube is 8.

3. D

To find the maximum number of rectangular blocks that can fit inside the given box, try to place the blocks in the box so that there is no space left over. Line up the blocks along each dimension of the box to see how many will fit. The blocks are 3 inches wide, so 9 of them can be lined up across the 27-inch width of the box. Similarly, the blocks are 12 inches wide, so 5 of them can be lined up across the 60-inch dimension of the box. Finally, the blocks are 8 inches high, so 8 of them can be placed along the 64-inch dimension of the box. The total number of blocks then $= 9 \times 5 \times 8 = 360$. Choice (D) is correct.

4. 72

The cube-shaped box has dimensions 12 inches by 12 inches by 12 inches, so you're essentially asked how many things that are 2 by 3 by 4 can fit into something 12 by 12 by 12:

$$\frac{12 \times 12 \times 12}{2 \times 3 \times 4} = 6 \times 4 \times 3 = 72$$

Medium

5. E

To find the volume of the cube, you need to know the length of an edge. The surface area of a cube equals 6 times the area of one face of the cube, or $6e^2$, where e is the length of an edge. Since you're given the surface area of the cube, plug it into the formula and solve for e :

$$6e^2 = 96$$
$$e^2 = 16$$
$$e = 4$$

So the length of an edge is 4. Since the volume of a cube equals the length of an edge cubed, the volume of this cube is 4^3, or 64, so choice (E) is correct.

6. C

To find the volume of the new cylinder, you have to find the area of its circular base. The volume of a cylinder is the area of the base $\times$ height, or $\pi r^2 \times h$. You're given the original height of the cylinder and its volume. So you can plug these values into the formula and solve for the area of the base:

$$\text{volume} = \pi r^2 h$$
$$72\pi = \pi r^2 \times 8$$
$$9\pi = \pi r^2$$

The area of the base equals 9π. Since the height of the new cylinder is 4 inches more, its height is $8 + 4$, or 12. The volume of the new cylinder equals $9\pi r^2 \times 12$, or 108π, and choice (C) is correct.

You could also use logic to solve this problem. If the height were increased by 8 inches, you'd double the volume of the cylinder—an increase of 72π cubic inches. Increasing the height by 4 inches will increase the volume by 50 percent of the original 72π, or 36π. So $36\pi + 72\pi = 108\pi$, and again, choice (C) is correct.

7. B

This figure is an unfamiliar solid, so we shouldn't try to calculate the volume directly. We are told that the solid in question is half of a cube. We can imagine the other half lying on top of the solid, forming a complete cube.

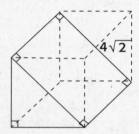

Notice that the diagonal with length $4\sqrt{2}$ and two of the cube's edges form an isosceles right triangle. In an isosceles right triangle, the hypotenuse is $\sqrt{2}$ times the length of a leg. Here the hypotenuse has length $4\sqrt{2}$, so the legs have length 4. So the volume of the whole cube is $4 \times 4 \times 4$, or 64. The volume of the solid in question is $\frac{1}{2}$ of this, or 32.

8. C

After it's poured, the volume of the milk in the cylinder will still be the same volume as the rectangular container. The volume of the rectangular container is $4 \times 9 \times 10$, or 360 cubic inches. The volume of a cylinder equals the area of its base times its height, or $\pi r^2 h$. Since the diameter is 6 inches, the radius, r, is 3 inches. Now we're ready to set up an equation to solve for h (which is the height of the milk):

Volume of milk = Volume of rectangular container

$$\pi(3)^2 h = 360$$

$$h = \frac{360}{9\pi} = \frac{40}{\pi}$$

Hard

9. C

Draw in *AE* and *AF* to get right triangle *AEF*.

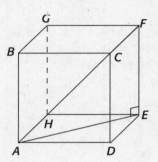

To find the diagonal *AF*, we can first find the lengths of *AE* and *EF* and then use the Pythagorean theorem. Since the cube has edge length 3, *EF* is 3. *AE* is the hypotenuse of right triangle *ADE*. $\triangle ADE$ is an isosceles right triangle, since legs *AD* and *DE* are edges of the cube and, therefore, both have length 3. Since the ratio of the length of a leg to the hypotenuse in an isosceles right triangle is 1 to $\sqrt{2}$, *AE* has length $3\sqrt{2}$.

Now, looking at triangle *AEF*, we can use the Pythagorean theorem to find *AF*. The theorem states that the hypotenuse squared equals the sum of the squares of the legs. So $AF^2 = AE^2 + EF^2$, or $AF^2 = (3\sqrt{2})^2 + 3^2 = (9 \times 2) + 9 = 18 + 9 = 27$. Therefore, $AF = \sqrt{27} = \sqrt{9 \times 3} = 3\sqrt{3}$.

10. 50

When the rectangular solid was cut into 2 identical cubes, 2 new faces were formed: 1 on each cube along the line of the cut. So the difference between the original surface area and the combined surface area of the resulting cubes is equal to the surface area of the 2 new faces. To find the area of each of these faces, you need to find the length of an edge of the cube. Since the rectangular block was divided into 2 equal cubes, the volume of each of these cubes is equal to $\frac{1}{2}$ the volume of the original solid, or 250 cubic inches ÷ 2 = 125 cubic inches. So an edge of one of these cubes has a length equal to the cube root of 125, which is 5. Therefore, the area of 1 face of the cube equals 5×5, or 25. So 2 of these faces have a total area of 2×25, or 50 square inches.

Important Math Concepts for the SAT

Chapter Twenty-One:
100 Essential Math Concepts

The math on the SAT covers a lot of ground—from arithmetic to algebra to geometry.

Don't let yourself be intimidated. We've highlighted the 100 most important concepts that you'll need for SAT Math and listed them in this chapter.

Use this list to remind yourself of the key areas you'll need to know. Do four concepts a day, and you'll be ready within a month. If a concept continually causes you trouble, circle it and refer back to it as you try to do the questions.

You've probably been taught most of these concepts in school already, so this list is a great way to refresh your memory.

NUMBER PROPERTIES

1. Number Categories

Integers are **whole numbers;** they include negative whole numbers and zero.

A **rational number** is a number that can be expressed as a **ratio of two integers. Irrational numbers** are real numbers—they have locations on the number line—but they **can't be expressed precisely as a fraction or decimal.** For the purposes of the SAT, the most important **irrational numbers** are $\sqrt{2}$, $\sqrt{3}$, and π.

2. Adding/Subtracting Signed Numbers

To **add a positive and a negative,** first ignore the signs and find the positive difference between the number parts. Then attach the sign of the original number with the larger number part. For example, to add 23 and −34, first ignore the minus sign and find the positive difference between 23 and 34—that's 11. Then attach the sign of the number with the larger number part—in this case it's the minus sign from the −34. So, $23 + (-34) = -11$.

Make **subtraction** situations simpler by turning them into addition. For example, you can think of $-17 - (-21)$ as $-17 + (+21)$.

To **add or subtract a string of positives and negatives,** first turn everything into addition. Then combine the positives and negatives so that the string is reduced to the sum of a single positive number and a single negative number.

3. Multiplying/Dividing Signed Numbers

To multiply and/or divide positives and negatives, treat the number parts as usual and **attach a minus sign if there were originally an odd number of negatives**. For example, to multiply −2, −3, and −5, first multiply the number parts: $2 \times 3 \times 5 = 30$. Then go back and note that there were *three*—an *odd* number—negatives, so the product is negative: $(-2) \times (-3) \times (-5) = -30$.

4. PEMDAS

When performing multiple operations, remember to perform them in the right order: **PEMDAS,** which means **Parentheses** first, then **Exponents,** then **Multiplication** and **Division** (left to right), and lastly **Addition** and **Subtraction** (left to right). In the expression $9 - 2 \times (5 - 3)^2 + 6 \div 3$, begin with the parentheses: $(5 - 3) = 2$. Then do the exponent: $2^2 = 4$. Now the expression is: $9 - 2 \times 4 + 6 \div 3$. Next do the multiplication and division to get: $9 - 8 + 2$, which equals 3. If you have difficulty remembering PEMDAS, use this sentence to recall it: **P**lease **E**xcuse **M**y **D**ear **A**unt **S**ally.

5. Counting Consecutive Integers

To count consecutive integers, **subtract the smallest from the largest and add 1.** To count the integers from 13 through 31, subtract: $31 - 13 = 18$. Then add 1: $18 + 1 = 19$.

NUMBER OPERATIONS AND CONCEPTS

6. Exponential Growth

If r is the ratio between consecutive terms, a_1 is the first term, a_n is the nth term, and S_n is the sum of the first n terms, then $a_n = a_1 r^{n-1}$ and $S_n = \dfrac{a_1 - a_1 r^n}{1 - r}$.

7. Union and Intersection of Sets

The things in a set are called elements or members. The union of Set A and Set B, sometimes expressed as $A \cup B$, is the set of elements that are in either or both of Set A and Set B. If Set $A = \{1, 2\}$ and Set $B = \{3, 4\}$, then $A \cup B = \{1, 2, 3, 4\}$. The intersection of Set A and Set B, sometimes expressed as $A \cap B$, is the set of elements common to both Set A and Set B. If Set $A = \{1, 2, 3\}$ and Set $B = \{3, 4, 5\}$, then $A \cap B = \{3\}$.

DIVISIBILITY

8. Factor/Multiple

The **factors** of integer n are the positive integers that divide into n with no remainder. The **multiples** of n are the integers that n divides into with no remainder. For example, 6 is a factor of 12, and 24 is a multiple of 12. 12 is both a factor and a multiple of itself, since $12 \times 1 = 12$ and $12 \div 1 = 12$.

9. Prime Factorization

To find the prime factorization of an integer, just keep breaking it up into factors until **all the factors are prime.** To find the prime factorization of 36, for example, you could begin by breaking it into 4×9: $36 = 4 \times 9 = 2 \times 2 \times 3 \times 3$.

10. Relative Primes

Relative primes are integers that have no common factor other than 1. To determine whether two integers are relative primes, break them both down to their prime factorizations. For example: $35 = 5 \times 7$, and $54 = 2 \times 3 \times 3 \times 3$. They have **no prime factors in common,** so 35 and 54 are relative primes.

11. Common Multiple

A common multiple is a number that is a multiple of two or more integers. You can always get a common multiple of two integers by **multiplying** them, but, unless the two numbers are relative primes, the product will not be the *least* common multiple. For example, to find a common multiple for 12 and 15, you could just multiply: $12 \times 15 = 180$.

To find the **least common multiple,** check out the **multiples of the larger integer** until you find one that's **also a multiple of the smaller.** To find the LCM of 12 and 15, begin by taking the multiples of 15: 15 is not divisible by 12; 30 is not; nor is 45. But the next multiple of 15, 60, *is* divisible by 12, so it's the LCM.

12. Greatest Common Factor (GCF)

To find the greatest common factor, break down both integers into their prime factorizations and multiply **all the prime factors they have in common.** $36 = 2 \times 2 \times 3 \times 3$, and $48 = 2 \times 2 \times 2 \times 2 \times 3$. What they have in common is two 2s and one 3, so the GCF is $2 \times 2 \times 3 = 12$.

13. Even/Odd

To predict whether a sum, difference, or product will be even or odd, just **take simple numbers like 1 and 2 and see what happens.** There are rules—"odd times even is even," for example—but there's no need to memorize them. What happens with one set of numbers generally happens with all similar sets.

14. Multiples of 2 and 4

An integer is divisible by 2 (even) if the **last digit is even.** An integer is divisible by 4 if the **last two digits form a multiple of 4.** The last digit of 562 is 2, which is even, so 562 is a multiple of 2. The last two digits form 62, which is *not* divisible by 4, so 562 is not a multiple of 4. The integer 512, however is divisible by four because the last two digits form 12, which is a multiple of 4.

15. Multiples of 3 and 9

An integer is divisible by 3 if the **sum of its digits is divisible by 3.** An integer is divisible by 9 if the **sum of its digits is divisible by 9.** The sum of the digits in 957 is 21, which is divisible by 3 but not by 9, so 957 is divisible by 3 but not by 9.

16. Multiples of 5 and 10

An integer is divisible by 5 if the **last digit is 5 or 0.** An integer is divisible by 10 if the **last digit is 0.** The last digit of 665 is 5, so 665 is a multiple of 5 but *not* a multiple of 10.

17. Remainders

The remainder is the **whole number left over after division.** 487 is 2 more than 485, which is a multiple of 5, so when 487 is divided by 5, the remainder will be 2.

FRACTIONS AND DECIMALS

18. Reducing Fractions

To reduce a fraction to lowest terms, **factor out and cancel** all factors the numerator and denominator have in common.

$$\frac{28}{36} = \frac{4 \times 7}{4 \times 9} = \frac{7}{9}$$

19. Adding/Subtracting Fractions

To add or subtract fractions, first find a **common denominator,** then add or subtract the numerators.

$$\frac{2}{15} + \frac{3}{10} = \frac{4}{30} + \frac{9}{30} = \frac{4+9}{30} = \frac{13}{30}$$

20. Multiplying Fractions

To multiply fractions, **multiply** the numerators and **multiply** the denominators.

$$\frac{5}{7} \times \frac{3}{4} = \frac{5 \times 3}{7 \times 4} = \frac{15}{28}$$

21. Dividing Fractions

To divide fractions, **invert** the second one and **multiply.**

$$\frac{1}{2} \div \frac{3}{5} = \frac{1}{2} \times \frac{5}{3} = \frac{1 \times 5}{2 \times 3} = \frac{5}{6}$$

22. Mixed Numbers and Improper Fractions

To convert a mixed number to an improper fraction, **multiply** the whole number part by the denominator, then **add** the numerator. The result is the new numerator (over the same denominator). To convert $7\frac{1}{3}$, first multiply 7 by 3, then add 1, to get the new numerator of 22. Put that over the same denominator, 3, to get $\frac{22}{3}$.

To convert an improper fraction to a mixed number, divide the denominator into the numerator to get a **whole number quotient with a remainder.** The quotient becomes the whole number part of the mixed number, and the remainder becomes the new numerator—with the same denominator. For example, to convert $\frac{108}{5}$, first divide 5 into 108, which yields 21 with a remainder of 3. Therefore, $\frac{108}{5} = 21\frac{3}{5}$.

23. Reciprocal

To find the reciprocal of a fraction, **switch the numerator and the denominator.** The reciprocal of $\frac{3}{7}$ is $\frac{7}{3}$. The reciprocal of 5 is $\frac{1}{5}$. The product of reciprocals is 1.

24. Comparing Fractions

One way to compare fractions is to **re-express them with a common denominator.** $\frac{3}{4} = \frac{21}{28}$ and $\frac{5}{7} = \frac{20}{28}$. $\frac{21}{28}$ is greater than $\frac{20}{28}$, so $\frac{3}{4}$ is greater than $\frac{5}{7}$. Another method is to **convert them both to decimals.** $\frac{3}{4}$ converts to .75 , and $\frac{5}{7}$ converts to approximately .714.

25. Converting Fractions and Decimals

To convert a fraction to a decimal, **divide the bottom into the top.** To convert $\frac{5}{8}$, divide 8 into 5, yielding .625.

To convert a decimal to a fraction, set the decimal over 1 and **multiply the numerator and denominator by 10** raised to the number of digits to the right of the decimal point.

To convert .625 to a fraction, you would multiply $\frac{.625}{1}$ by $\frac{10^3}{10^3}$ or $\frac{1000}{1000}$. Then simplify: $\frac{625}{1000} = \frac{5 \times 125}{8 \times 125} = \frac{5}{8}$.

26. Repeating Decimal

To find a particular digit in a repeating decimal, note the **number of digits in the cluster that repeats.** If there are 2 digits in that cluster, then every second digit is the same. If there are 3 digits in that cluster, then every third digit is the same. And so on. For example, the decimal equivalent of $\frac{1}{27}$ is .037037037…, which is best written $.\overline{037}$. There are 3 digits in the repeating cluster, so every third digit is the same: 7. To find the 50th digit, look for the multiple of 3 just less than 50—that's 48. The 48th digit is 7, and with the 49th digit the pattern repeats with 0. The 50th digit is 3.

27. Identifying the Parts and the Whole

The key to solving most fractions and percents story problems is to identify the part and the whole. Usually you'll find the **part** associated with the verb *is/are* and the **whole** associated with the word *of.* In the sentence, "Half of the boys are blonds," the whole is the boys ("*of the* boys"), and the part is the blonds ("*are* blonds").

PERCENTS

28. Percent Formula

Whether you need to find the part, the whole, or the percent, use the same formula:

Part = Percent × Whole

Example: What is 12 percent of 25?
Setup: Part = .12 × 25

Example: .15 is 3 percent of what number?
Setup: 15 = .03 × Whole

Example: 45 is what percent of 9?
Setup: 45 = Percent × 9

29. Percent Increase and Decrease

To increase a number by a percent, **add the percent to 100 percent,** convert to a decimal, and multiply. To increase 40 by 25 percent, add 25 percent to 100 percent, convert 125 percent to 1.25, and multiply by 40. 1.25 × 40 = 50.

30. Finding the Original Whole

To find the **original whole before a percent increase or decrease,** set up an equation. Think of the result of a 15 percent increase over x as $1.15x$.

Example: After a 5 percent increase, the population was 59,346. What was the population before the increase?
Setup: $1.05x = 59,346$

31. Combined Percent Increase and Decrease

To determine the combined effect of multiple percent increases and/or decreases, **start with 100 and see what happens.**

Example: A price went up 10 percent one year, and the new price went up 20 percent the next year. What was the combined percent increase?
Setup: First year: 100 + (10 percent of 100) = 110. Second year: 110 + (20 percent of 110) = 132. That's a combined 32 percent increase.

RATIOS, PROPORTIONS, AND RATES

32. Setting up a Ratio

To find a ratio, put the number associated with the word *of* **on top** and the quantity associated with the word *to* **on the bottom** and reduce. The ratio of 20 oranges to 12 apples is $\frac{20}{12}$, which reduces to $\frac{5}{3}$.

33. Part-to-Part Ratios and Part-to-Whole Ratios

If the parts add up to the whole, a part-to-part ratio can be turned into two part-to-whole ratios by putting **each number in the original ratio over the sum of the numbers.** If the ratio of males to females is 1 to 2, then the males-to-people ratio is $\frac{1}{1+2} = \frac{1}{3}$ and the females-to-people ratio is $\frac{2}{1+2} = \frac{2}{3}$. In other words, $\frac{2}{3}$ of all the people are female.

34. Solving a Proportion

To solve a proportion, **cross multiply:**

$$\frac{x}{5} = \frac{3}{4}$$

$$4x = 3 \times 5$$

$$x = \frac{15}{4} = 3.75$$

35. Rate

To solve a rates problem, **use the units** to keep things straight.

Example: If snow is falling at the rate of one foot every four hours, how many inches of snow will fall in seven hours?

Setup:

$$\frac{1 \text{ foot}}{4 \text{ hours}} = \frac{x \text{ inches}}{7 \text{ hours}}$$

$$\frac{12 \text{ inches}}{4 \text{ hours}} = \frac{x \text{ inches}}{7 \text{ hours}}$$

$$4x = 12 \times 7$$

$$x = 21$$

36. Average Rate

Average rate is *not* simply the average of the rates.

$$\text{Average } A \text{ per } B = \frac{\text{Total } A}{\text{Total } B}$$

$$\text{Average Speed} = \frac{\text{Total distance}}{\text{Total time}}$$

To find the average speed for 120 miles at 40 mph and 120 miles at 60 mph, **don't just average the two speeds.** First figure out the total distance and the total time. The total distance is 120 + 120 = 240 miles. The times are two hours for the first leg and three hours for the second leg, or five hours total. The average speed, then, is $\frac{240}{5} = 48$ miles per hour.

AVERAGES

37. Average Formula

To find the average of a set of numbers, **add them up and divide by the number of numbers.**

$$\text{Average} = \frac{\text{Sum of the terms}}{\text{Number of terms}}$$

To find the average of the 5 numbers 12, 15, 23, 40, and 40, first add them: $12 + 15 + 23 + 40 + 40 = 130$. Then divide the sum by 5: $130 \div 5 = 26$.

38. Average of Evenly Spaced Numbers

To find the average of evenly spaced numbers, just **average the smallest and the largest.** The average of all the integers from 13 through 77 is the same as the average of 13 and 77:

$$\frac{13 + 77}{2} = \frac{90}{2} = 45$$

39. Using the Average to Find the Sum

$$\text{Sum} = (\text{Average}) \times (\text{Number of terms})$$

If the average of 10 numbers is 50, then they add up to 10×50, or 500.

40. Finding the Missing Number

To find a missing number when you're given the average, **use the sum.** If the average of 4 numbers is 7, then the sum of those 4 numbers is 4×7, or 28. Suppose that 3 of the numbers are 3, 5, and 8. These 3 numbers add up to 16 of that 28, which leaves 12 for the fourth number.

41. Median and Mode

The median of a set of numbers is the **value that falls in the middle of the set.** If you have 5 test scores, and they are 88, 86, 57, 94, and 73, you must first list the scores in increasing or decreasing order: 57, 73, 86, 88, 94.

The median is the middle number, or 86. If there is an even number of values in a set (6 test scores, for instance), simply take the average of the 2 middle numbers.

The mode of a set of numbers is the **value that appears most often.** If your test scores were 88, 57, 68, 85, 99, 93, 93, 84, and 81, the mode of the scores would be 93 because it appears more often than any other score. If there is a tie for the most common value in a set, the set has more than one mode.

POSSIBILITIES AND PROBABILITY

42. Counting the Possibilities

The fundamental counting principle: If there are **m ways** one event can happen and **n ways** a second event can happen, then there are **$m \times n$ ways** for the 2 events to happen. For example, with 5 shirts and 7 pairs of pants to choose from, you can have $5 \times 7 = 35$ different outfits.

43. Probability

$$\text{Probability} = \frac{\text{Favorable Outcomes}}{\text{Total Possible Outcomes}}$$

For example, if you have 12 shirts in a drawer and 9 of them are white, the probability of picking a white shirt at random is $\frac{9}{12} = \frac{3}{4}$. This probability can also be expressed as .75 or 75%.

POWERS AND ROOTS

44. Multiplying and Dividing Powers

To multiply powers with the same base, **add the exponents and keep the same base:**

$$x^3 \times x^4 = x^{3+4} = x^7$$

To divide powers with the same base, **subtract the exponents and keep the same base:**

$$y^{13} \div y^8 = y^{13-8} = y^5$$

45. Raising Powers to Powers

To raise a power to a power, **multiply the exponents:**

$$(x^3)^4 = x^{3 \times 4} = x^{12}$$

46. Simplifying Square Roots

To simplify a square root, **factor out the perfect squares** under the radical, unsquare them, and put the result in front.

$$\sqrt{12} = \sqrt{4 \times 3} = \sqrt{4} \times \sqrt{3} = 2\sqrt{3}$$

47. Adding and Subtracting Roots

You can add or subtract radical expressions **when the part under the radicals is the same:**

$$2\sqrt{3} + 3\sqrt{3} = 5\sqrt{3}$$

Don't try to add or subtract when the radical parts are different. There's not much you can do with an expression like:

$$3\sqrt{5} + 3\sqrt{7}$$

48. Multiplying and Dividing Roots

The product of square roots is equal to the **square root of the product:**

$$\sqrt{3} \times \sqrt{5} = \sqrt{3 \times 5} = \sqrt{15}$$

The quotient of square roots is equal to the **square root of the quotient:**

$$\frac{\sqrt{6}}{\sqrt{3}} = \sqrt{\frac{6}{3}} = \sqrt{2}$$

49. Negative Exponent and Rational Exponent

To find the value of a number raised to a negative exponent, simply rewrite the number, without the negative sign, as the bottom of a fraction with 1 as the numerator of the fraction: $3^{-2} = \frac{1}{3^2} = \frac{1}{9}$. If x is a positive number and a is a nonzero number, then $x^{\frac{1}{a}} = \sqrt[a]{x}$. So $4^{\frac{1}{2}} = \sqrt[2]{4} = 2$. If p and q are integers, then $x^{\frac{p}{q}} = \sqrt[q]{x^p}$. So $4^{\frac{3}{2}} = \sqrt[2]{4^3} = \sqrt{64} = 8$.

ABSOLUTE VALUE

50. Determining Absolute Value

The absolute value of a number is the distance of the number from zero on the number line. Because absolute value is a distance, it is always positive. The absolute value of 7 is 7; this is expressed $|7| = 7$. Similarly, the absolute value of -7 is 7: $|-7| = 7$. Every positive number is the absolute value of 2 numbers: itself and its negative.

ALGEBRAIC EXPRESSIONS

51. Evaluating an Expression

To evaluate an algebraic expression, **plug in** the given values for the unknowns and calculate according to **PEMDAS.** To find the value of $x^2 + 5x - 6$ when $x = -2$, plug in -2 for x: $(-2)^2 + 5(-2) - 6 = -12$.

52. Adding and Subtracting Monomials

To combine like terms, **keep the variable part unchanged while adding or subtracting the coefficients:**

$$2a + 3a = (2 + 3)a = 5a$$

53. Adding and Subtracting Polynomials

To add or subtract polynomials, **combine like terms.**

$$(3x^2 + 5x - 7) - (x^2 + 12) =$$
$$(3x^2 - x^2) + 5x + (-7 - 12) =$$
$$2x^2 + 5x - 19 =$$

54. Multiplying Monomials

To multiply monomials, **multiply the coefficients and the variables separately:**

$$2a \times 3a = (2 \times 3)(a \times a) = 6a^2$$

55. Multiplying Binomials—FOIL

To multiply binomials, use **FOIL.** To multiply $(x + 3)$ by $(x + 4)$, first multiply the **F**irst terms: $x \times x = x^2$. Next the **O**uter terms: $x \times 4 = 4x$. Then the **I**nner terms: $3 \times x = 3x$. And finally the **L**ast terms: $3 \times 4 = 12$. Then add and combine like terms:

$$x^2 + 4x + 3x + 12 = x^2 + 7x + 12$$

56. Multiplying Other Polynomials

FOIL works only when you want to multiply two binomials. If you want to multiply polynomials with more than two terms, make sure you **multiply each term in the first polynomial by each term in the second.**

$$(x^2 + 3x + 4)(x + 5) =$$
$$x^2(x + 5) + 3x(x + 5) + 4(x + 5) =$$
$$x^3 + 5x^2 + 3x^2 + 15x + 4x + 20 =$$
$$x^3 + 8x^2 + 19x + 20$$

After multiplying two polynomials together, the number of terms in your expression before simplifying should equal the number of terms in one polynomial multiplied by the number of terms in the second. In the example, you should have $3 \times 2 = 6$ terms in the product before you simplify like terms.

FACTORING ALGEBRAIC EXPRESSIONS

57. Factoring out a Common Divisor

A factor common to all terms of a polynomial can be **factored out.** All three terms in the polynomial $3x^3 + 12x^2 - 6x$ contain a factor of $3x$. Pulling out the common factor yields $3x(x^2 + 4x - 2)$.

58. Factoring the Difference of Squares

One of the test maker's favorite factorables is the **difference of squares.**

$$a^2 - b^2 = (a - b)\ (a + b)$$

$x^2 - 9$, for example, factors to $(x - 3)(x + 3)$.

59. Factoring the Square of a Binomial

Recognize polynomials that are squares of binomials:

$$a^2 + 2ab + b^2 = (a + b)^2$$
$$a^2 - 2ab + b^2 = (a - b)^2$$

For example, $4x^2 + 12x + 9$ factors to $(2x + 3)^2$, and $n^2 - 10n + 25$ factors to $(n - 5)^2$.

60. Factoring Other Polynomials—FOIL in Reverse

To factor a quadratic expression, **think about what binomials you could use FOIL on to get that quadratic expression.** To factor $x^2 - 5x + 6$, think about what First terms will produce x^2, what Last terms will produce $+6$, and what Outer and Inner terms will produce $-5x$. Some common sense—and a little trial and error—lead you to $(x - 2)(x - 3)$.

61. Simplifying an Algebraic Fraction

Simplifying an algebraic fraction is a lot like simplifying a numerical fraction. The general idea is to **find factors common to the numerator and denominator and cancel them.** Thus, simplifying an algebraic fraction begins with factoring.

For example, to simplify $\dfrac{x^2 - x - 12}{x^2 - 9}$, first factor the numerator and denominator:

$$\frac{x^2 - x - 12}{x^2 - 9} = \frac{(x - 4)(x + 3)}{(x - 3)(x + 3)}$$

Canceling $x + 3$ from the numerator and denominator leaves you with $\dfrac{x - 4}{x - 3}$.

SOLVING EQUATIONS

62. Solving a Linear Equation

To solve an equation, do whatever is necessary to both sides to **isolate the variable.** To solve the equation $5x - 12 = -2x + 9$, first get all the x's on one side by adding $2x$ to both sides: $7x - 12 = 9$. Then add 12 to both sides: $7x = 21$. Then divide both sides by 7: $x = 3$.

63. Solving "In Terms Of"

To solve an equation for one variable **in terms of** another means to **isolate the one variable on one side of the equation,** leaving an expression containing the other variable on the other side of the equation. To solve the equation $3x - 10y = -5x + 6y$ for x in terms of y, isolate x:

$$3x - 10y = -5x + 6y$$

$$3x + 5x = 6y + 10y$$

$$8x = 16y$$

$$x = 2y$$

64. Translating from English into Algebra

To translate from English into algebra, look for the key words and systematically turn phrases into algebraic expressions and sentences into equations. Be careful about order, especially when subtraction is called for.

Example: The charge for a phone call is r cents for the first 3 minutes and s cents for each minute thereafter. What is the cost, in cents, of a phone call lasting exactly t minutes? ($t > 3$)

Setup: The charge begins with r, and then something more is added, depending on the length of the call. The amount added is s times the number of minutes past 3 minutes. If the total number of minutes is t, then the number of minutes past 3 is $t - 3$. So the charge is $r + s(t - 3)$.

65. Solving a Quadratic Equation

To solve a quadratic equation, put it in the "$ax^2 + bx + c = 0$" form, **factor** the left side (if you can), and set each factor equal to 0 separately to get the two solutions. To solve $x^2 + 12 = 7x$, first rewrite it as $x^2 - 7x + 12 = 0$. Then factor the left side:

$$(x - 3)(x - 4) = 0$$

$$x - 3 = 0 \text{ or } x - 4 = 0$$

$$x = 3 \text{ or } 4$$

66. Solving a System of Equations

You can solve for 2 variables only if you have 2 distinct equations. 2 forms of the same equation will not be adequate. **Combine the equations** in such a way that **one of the variables cancels out.** To solve the 2 equations $4x + 3y = 8$ and $x + y = 3$, multiply both sides of the second equation by -3 to get: $-3x - 3y = -9$. Now add the 2 equations; the $3y$ and the $-3y$ cancel out, leaving: $x = -1$. Plug that back into either one of the original equations and you'll find that $y = 4$.

67. Solving an Inequality

To solve an inequality, do whatever is necessary to both sides to **isolate the variable.** Just remember that when you **multiply or divide both sides by a negative number,** you must **reverse the sign.** To solve $-5x + 7 < -3$, subtract 7 from both sides to get: $-5x < -10$. Now divide both sides by -5, remembering to reverse the sign: $x > 2$.

68. Radical Equations

A radical equation contains at least one radical expression. Solve radical equations by using standard rules of algebra. If $5\sqrt{x} - 2 = 13$, then $5\sqrt{x} = 15$ and $\sqrt{x} = 3$, so $x = 9$.

FUNCTIONS

69. Function Notation and Evaluation

Standard function notation is written $f(x)$ and read "f of 4." To evaluate the function $f(x) = 2x + 3$ for $f(4)$, replace x with 4 and simplify: $f(4) = 2(4) + 3 = 11$.

70. Direct and Inverse Variation

In direct variation, $y = kx$, where k is a nonzero constant. In direct variation, the variable y changes directly as x does. If a unit of Currency A is worth 2 units of Currency B, then $A = 2B$. If the number of units of B were to double, the number of units of A would double, and so on for halving, tripling, etc. In inverse variation, $xy = k$, where x and y are variables and k is a constant. A famous inverse relationship is $rate \times time = distance$, where distance is constant. Imagine having to cover a distance of 24 miles. If you were to travel at 12 miles per hour, you'd need 2 hours. But if you were to halve your rate, you would have to double your time. This is just another way of saying that rate and time vary inversely.

71. Domain and Range of a Function

The domain of a function is the set of values for which the function is defined. For example, the domain of $f(x) = \dfrac{1}{1 - x^2}$ is all values of x except 1 and -1, because for those values the denominator has a value of 0 and is therefore undefined. The range of a function is the set of outputs or results of the function. For example, the range of $f(x) = x^2$ is all numbers greater than all or equal to zero, because x^2 cannot be negative.

COORDINATE GEOMETRY

72. Finding the Distance Between Two Points

To find the distance between points, **use the Pythagorean theorem** or **special right triangles.** The difference between the x's is one leg and the difference between the y's is the other.

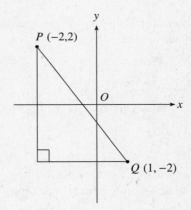

In the figure above, PQ is the hypotenuse of a 3-4-5 triangle, so $PQ = 5$.

You can also use the **distance formula:**

$$d = \sqrt{(x_1 - x_2)^2 + (y_1 + y_2)^2}$$

To find the distance between $R(3, 6)$ and $S(5, -2)$:

$$d = \sqrt{(3 - 5)^2 + [6 - (-2)^2}$$

$$= \sqrt{(-2)^2 + (8)^2}$$

$$= \sqrt{68} = 2\sqrt{17}$$

73. Using Two Points to Find the Slope

$$\text{Slope} = \frac{\text{Change in } y}{\text{Change in } x} = \frac{\text{Rise}}{\text{Run}}$$

The slope of the line that contains the points $A(2, 3)$ and $B(0, -1)$ is:

$$\frac{y_A - y_B}{x_A - x_B} = \frac{3 - (-1)}{2 - 0} = \frac{4}{2} = 2$$

74. Using an Equation to Find the Slope

To find the slope of a line from an equation, put the equation into the **slope-intercept** form:

$$y = mx + b$$

The **slope is m**. To find the slope of the equation $3x + 2y = 4$, rearrange it:

$$3x + 2y = 4$$

$$2y = -3x + 4$$

$$y = -\frac{3}{2}x + 2$$

The slope is $-\frac{3}{2}$.

75. Using an Equation to Find an Intercept

To find the y-intercept, you can either put the equation into $y = mx + b$ (slope-intercept) form—in which case b is the y-intercept—or you can just **plug $x = 0$** into the equation and **solve for y**. To find the x-intercept, **plug $y = 0$** into the equation and **solve for x**.

LINES AND ANGLES

76. Intersecting Lines

When two lines intersect, **adjacent angles are supplementary and vertical angles are equal.**

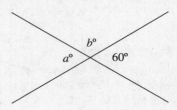

In the figure above, the angles marked $a°$ and $b°$ are adjacent and supplementary, so $a + b = 180$. Furthermore, the angles marked $a°$ and $60°$ are vertical and equal, so $a = 60$.

77. Parallel Lines and Transversals

A transversal across parallel lines forms **four equal acute angles and four equal obtuse angles.**

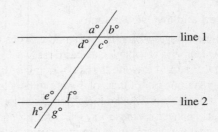

In the figure above, line 1 is parallel to line 2. Angles a, c, e, and g are obtuse, so they are all equal. Angles b, d, f, and h are acute, so they are all equal.

Furthermore, **any of the acute angles is supplementary to any of the obtuse angles.** Angles a and h are supplementary, as are b and e, c and f, and so on.

TRIANGLES—GENERAL

78. Interior and Exterior Angles of a Triangle

The 3 angles of any triangle **add up to 180 degrees.**

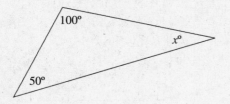

In the figure above, $x + 50 + 100 = 180$, so $x = 30$.

An exterior angle of a triangle is equal to the **sum of the remote interior angles.**

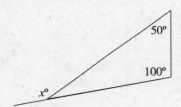

In the figure above, the exterior angle labeled $x°$ is equal to the sum of the remote angles: $x = 50 + 100 = 150$.

The 3 exterior angles of a triangle add up to 360 degrees.

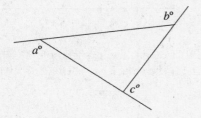

In the figure above, $a + b + c = 360$.

79. Similar Triangles

Similar triangles have the same shape: **corresponding angles are equal and corresponding sides are proportional.**

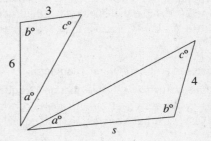

The triangles above are similar because they have the same angles. The 3 corresponds to the 4 and the 6 corresponds to the s.

$$\frac{3}{4} = \frac{6}{s}$$

$$3s = 24$$

$$s = 8$$

80. Area of a Triangle

$$\text{Area of Triangle} = \frac{1}{2}(\text{base})(\text{height})$$

The height is the perpendicular distance between the side that's chosen as the base and the opposite vertex.

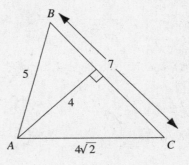

In the triangle above, 4 is the height when the 7 is chosen as the base.

$$\text{Area} = \frac{1}{2}bh = \frac{1}{2}(7)(4) = 14$$

81. Triangle Inequality Theorem

The length of one side of a triangle must be **greater than the difference and less than the sum** of the lengths of the other two sides. For example, if it is given that the length of one side is 3 and the length of another side is 7, then you know that the length of the third side must be greater than $7 - 3 = 4$ and less than $7 + 3 = 10$.

82. Isosceles and Equilateral Triangles

An isosceles triangle is a triangle that has **2 equal sides.** Not only are 2 sides equal, but the angles opposite the equal sides, called **base angles**, are also equal.

Equilateral triangles are triangles in which **all 3 sides are equal.** Since all the sides are equal, all the angles are also equal. All 3 angles in an equilateral triangle measure 60 degrees, regardless of the lengths of sides.

RIGHT TRIANGLES

83. Pythagorean Theorem

For all right triangles:

$$(\text{leg}_1)^2 + (\text{leg}_2)^2 = (\text{hypotenuse})^2$$

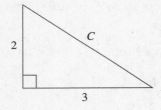

If one leg is 2 and the other leg is 3, then:

$$2^2 + 3^2 = c^2$$
$$c^2 = 4 + 9$$
$$c = \sqrt{13}$$

84. The 3-4-5 Triangle

If a right triangle's leg-to-leg ratio is 3:4, or if the leg-to-hypotenuse ratio is 3:5 or 4:5, it's a 3-4-5 triangle and you don't need to use the Pythagorean theorem to find the third side. Just figure out what multiple of 3-4-5 it is.

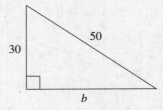

In the right triangle shown, one leg is 30 and the hypotenuse is 50. This is 10 times 3-4-5. The other leg is 40.

85. The 5-12-13 Triangle

If a right triangle's leg-to-leg ratio is 5:12, or if the leg-to-hypotenuse ratio is 5:13 or 12:13, then it's a 5-12-13 triangle and you don't need to use the Pythagorean theorem to find the third side. Just figure out what multiple of 5-12-13 it is.

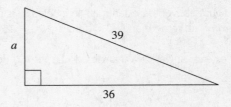

Here one leg is 36 and the hypotenuse is 39. This is 3 times 5-12-13. The other leg is 15.

86. The 30-60-90 Triangle

The sides of a 30-60-90 triangle are in a ratio of $x : x\sqrt{3} : 2x$. You don't need the Pythagorean theorem.

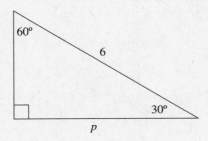

If the hypotenuse is 6, then the shorter leg is half that, or 3; and then the longer leg is equal to the short leg times $\sqrt{3}$, or $3\sqrt{3}$.

87. The 45-45-90 Triangle

The sides of a 45-45-90 triangle are in a ratio of $x : x : x\sqrt{2}$.

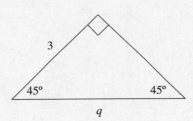

If one leg is 3, then the other leg is also 3, and the hypotenuse is equal to a leg times $\sqrt{2}$, or $3\sqrt{2}$.

OTHER POLYGONS

88. Characteristics of a Rectangle

A rectangle is a **four-sided figure with four right angles.** Opposite sides are equal. Diagonals are equal.

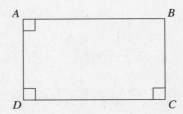

Quadrilateral *ABCD* above is shown to have three right angles. The fourth angle therefore also measures 90 degrees, and *ABCD* is a rectangle. The perimeter of a rectangle is equal to the sum of the lengths of the four sides, which is equivalent to 2(length + width).

Area of Rectangle = length × width

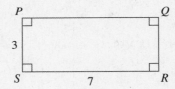

The area of a 7-by-3 rectangle is $7 \times 3 = 21$.

89. Characteristics of a Parallelogram

A parallelogram has **two pairs of parallel sides.** Opposite sides are equal. Opposite angles are equal. Consecutive angles add up to 180 degrees.

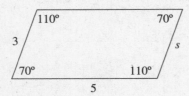

In the figure above, s is the length of the side opposite the 3, so s = 3.

Area of Parallelogram = base × height

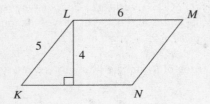

In parallelogram KLMN above, 4 is the height when LM or KN is used as the base. Base × height = 6 × 4 = 24.

90. Characteristics of a Square

A square is a **rectangle with four equal sides.**

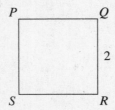

If PQRS is a square, all sides are the same length as QR. The perimeter of a square is equal to four times the length of one side.

Area of Square = (Side)²

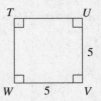

The square above, with sides of length 5, has an area of $5^2 = 25$.

91. Interior Angles of a Polygon

The **sum of the measures of the interior angles of a polygon = (n − 2) × 180,** where n is the number of sides.

Sum of the Angles = (n − 2) × 180

The eight angles of an octagon, for example, add up to $(8 − 2) \times 180 = 1{,}080$.

CIRCLES

92. Circumference of a Circle

Circumference = 2πr

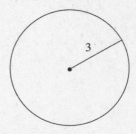

In the circle above, the radius is 3, and so the circumference is $2\pi(3) = 6\pi$.

93. Length of an Arc

An **arc** is a piece of the circumference. If n is the degree measure of the arc's central angle, then the formula is:

$$\text{Length of an Arc} = \left(\frac{n}{360}\right)(2\pi r)$$

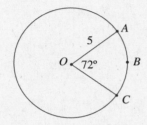

In the figure above, the radius is 5 and the measure of the central angle is 72 degrees. The arc length is $\frac{72}{360}$ or $\frac{1}{5}$ of the circumference:

$$\left(\frac{72}{360}\right)(2\pi)(5) = \left(\frac{1}{5}\right)(10\pi) = 2\pi$$

94. Area of a Circle

$$\text{Area of a Circle} = \pi r^2$$

The area of the circle is $\pi(4)^2 = 16\pi$.

95. Area of a Sector

A **sector** is a piece of the area of a circle. If n is the degree measure of the sector's central angle, then the formula is:

$$\text{Area of a Sector} = \left(\frac{n}{360}\right)(\pi r^2)$$

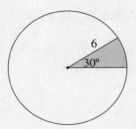

In the figure above, the radius is 6 and the measure of the sector's central angle is 30 degrees. The sector has $\frac{30}{360}$ or $\frac{1}{12}$ of the area of the circle:

$$\left(\frac{30}{360}\right)(\pi)(6^2) = \left(\frac{1}{12}\right)(36\pi) = 3\pi$$

96. Tangency

When a line is tangent to a circle, the radius of the circle is perpendicular to the line at the point of contact.

SOLIDS

97. Surface Area of a Rectangular Solid

The surface of a rectangular solid consists of three pairs of identical faces. To find the surface area, find the area of each face and add them up. If the length is l, the width is w, and the height is h, the formula is:

$$\text{Surface Area} = 2lw + 2wh + 2lh$$

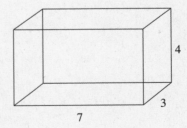

The surface area of the box above is:
$$2 \times 7 \times 3 + 2 \times 3 \times 4 + 2 \times 7 \times 4 = 42 + 24 + 56 = 122$$

98. Volume of a Rectangular Solid

Volume of a Rectangular Solid = *lwh*

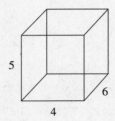

The volume of a 4-by-5-by-6 box is

$4 \times 5 \times 6 = 120$

A cube is a rectangular solid with length, width, and height all equal. If e is the length of an edge of a cube, the volume formula is:

Volume of a Cube = e^3

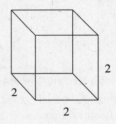

The volume of this cube is $2^3 = 8$.

99. Volume of a Cylinder

Volume of a Cylinder = $\pi r^2 h$

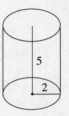

In the cylinder above, $r = 2$, $h = 5$, so:

Volume $= \pi(2^2)(5) = 20\pi$

100. Finding the Midpoint

The midpoint of two points on a line segment is the average of the x-coordinates of the endpoints and the average of the y-coordinates of the endpoints. If the endpoints are (x_1, y_1) and (x_2, y_2), the midpoint is $\left(\dfrac{x_1 + x_2}{2}, \dfrac{y_1 + y_2}{2}\right)$. The midpoint of (3, 5) and (9, 1) is $\left(\dfrac{3 + 9}{2}, \dfrac{5 + 1}{2}\right)$.

Practice Tests and Explanations

Before taking these practice tests, find a quiet room where you can work uninterrupted for 70 minutes. Make sure you have a comfortable desk, your calculator, and several No. 2 pencils.

Use the answer sheet on the following page to record your answers. You can tear it out or photocopy it.

Once you start this practice test, don't stop until you've finished. Remember—you can review any question within a section, but you may not go backward or forward to a different section.

Good luck.

Note: At the time of printing, the College Board had not yet officially released the New SAT, therefore the precise number of questions you may see in a given section is not yet known. The number of questions that appear in the practice tests that follow is based on the sample test released on the College Board website.

Practice Test A
Answer Sheet

Remove (or photocopy) this answer sheet and use it to complete the practice test. See the answer key following the test when finished. The "Compute Your Score" section at the back of the book will show you how to find your score.

Start with number 1 for each section.

SECTION 1

1. Ⓐ Ⓑ Ⓒ Ⓓ Ⓔ   7. Ⓐ Ⓑ Ⓒ Ⓓ Ⓔ   13. Ⓐ Ⓑ Ⓒ Ⓓ Ⓔ   19. Ⓐ Ⓑ Ⓒ Ⓓ Ⓔ
2. Ⓐ Ⓑ Ⓒ Ⓓ Ⓔ   8. Ⓐ Ⓑ Ⓒ Ⓓ Ⓔ   14. Ⓐ Ⓑ Ⓒ Ⓓ Ⓔ   20. Ⓐ Ⓑ Ⓒ Ⓓ Ⓔ
3. Ⓐ Ⓑ Ⓒ Ⓓ Ⓔ   9. Ⓐ Ⓑ Ⓒ Ⓓ Ⓔ   15. Ⓐ Ⓑ Ⓒ Ⓓ Ⓔ
4. Ⓐ Ⓑ Ⓒ Ⓓ Ⓔ   10. Ⓐ Ⓑ Ⓒ Ⓓ Ⓔ   16. Ⓐ Ⓑ Ⓒ Ⓓ Ⓔ
5. Ⓐ Ⓑ Ⓒ Ⓓ Ⓔ   11. Ⓐ Ⓑ Ⓒ Ⓓ Ⓔ   17. Ⓐ Ⓑ Ⓒ Ⓓ Ⓔ
6. Ⓐ Ⓑ Ⓒ Ⓓ Ⓔ   12. Ⓐ Ⓑ Ⓒ Ⓓ Ⓔ   18. Ⓐ Ⓑ Ⓒ Ⓓ Ⓔ

right in section 1

wrong in section 1

SECTION 2

1. Ⓐ Ⓑ Ⓒ Ⓓ Ⓔ   3. Ⓐ Ⓑ Ⓒ Ⓓ Ⓔ   5. Ⓐ Ⓑ Ⓒ Ⓓ Ⓔ   7. Ⓐ Ⓑ Ⓒ Ⓓ Ⓔ
2. Ⓐ Ⓑ Ⓒ Ⓓ Ⓔ   4. Ⓐ Ⓑ Ⓒ Ⓓ Ⓔ   6. Ⓐ Ⓑ Ⓒ Ⓓ Ⓔ   8. Ⓐ Ⓑ Ⓒ Ⓓ Ⓔ

right in section 2

wrong in section 2

9.   10.   11.   12.   13.

14.   15.   16.   17.   18.

Remove (or photocopy) this answer sheet and use it to complete the practice test.

Start with number 1 for each section.

SECTION

3

1. Ⓐ Ⓑ Ⓒ Ⓓ Ⓔ   5. Ⓐ Ⓑ Ⓒ Ⓓ Ⓔ   9. Ⓐ Ⓑ Ⓒ Ⓓ Ⓔ   13. Ⓐ Ⓑ Ⓒ Ⓓ Ⓔ

2. Ⓐ Ⓑ Ⓒ Ⓓ Ⓔ   6. Ⓐ Ⓑ Ⓒ Ⓓ Ⓔ   10. Ⓐ Ⓑ Ⓒ Ⓓ Ⓔ   14. Ⓐ Ⓑ Ⓒ Ⓓ Ⓔ

3. Ⓐ Ⓑ Ⓒ Ⓓ Ⓔ   7. Ⓐ Ⓑ Ⓒ Ⓓ Ⓔ   11. Ⓐ Ⓑ Ⓒ Ⓓ Ⓔ   15. Ⓐ Ⓑ Ⓒ Ⓓ Ⓔ

4. Ⓐ Ⓑ Ⓒ Ⓓ Ⓔ   8. Ⓐ Ⓑ Ⓒ Ⓓ Ⓔ   12. Ⓐ Ⓑ Ⓒ Ⓓ Ⓔ   16. Ⓐ Ⓑ Ⓒ Ⓓ Ⓔ

right in
section 3

wrong in
section 3

Practice Test A

SECTION ONE

Time—25 Minutes
20 Questions

Solve each of the following problems, decide which is the best answer choice, and darken the corresponding oval on the answer sheet. Use available space in the test booklet for scratchwork.*

Notes:

(1) Calculator use is permitted.

(2) All numbers used are real numbers.

(3) Figures are provided for some problems. All figures are drawn to scale and lie in a plane UNLESS otherwise indicated.

(4) Unless otherwise specified, the domain of any function f is assumed to be the set of all real numbers x for which $f(x)$ is a real number.

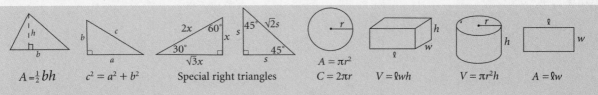

$A = \frac{1}{2}bh$ $c^2 = a^2 + b^2$ Special right triangles $A = \pi r^2$ $C = 2\pi r$ $V = \ell wh$ $V = \pi r^2 h$ $A = \ell w$

The sum of the degree measures of the angles in a triangle is 180.
The number of degrees of arc in a circle is 360.
A straight angle has a degree measure of 180.

1. What is the smallest positive integer that is evenly divisible by both 21 and 9?

(A) 189

(B) 126

(C) 63

(D) 42

(E) 21

2. Which of the following elements is in the union of the sets {1, 4, 9, 12} and {2, 4, 6, 8}?

 I. 2
 II. 4
 III. 12

(A) I only

(B) II only

(C) I and II

(D) II and III

(E) I, II, and III

GO ON TO THE NEXT PAGE

*The directions on the actual SAT will vary slightly.

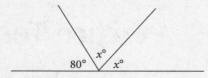

3. In the figure above, what is the value of x ?

    (A) 40

    (B) 50

    (C) 60

    (D) 80

    (E) 100

4. At a certain photography store it costs Pete $1.65 for the first print of a photograph and $0.85 for each additional print. How many prints of a particular photograph can Pete get for $20?

    (A) 19

    (B) 20

    (C) 21

    (D) 22

    (E) 23

5. If $m(x) = \dfrac{x + 4}{x - 4}$ for all values of $x \neq 4$ and $m(y) = -3$, what is the value of y?

    (A) −5

    (B) −3

    (C) 1

    (D) 2

    (E) 3

6. A laboratory has 55 rabbits, some white and the rest brown. Which of the following could be the ratio of white rabbits to brown rabbits in the lab?

    (A) 3:8

    (B) 5:11

    (C) 3:4

    (D) 3:1

    (E) 5:1

7. If $k^{\frac{1}{3}} = \dfrac{k}{4}$ and $k \neq 0$, then what is the value of k^2?

    (A) 2

    (B) 7

    (C) 8

    (D) 16

    (E) 64

8. For all x and y, $(x + 1)(y + 1) - x - y =$

    (A) $xy - x - y + 1$

    (B) $xy + 1$

    (C) $-x - y + 1$

    (D) $x^2 + y^2 - 1$

    (E) 1

9. What percent of 4 is $\dfrac{2}{3}$ of 8?

    (A) 25%

    (B) $66\dfrac{2}{3}\%$

    (C) 120%

    (D) $133\dfrac{1}{3}\%$

    (E) 150%

GO ON TO THE NEXT PAGE

KAPLAN

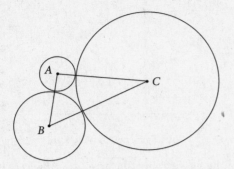

Contribution to Charity	Number of People
$10	4
$15	3
$20	2
$25	4
$30	2

10. If points *A*, *B*, and *C* are the centers of the above circles, and the circles have radii of 2, 3, and 4, respectively, what is the perimeter of triangle *ABC*? The circles are tangent to each other.

(A) 18

(B) 12

(C) 3π

(D) 9

(E) 6

11. If *n* is an odd number, which of the following must be even?

(A) $\dfrac{n+1}{2}$

(B) $\dfrac{n-1}{2}$

(C) $n^2 + 2n$

(D) $2n + 2$

(E) $3n^2 - 2n$

12. The contributions of 15 people to a certain charity are shown above. What is the difference between the median contribution and the average (arithmetic mean) contribution?

(A) $5

(B) $4

(C) $3

(D) $2

(E) $1

13. If $m \blacktriangle n$ is defined by the equation

$$m \blacktriangle n = \frac{m^2 - n + 1}{mn}, \text{ for all nonzero } m \text{ and } n,$$

then $3 \blacktriangle 1 =$

(A) $\dfrac{9}{4}$

(B) 3

(C) $\dfrac{11}{3}$

(D) 6

(E) 9

GO ON TO THE NEXT PAGE

KAPLAN

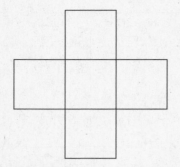

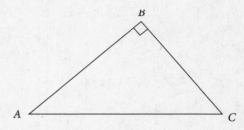

Note: Figure not drawn to scale.

14. The figure above is made of 5 squares of equal area. If the area of the figure is 20, what is the perimeter of the figure?

(A) 24

(B) 30

(C) 36

(D) 48

(E) 100

15. What is the radius of the largest sphere that can be placed inside a cube of volume 64?

(A) $6\sqrt{2}$

(B) 8

(C) 4

(D) $2\sqrt{2}$

(E) 2

16. In the figure above, the area of $\triangle ABC$ is 6. If the length of BC is $\frac{1}{3}$ the length of AB, then $AC =$

(A) $\sqrt{2}$

(B) 2

(C) 4

(D) 6

(E) $2\sqrt{10}$

17. If $d = \dfrac{c - b}{a - b}$, then $b =$

(A) $\dfrac{c - d}{a - d}$

(B) $\dfrac{c + d}{a + d}$

(C) $\dfrac{ca - d}{ca + d}$

(D) $\dfrac{c - ad}{1 - d}$

(E) $\dfrac{c + ad}{d - 1}$

GO ON TO THE NEXT PAGE

KAPLAN

18. If snow falls at the rate of x centimeters per minute, how many hours would it take y centimeters to fall?

    (A) $\dfrac{x}{60y}$

    (B) $\dfrac{y}{60x}$

    (C) $\dfrac{60x}{y}$

    (D) $\dfrac{60y}{x}$

    (E) $60xy$

20. A motorist travels 90 miles at a rate of 20 miles per hour. If he returns the same distance at a rate of 40 miles per hour, what is his average speed for the entire trip, in miles per hour?

    (A) 20

    (B) $\dfrac{65}{3}$

    (C) $\dfrac{80}{3}$

    (D) 30

    (E) $\dfrac{130}{3}$

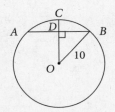

Note: Figure not drawn to scale.

19. In the figure above, if AB has a length of 16 and OB has a length of 10, what is the length of CD?

    (A) 4
    (B) $2\sqrt{3}$
    (C) $8 - \sqrt{35}$
    (D) 2
    (E) $8 - \sqrt{39}$

IF YOU FINISH BEFORE TIME IS CALLED, YOU MAY CHECK YOUR WORK ON THIS SECTION ONLY. DO NOT TURN TO ANY OTHER SECTION IN THE TEST. STOP

SECTION TWO

Time—25 Minutes
18 Questions

Solve each of the following problems, decide which is the best answer choice, and darken the corresponding oval on the answer sheet. Use available space in the test booklet for scratchwork.*

Notes:

(1) Calculator use is permitted.

(2) All numbers used are real numbers.

(3) Figures are provided for some problems. All figures are drawn to scale and lie in a plane UNLESS otherwise indicated.

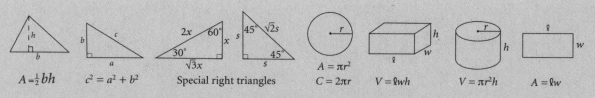

$A = \frac{1}{2}bh$ $c^2 = a^2 + b^2$ Special right triangles $A = \pi r^2$ $C = 2\pi r$ $V = \ell wh$ $V = \pi r^2 h$ $A = \ell w$

The sum of the degree measures of the angles in a triangle is 180.
The number of degrees of arc in a circle is 360.
A straight angle has a degree measure of 180.

1. If $f(x) = x^3 + 6$, what is the value of $f(3)$?

(A) −3
(B) 15
(C) 33
(D) 39
(E) 729

2. If the maximum value of $r(x)$ is 6, what is the maximum value of $r(x + 4)$?

(A) −2
(B) 2
(C) 4
(D) 6
(E) 10

*The directions on the actual SAT will vary slightly.

GO ON TO THE NEXT PAGE

KAPLAN

3. Set *J* is the set of all positive even integers and set *K* is the set of all numbers between −2 and 2, inclusive. Which of the following represents the intersection of *J* and *K*?

(A) all integers

(B) all positive integers

(C) all positive even integers

(D) {2}

(E) {0,2}

4. If $|-3x - 7| = 5$, $x =$

(A) $-\dfrac{2}{3}$

(B) −4

(C) $-\dfrac{2}{3}$ or −4

(D) $\dfrac{2}{3}$ or −4

(E) 4

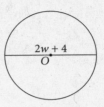

5. If the area of the circle with center *O* shown above is 16π, what is the value of *w*?

(A) 2

(B) 3

(C) 4

(D) 8

(E) 16

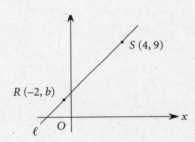

Note: Figure not drawn to scale.

6. In the figure above, the slope of line ℓ is $\dfrac{4}{3}$. What is the value of *b* ?

(A) −2

(B) −1

(C) 1

(D) 2

(E) 3

GO ON TO THE NEXT PAGE

KAPLAN

7. A factory cut its labor force by 16 percent, but then increased it by 25 percent of the new amount. What was the overall change in the size of the workforce?

   (A) A 5% decrease

   (B) No net change

   (C) A 5% increase

   (D) A 9% increase

   (E) A 10% increase

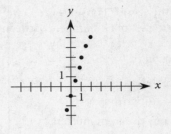

8. Which of the following lines best fits the points in the figure above?

   (A) $y = x - 1$

   (B) $y = 3x - 1$

   (C) $y = 1 - 3x$

   (D) $y = 1 - x$

   (E) $y = x + 3$

GO ON TO THE NEXT PAGE

DIRECTIONS FOR STUDENT-PRODUCED RESPONSE QUESTIONS

For each of the questions below (9–18), solve the problem and indicate your answer by darkening the ovals in the special grid. For example:

Answer: 1.25 or $\frac{5}{4}$ or 5/4

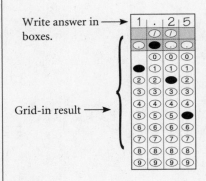

Write answer in boxes.

Grid-in result

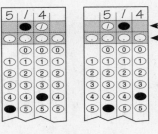

Fraction line
Decimal point

Either position is correct.

You may start your answers in any column, space permitting. Columns not needed should be left blank.

- It is recommended, though not required, that you write your answer in the boxes at the top of the columns. However, you will receive credit only for darkening the ovals correctly.

- Grid only one answer to a question, even though some problems have more than one correct answer.

- Darken no more than one oval in a column.

- No answers are negative.

- Mixed numbers cannot be gridded. For example: the number $1\frac{1}{4}$ must be gridded as 1.25 or 5/4.

  (If 1 1 / 4 is gridded, it will be interpreted as $\frac{11}{4}$ not $1\frac{1}{4}$.)

- Decimal Accuracy: Decimal answers must be entered as accurately as possible. For example, if you obtain an answer such as 0.1666..., you should record the result as .166 or .167. **Less accurate values such as .16 or .17 are not acceptable.**

Acceptable ways to grid $\frac{1}{6}$ = .1666...

KAPLAN

9. A certain book costs $12 more in hardcover than softcover. If the softcover price is $\frac{2}{3}$ of the hardcover price, how much does the book cost, in dollars, in hardcover? (Ignore the dollar sign when gridding your answer.)

10. If $4a - 1 = 64$, what is the value of $6a$?

11. The average (arithmetic mean) of six numbers is $7\frac{1}{2}$. If the average of 4 of these numbers is 2, what is the average of the other 2 numbers?

12. In a certain dairy store, $\frac{1}{3}$ of all the yogurts are fruit flavored. If $\frac{1}{8}$ of all yogurts are peach flavored, what fraction of the fruit flavored yogurts are peach flavored?

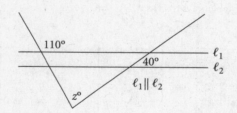

13. In the figure above, what is the value of z?

14. If m and n are prime numbers such that the sum of m and n is greater than 20 and the product of m and n is less than 50, what is a possible value of mn?

15. What is the area of a triangle with vertices $(2, 3)$, $(8, 3)$, and $(13, 6)$ in the xy-plane?

16. If $y > 0$ and x is $2\frac{1}{2}$ percent of y, then y is what percent of x? (Ignore the percent sign when gridding your answer.)

17. For how many positive integers x is $\frac{130}{x}$ an integer?

18. The area of a circle is 16π square inches. What is the area, in square inches, of the largest square that can be drawn within this circle?

IF YOU FINISH BEFORE TIME IS CALLED, YOU MAY CHECK YOUR WORK ON THIS SECTION ONLY. DO NOT TURN TO ANY OTHER SECTION IN THE TEST. **STOP**

KAPLAN

SECTION THREE

Time—20 Minutes
16 Questions

Solve each of the following problems, decide which is the best answer choice, and darken the corresponding oval on the answer sheet. Use available space in the test booklet for scratchwork.*

Notes:

(1) Calculator use is permitted.

(2) All numbers used are real numbers.

(3) Figures are provided for some problems. All figures are drawn to scale and lie in a plane UNLESS otherwise indicated.

(4) Unless otherwise specified, the domain of any function f is assumed to be the set of all real numbers x for which $f(x)$ is a real number.

Reference Information

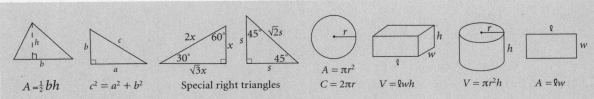

$A = \frac{1}{2}bh$ $c^2 = a^2 + b^2$ Special right triangles $A = \pi r^2$ $C = 2\pi r$ $V = \ell w h$ $V = \pi r^2 h$ $A = \ell w$

The sum of the degree measures of the angles in a triangle is 180.
The number of degrees of arc in a circle is 360.
A straight angle has a degree measure of 180.

1. A machine places caps on 7 bottles every 3 seconds. At this rate, how many bottles will the machine place a cap on in one minute?

   (A) 14
   (B) 21
   (C) 140
   (D) 210
   (E) 420

2. If the 3-digit number $5W2$ is evenly divisible by 8, which of the following could be the value for the digit W?

   (A) 2
   (B) 3
   (C) 4
   (D) 5
   (E) 6

3. If $\dfrac{3}{11} + \dfrac{3}{11} + \dfrac{3}{11} = \dfrac{x}{33}$, what is the value of $\dfrac{x}{3}$?

   (A) 27
   (B) 9
   (C) 6
   (D) 3
   (E) 1

*The directions on the actual SAT will vary slightly.

GO ON TO THE NEXT PAGE

KAPLAN

4. If $gh > 0$, which of the following must be true?

    (A) $\dfrac{g}{h} > 0$

    (B) $\dfrac{h}{g} < 0$

    (C) $g + h > 0$

    (D) $g - h > 0$

    (E) $g + h < 0$

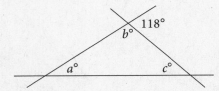

Note: Figure not drawn to scale.

5. In the figure above, what is the value of $a + c - b$?

    (A) 45
    (B) 56
    (C) 59
    (D) 62
    (E) 64

6. The first term of a certain sequence is 5. If every term after the first term is 3 less than 2 times the term immediately preceding it, what is the difference between the third and fourth terms?

    (A) 8
    (B) 11
    (C) 16
    (D) 19
    (E) 32

7. The sum of 2 positive numbers x and z is 50. If x is greater than 10 more than 4 times z, which of the following includes the entire range of values for z?

    (A) $0 < z < 4$
    (B) $0 < z < 8$
    (C) $0 < z < 10$
    (D) $8 < z < 10$
    (E) $8 < z < 50$

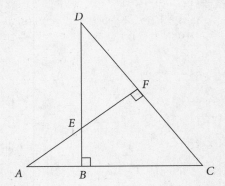

Note: Figure not drawn to scale.

8. In the figure above, if $AC = 12$, $DC = 18$, and $DB = 15$, what is the length of AF?

    (A) 8
    (B) 9
    (C) 10
    (D) 11
    (E) 12

9. If 1 clank = 7 bops and 2 bops = 1 fig, how many clanks are equal to 28 figs?

    (A) 3.5
    (B) 8
    (C) 9
    (D) 14
    (E) 28

GO ON TO THE NEXT PAGE

KAPLAN

10. A radioactive chemical decays 20 percent each day. If 48 pounds of this chemical remain today, how many pounds of this chemical were present two days ago?

   (A) 75
   (B) 72
   (C) 70
   (D) 66
   (E) 60

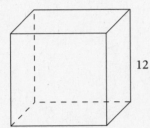

11. The figure above is a cube with an edge of 12. If this cube is divided into smaller rectangular solids with dimensions 2 by 2 by 4, how many times greater is the combined surface areas of all these smaller rectangular solids than the surface area of the larger cube?

   (A) 16
   (B) 12
   (C) 10
   (D) 8
   (E) 5

12. If k is a positive integer less than 17, what is the total number of possible integral solutions for the equation $x^2 + 8x + k = 0$?

   (A) 4
   (B) 5
   (C) 6
   (D) 7
   (E) 8

13. In the equation $y^3 = kx$, $x = 9$ when $y = 3$ and k is a constant. What is the value of y when $x = 72$?

   (A) 3
   (B) 6
   (C) 8
   (D) 9
   (E) 12

14. If $f(x) = |\, 6x^2 + 3x \,|$, what is $f(-3)$?

   (A) −45
   (B) 12
   (C) 18
   (D) 30
   (E) 45

15. In a certain geometric sequence, each term after the first is the result of multiplying the previous term by some positive number. If the third term in the sequence is $36x$, and the first term is $9x$, which of the following represents the seventh term?

   (A) $126x$
   (B) $273x$
   (C) $454x$
   (D) $576x$
   (E) $12{,}823x$

16. If N is the square of a positive integer, which of the following must be equal to the square of the next greater integer?

   (A) $\sqrt{N+1}$
   (B) $N + 1$
   (C) $N^2 + 1$
   (D) $N^2 + 2N + 1$
   (E) $N + 2\sqrt{N} + 1$

IF YOU FINISH BEFORE TIME IS CALLED, YOU MAY CHECK YOUR WORK ON THIS SECTION ONLY. DO NOT TURN TO ANY OTHER SECTION IN THE TEST.

STOP

KAPLAN

Practice Test A: **Answer Key**

SECTION ONE

1. C
2. E
3. B
4. D
5. D
6. A
7. E
8. B
9. D
10. A
11. D
12. E
13. B
14. A
15. E
16. E
17. D
18. B
19. A
20. C

SECTION TWO

1. C
2. D
3. D
4. C
5. A
6. C
7. C
8. B
9. 36
10. 97.5
11. 18.5 or $\dfrac{37}{2}$
12. $\dfrac{3}{8}$ or .375
13. 70
14. 38 or 46
15. 9
16. 4000
17. 8
18. 32

SECTION THREE

1. C
2. D
3. B
4. A
5. B
6. A
7. B
8. C
9. B
10. A
11. E
12. D
13. B
14. E
15. D
16. E

Answers and Explanations

SECTION ONE

1. C

The fastest method is to start with the smallest answer choice and test each one for divisibility. Choice (E) is divisible by 21, but not by 9. Similarly, choice (D) is 2 × 21, but it is not divisible by 9. Choice (C), 63, is divisible by both 21 (21 × 3 = 63) and 9 (9 × 7 = 63). Since the remaining answer choices are larger, this must be the correct answer.

A more mathematical approach is to find the prime factors of 9 and 21, and, by eliminating shared factors, find the least common multiple. Breaking each into prime factors:

$$21 = 3 \times 7$$
$$9 = 3 \times 3$$

We can drop one factor of 3 from the 9, since it is already present in the factors of 21. The least common multiple is 3 × 3 × 7, or 63.

2. E

The union of two sets consists of all the numbers that appear in either or both sets. Since 2, 4, and 12 each appear in at least one of these sets, they are all in the union.

3. B

Since the three marked angles form a straight angle, the sum of their measures is 180°. So we can set up an equation to solve for x :

$$x + x + 80 = 180$$
$$2x + 80 = 180$$
$$2x = 100$$
$$x = 50$$

4. D

The first print uses up $1.65 of the $20 Pete has available. This leaves him $20 − $1.65 or $18.35 for the rest of the prints, at a rate of $0.85 per print. Divide 0.85 into 18.35 to find out how many additional prints can be purchased. It comes out to 21 prints (with change left over), and that, plus the first print, means he can buy 22 prints all together.

5. D

Set $m(y)$ equal to -3, then solve for y:

$$m(y) = \frac{y + 4}{y - 4} = -3$$
$$y + 4 = -3(y - 4)$$
$$y + 4 = -3y + 12$$
$$4y = 8$$
$$y = 2$$

Backsolving also works well here.

6. A

There are 55 rabbits in the laboratory. So the sum of the terms in the ratio must be a factor of 55. There are only four factors of 55: 1, 5, 11, and 55. The only answer choice with terms that add up to one of these numbers is choice (A): the sum of the terms in a 3:8 ratio is 11.

7. E

First, solve for k, but don't forget that you're really looking for k^2.

$$k^{\frac{1}{3}} = \frac{k}{4}$$
$$4k^{\frac{1}{3}} = k$$
$$4 = k^{\frac{2}{3}}$$
$$k = 4^{\frac{3}{2}} = 2^3 = 8$$
$$k^2 = 8^2 = 64$$

Backsolving is also a good method here—just remember that the answer choices are k^2, not just k.

8. B

To simplify the expression, first use the FOIL method (**F**irst terms, **O**uter terms, **I**nner terms, and **L**ast terms) to multiply the binomials $x + 1$ and $y + 1$. Then combine terms:

$$(x + 1)(y + 1) = xy + x + y + 1$$

$$(x + 1)(y + 1) - x - y = xy + x + y + 1 - x - y$$

$$= xy + 1$$

9. D

First, translate the words into algebra: *of* means "times," *is* means "equals." Call the percent you're looking for p :

$$\frac{2}{3} \times 8 = p \times 4$$

$$\frac{\frac{2}{3} \times 8}{4} = p$$

$$\frac{16}{3} \times \frac{1}{4} = p$$

$$\frac{4}{3} = p$$

To convert $\frac{4}{3}$ to a percent, multiply by 100%:

$$\frac{4}{3} = \frac{4}{3} \times 100\% = \frac{400}{3}\% = 133\frac{1}{3}\%$$

10. A

Each side of triangle *ABC* connects the centers of two tangent circles, and each side passes through the point where the circumferences of the circles touch. Therefore, each side is composed of the radii of two of the circles: *AB* is made up of a radius of *A* and a radius of *B*, *BC* is made up of a radius of *B* and a radius of *C*, and *AC* is made up of a radius of *A* and a radius of *C*. The sum of the lengths of these sides is the perimeter of the triangle. Since we have two radii of each circle, the perimeter is twice the sum of the radii: $2(2 + 3 + 4) = 18$.

11. D

The simplest approach here is to pick an odd value for *n*, such as 3. When working with addition, subtraction, or multiplication, *any* odd or even number will behave the same way (in terms of whether the *result* is odd or even). In this particular problem we have to be careful, though, because two answer choices involve division, and the problem asks for a choice that *must* be even. If choices (A) or (B) produce an even result, we'll have to make sure there's not another possibility.

Choice (A): $\frac{n + 1}{2} = \frac{3 + 1}{2} = \frac{4}{2} = 2$. Even. But this choice involves division, so we need to try another value, such as 1: $\frac{1 + 1}{2} = \frac{2}{2} = 1$. So this doesn't have to be even, and that means it's not the correct answer.

Choice (B): $\frac{n - 1}{2} = \frac{3 - 1}{2} = \frac{2}{2} = 1$. Not even, so this choice can't be correct.

Choice (C): $n^2 + 2n = 3^2 + 2(3) = 9 + 6 = 15$. No.

Choice (D): $2n + 2 = 2(3) + 2 = 6 + 2 = 8$. Even. Since no division is involved, we can safely assume any odd value for *n* will cause the result here to be even. So this is the correct choice.

Just for practice:

Choice (E): $3n^2 - 2n = 3(3)^2 - 2(3) = 21$. As expected, it doesn't produce an even result.

12. E

The median is the middle term in a group of terms arranged in numerical order. Since there were 15 contributions made, the median contribution will be the eighth term. The eighth term coincides with a $20 contribution, so the median contribution is $20. Remember that average $= \frac{\text{sum of the terms}}{\text{number of terms}}$. You know there were 15 contributions, so all you need to find is the total amount of contributions:

$(4 \times \$10) + (3 \times \$15) + (2 \times \$20) + (4 \times \$25) +$ $(2 \times \$30) = \$285$. So the average $= \dfrac{\$285}{15}$, or \$19. So the difference between the median contribution and the average contribution is $\$20 - \$19$, or \$1, and choice (E) is correct.

13. B

Here we have a symbolism problem, involving a symbol—▲—that doesn't exist in mathematics. All you need to do is follow the directions given in the definition of this symbol. To find the value of 3 ▲ 1, plug 3 and 1 into the formula given for m ▲ n, substituting 3 for m and 1 for n. Then the equation becomes:

$$3 \text{ ▲ } 1 = \frac{(3)^2 - (1) + 1}{(3)(1)}$$

$$= \frac{9}{3}$$

$$= 3$$

14. A

Each of these squares must have an area equal to one-fifth of the area of the whole figure: $\dfrac{1}{5} \times 20 = 4$. For squares, area = side^2, or $\sqrt{\text{area}}$ = side. Since $\sqrt{4} = 2$, the length of each side of each square must be 2.

The perimeter consists of 3 sides from each of 4 squares, for a total of 3×4, or 12 sides. Each side has a length of 2, for a total perimeter of 12×2, or 24.

15. E

It may be helpful to draw a quick diagram, like this one:

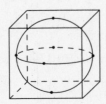

The sphere will touch the cube at six points. Each point will be an endpoint of a diameter and will be at the center of one of the cubic faces. (Imagine putting a beach ball inside a tight-fitting, cube-shaped box.) Therefore the diameter extends directly from one face of the cube to the other, and is perpendicular to both faces that it touches. This means that the diameter must have the same length as an edge of the cube. The cube's volume is 64, so the length of each edge is the cube root of 64, or 4. So the diameter of the sphere is 4, which means that the radius is 2.

16. E

The area of any right triangle equals $\dfrac{1}{2}$ the product of the legs. Since AB is 3 times as long as BC, we can call the length of BC x, and the length of AB $3x$. The area of the triangle is one-half their product, or $\dfrac{1}{2}(x)(3x)$. Since we know the area is 6, we can say:

$$\frac{1}{2}(x)(3x) = 6$$

$$3x^2 = 12$$

$$x^2 = 4$$

$$x = 2$$

So BC has a length of 2. AB, which is $3x$, is 6. Now use the Pythagorean theorem to find AC.

$$AC^2 = AB^2 + BC^2$$

$$AC^2 = (6)^2 + (2)^2$$

$$AC^2 = 36 + 4$$

$$AC = \sqrt{40} = \sqrt{4} \times \sqrt{10}.$$

$$= 2\sqrt{10}.$$

17. D

Solve for b in terms of a, c, and d. First, multiply both sides by $(a - b)$:

$$d = \frac{c - b}{a - b}$$

$$d(a - b) = c - b$$

Distribute the d:

$$da - db = c - b$$

Gather the b factors on one side and factor out:

$$b - db = c - da$$

$$b(1 - d) = c - da$$

Divide both sides by $1 - d$ to isolate b:

$$b = \frac{c - ad}{1 - d}$$

This equation could have been solved differently to arrive at $b = \frac{da - c}{d - 1}$, which is not an answer choice. However, if you multiply this fraction by $\frac{-1}{-1}$: $\frac{-1(da - c)}{-1(d - 1)} = \frac{c - da}{1 - d}$, which is choice (D).

18. B

The easiest method to solve this problem is to pick numbers. Choose numbers that will be easy to work with. Let $x = 2$, that is, say that the snow falls at a rate of 2 centimeters per minute. Let $y = 60$, since there are a lot of 60s to divide by in the answer choices. Now we figure out how many hours it would take for 60 centimeters to fall at this rate. At 2 centimeters per minute, 60 centimeters would fall in half an hour.

Next, let's plug 2 and 60 into each answer choice and see which one equals half an hour. (When using this method, remember that more than one answer choice *could* have the right value depending on the numbers we happen to pick, so we need to try them all. If more than one works, we try different values until only one choice works.)

Choice (A): $\frac{2}{(60)(60)} = \frac{1}{1,800}$. Discard.

Choice (B): $\frac{60}{(60)(2)} = \frac{60}{120} = \frac{1}{2}$. Choice (B) is probably correct, but we have to make sure by checking the other choices.

Choice (C): $\frac{(60)(2)}{60} = 2$. Discard.

Choice (D): $\frac{(60)(60)}{2} = 1,800$. Discard.

Choice (E): $(60)(2)(60) = 7,200$. Since none of the other choices yields $\frac{1}{2}$, choice (B) is indeed the correct answer.

19. A

We're looking for the length of CD. Note that OC is a radius of the circle, so if we knew the lengths of OC and OD, we could find CD, since $CD = OC - OD$. We're given that OB has a length of 10, which means the circle has a radius of 10, and therefore OC is 10. All that remains is to find OD and subtract.

The only other piece of information we have to work with is that AB has length 16. If we connect O and A, we create two right triangles, ADO and BDO:

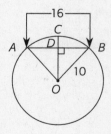

Since both these right triangles have a radius as the hypotenuse and both have leg OD in common, they must be equal in size. Therefore, the other legs, AD and DB, must also be equal. That means that D is the midpoint of AB, so

DB is $\frac{1}{2}$(16), or 8. So right triangle BDO has a hypotenuse of 10 and a leg of 8; thus its other leg has length 6. If you didn't recognize this as a 6-8-10 Pythagorean Triplet—a multiple of the 3-4-5 triangle—you could have used the Pythagorean theorem to find the length of OD. So OD has length 6, and $CD = 10 - 6 = 4$.

20. C

Since he traveled the same distance both ways, it's tempting to think we can simply average the speeds to find the answer. But rates can't be averaged in that way. It's necessary to compute the total distance and the total time and use these numbers in the average formula.

Total miles: He travels 90 miles there and 90 miles back, for a total of 180 miles. To find the total time, we must calculate the time for each part of the trip, and then add them together. Going there, he travels 90 miles at 20 miles per hour.

Since rate × time = distance, time = $\frac{\text{distance}}{\text{rate}}$. So it takes him $\frac{90 \text{ miles}}{20 \text{ miles per hour}} = \frac{9}{2}$ hours to travel there. Coming back, he travels 90 miles at 40 miles per hour, so it takes him $\frac{90}{40} = \frac{9}{4}$ hours to return home.

The total time spent was therefore $\frac{9}{2} + \frac{9}{4} = \frac{18}{4} + \frac{9}{4} = \frac{27}{4}$, or $6\frac{3}{4}$ hours.

So his average speed for the whole trip was

$\frac{\text{Total miles}}{\text{Total hours}} = \frac{180 \text{ miles}}{\frac{27}{4} \text{ hours}} = \left(180 \times \frac{4}{27}\right) = \frac{80}{3}$ miles per hour.

SECTION TWO

1. C

All you need to do here is plug $x = 3$ into the function: $f(3) = 3^3 + 6 = 27 + 6 = 33$

2. D

The graph of $r(x + 4)$ will appear to be the graph of $r(x)$ shifted 4 units to the left. Since the graph has only moved horizontally, the maximum and minimum values will be the same. Since the maximum value of $r(x)$ is 6, so is the maximum value of $r(x + 4)$.

3. D

Set J is {2, 4, 6, …} and Set K is all values from -2 to 2, including the endpoints themselves. The only number that is both a positive even integer and in the range is 2.

4. C

If $|-3x - 7| = 5$, then $-3x - 7 = 5$ or $-3x - 7 = -5$. Solve for x:

$-3x = 12$ or $-3x = 2$

$x = -4$ or $x = -\frac{2}{3}$

5. A

The area of a circle is π times the square of the radius. In this diagram, we are not given the radius, but we are given the diameter, which is twice the radius. If the area of the circle is 16π, the radius must be 4. The diameter, then, must be 8. So $2w + 4 = 8$, $2w = 4$, and $w = 2$, which is (A). You could also solve this problem by Backsolving, plugging each answer choice in for w and then solving for the area of the circle.

6.   C

The slope of a line is defined as *rise over run,* which means the difference between the *y*-coordinates of any two points on the line, divided by the difference between the *x*-coordinates of the same two points. We're given the value of the slope and three of the four coordinates, so we can write an equation to solve for the missing coordinate. Since both coordinates of point *S* will be greater than those of point *R,* we'll put those numbers first when we compute the difference:

$$\frac{9-b}{4-(-2)} = \frac{4}{3}$$

$$\frac{9-b}{6} = \frac{4}{3}$$

$$6\left(\frac{9-b}{6}\right) = 6\left(\frac{4}{3}\right)$$

$$9 - b = 8$$

$$-b = -1$$

$$b = 1$$

7.   C

Many students will assume that a loss of 16 percent followed by an increase of 25 percent adds up to an overall increase of 25 − 16, or 9 percent. This works if both percents are percents of the same amount. But the 25 percent is a percent of a *different* amount. To find the actual result, assume a starting value of 100 (since we're working with percents) and see what happens.

If the factory cuts its labor force by 16 percent, it eliminates 16 percent of 100 jobs, or 16 jobs, leaving a work force of 100 − 16, or 84 people. It then increases this work force by 25 percent. Twenty-five percent of 84 is the same as $\frac{1}{4}$ of 84, or 21. So the factory adds 21 jobs to the 84 it had, for a total of 105 jobs. Since the factory started with 100 jobs and finished with 105, it gained 5

jobs overall. This represents $\frac{5}{100}$, or 5 percent, of the total we started with. So there was a 5 percent overall increase after both changes were made.

8.   B

The standard form of the equation of a line is $y = mx + b$, where m is the slope and b is the *y*-intercept. Consider the slope and *y*-intercept of a line that passes through the points in the graph—how steeply does it go up or down as it goes the right? Where does it cross the *y*-axis? This line goes up steeply as it goes to the right, so it must have a fairly large positive slope. It crosses the *y*-axis around $y = -1$. So you need to find a line in the answer choices with a y-intercept of −1 and a fairly large positive slope. The only choice that fits is (B). Check your answer by plugging a few points from the graph into the equation to be sure they fit.

9.   36

The price of the softcover is $\frac{2}{3}$ the price of the hardcover. So the difference between the prices—the extra money you pay to get the hardcover edition—must be the remaining third of the hardcover price. That amount is $12. If $12 is $\frac{1}{3}$ the cost of the hardcover, the full cost must be 3 times that, or $36.

10. 97.5

Solve the given equation for *a*:

$$4a - 1 = 64$$

$$4a = 65$$

$$a = 16.25$$

So $6a = 97.5$

11. 18.5 or $\frac{37}{2}$

To solve a problem like this we have to use the formula for average (average = the sum of terms ÷ the number of terms, or, restated in the way most useful for this problem, average × the number of terms = the sum of the terms) to find the sum of each set of terms. If the average of 6 numbers is $7\frac{1}{2}$, then the sum of the 6 terms must be 6 times $7\frac{1}{2}$, or 45. If the average of 4 of those numbers is 2, then the sum of those 4 numbers must be 4 times 2, or 8. If those 4 numbers add up to only 8, then the other 2 numbers in the group of 6 must account for the rest of the overall total of 45. Taking away 8 from 45 leaves 37, so that must be the sum of the 2 remaining numbers. To find their average, we simply divide by 2, for a result of $\frac{37}{2}$, or 18.5.

12. $\frac{3}{8}$ or .375

Since $\frac{1}{3}$ of all the yogurts are fruit flavored and $\frac{1}{8}$ are peach, we need to ask, $\frac{1}{8}$ is what fraction of $\frac{1}{3}$? To find that, we simply divide $\frac{1}{8}$ by $\frac{1}{3}$. Dividing by a fraction is the same as multiplying by the reciprocal of the fraction, so $\frac{1}{8}$ ÷ $\frac{1}{3}$ is the same as $\frac{1}{8} \times \frac{3}{1}$, or $\frac{3}{8}$.

13. 70

Neither one of the two marked angles can tell us the value of z by itself, but angle z is an interior angle of a triangle, and the marked angles can help us find the value of the other two interior angles. The angle marked 40 degrees is a vertical angle to one of the interior angles of the triangle, so that interior angle must also have a measure of 40 degrees. Since ℓ_1 and ℓ_2 are parallel and the two lines that form angle z are transversals, all the obtuse angles formed by the line on the left are equal. That means the obtuse angle right above $\angle z$ on the left is 110 degrees. And that angle, in turn, is supplementary to the remaining interior angle. So the remaining interior angle has a measure of 180 − 110, or 70 degrees.

Now we have the measure of two of the three interior angles. Since they must add up to 180 degrees, we can write an equation: $40 + 70 + z = 180$, and then $110 + z = 180$. Subtracting 110 from both sides gives us $z = 70$.

14. 38 or 46

If you list the first several prime numbers—2, 3, 5, 7, 11, 13, 17, 19, 23, 29—you can see that there aren't many pairs that will work. Lots of pairs add up to more than 20, but most have products much greater than 50. In fact, the only way to keep the product under 50 is to combine a prime number close to 20 with 2. But two pairs of prime numbers *will* work. 2 and 19 sum to 21 and their product is 38, less than 50. Likewise, 2 and 23 sum to 25, but have a product of only 46. But the next prime after 23, 29, breaks the 50 limit when multiplied by 2. So the only pairs that work are 2 and 19, and 2 and 23, with products of 38 and 46, respectively.

15. 9

You'll probably find it helpful to draw a diagram for this one. If you do, you'll see that the triangle in question has a base that runs from (2, 3) to (8, 3), parallel to the *x*-axis. Since it is parallel to the *x*-axis, we can find the length of the base by subtracting the *x*-coordinates: $8 - 2 = 6$, and that's the length of the base.

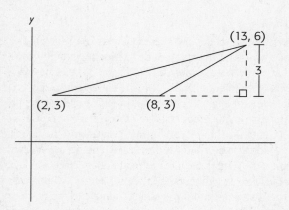

To find the area, we need both the base and height. The vertex of this triangle is off to one side, but all we need to know is the vertical distance from the base to the vertex, and the *y*-coordinates of the points make this easy to find. The base line is parallel to the *x*-axis, so the whole line is at a height of 3, measured along the *y*-axis. The vertex of the triangle has a *y*-coordinate of 6, or 3 units above the base, measured vertically. So the base is 6 and the height is 3.

Area $= \frac{1}{2}$ base times height, or $\frac{1}{2} \times 6 \times 3 = 9$.

16. 4000

This question is easily solved by picking numbers. If we let $y = 100$, then *x* is $2\frac{1}{2}$ percent of 100, or 2.5. Now what percent of 2.5 is 100? Percent $= \frac{\text{part}}{\text{whole}} \times 100\% = \frac{100}{2.5}$ $\times 100\% = 40 \times 100\% = 4,000\%$.

17. 8

$\frac{130}{x}$ will be an integer whenever *x* is a factor of 130. So we need to find *every number* that's a factor of 130. Perhaps the best approach is to break down 130 into its prime factorization. Obviously $130 = 13 \times 10$. Thirteen is prime, but we can break down 10 into 5×2. So the prime factorization of 130 is $13 \times 5 \times 2$. That doesn't mean the correct

answer is 3, though; these are just the *prime* factors. We can find other factors by multiplying the prime factors together in different combinations: $5 \times 2 = 10$, and 10 is a factor; $5 \times 13 = 65$, and 65 is a factor; $13 \times 2 = 26$, another factor. Also, 130 and 1 are factors of 130. So any of these 8 numbers, divided into 130, will produce an integer value.

18. 32

The largest square that can be drawn within a circle is a square that's inscribed in the circle. Draw a diagram:

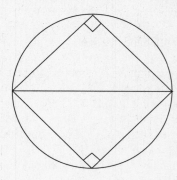

Note that the diagonal of the square is a diameter of the circle. We can find this length from the area of the circle. Since area $= \pi r^2 = 16\pi$, in this case $r^2 = 16$, so the radius of the circle is 4. The diameter is double that, or 8.

So a diagonal of the square has a length of 8. The diagonal divides the square into 2 isosceles right triangles, so the ratio of the diagonal to a side of the square is $\sqrt{2}:1$. Since the diagonal is the length of a side times $\sqrt{2}$, the side is the length of the diagonal *divided by* $\sqrt{2}$. In this case, that means $\frac{8}{\sqrt{2}}$.

Now that we know the length of a side, it's easy to find the area of the square by squaring that side:

$$\left(\frac{8}{\sqrt{2}}\right) = \frac{8^2}{(\sqrt{2})^2} = \frac{64}{2} = 32.$$

SECTION THREE

1. C

You know that the machine can cap 7 bottles in 3 seconds. Since there are 20 three-second periods in 1 minute, the number of bottles capped in 1 minute is $7(20) = 140$.

2. D

Any number that is divisible by 8 must also be divisible by 4. A number is divisible by 4 if its last two digits form a number that is divisible by 4; the only answer choices for W that will make $5W2$ divisible by 4 are 3 and 5 (since 32 and 52 are both divisible by 4). Dividing 532 and 552 by 8, you see that only 552 leaves no remainder, so W must be 5, answer choice (D).

3. B

Add the terms on the left side of the equation: $\dfrac{9}{11} = \dfrac{x}{33}$

Multiply both sides by 33:

$$\frac{9}{11} \times 33 = x$$

Simplify: $27 = x$.

So $\qquad \dfrac{x}{3} = \dfrac{27}{3} = 9$.

4. A

For the product gh to be positive, g and h are either both positive or both negative (since a negative times a negative is a positive). Looking at the answer choices, (A) says $\dfrac{g}{h}$ is positive. If g and h are both positive, this will be true; if g and h are both negative this will also be true. So choice (A) must be correct.

5. B

The angle marked 118 degrees is an exterior angle of the triangle, so its measure is equal to the sum of the 2 non-adjacent interior angles. This means $a + c = 118$. Angle b is supplementary to the 118 degree angle, so $b = 62$. So $a + c - b = 118 - 62 = 56$, answer choice (B).

6. A

Every term after the first term in this sequence is 3 less than 2 times the term before it, or $2n - 3$, where n represents the term before it. Since the first term is 5, the second term is $2(5) - 3 = 7$. The third term is $2(7) - 3 = 11$. So the fourth term is $2(11) - 3 = 19$. Therefore, the difference between the third term and the fourth terms is $19 - 11 = 8$.

7. B

According to the given information, $x + z = 50$ and $x > 4z + 10$. To find the range of values of z, solve for x in terms of z in the first equation:

$$x + z = 50$$
$$x = 50 - z$$

Now plug this expression for x into the inequality and solve for z :

$$x > 4z + 10$$
$$50 - z > 4z + 10$$
$$40 > 5z$$
$$8 > z$$

Since you're given that z is positive, it must be greater than 0. Therefore, $0 < z < 8$.

KAPLAN

8. C

Draw *AD* as shown below to create △*ADC*:

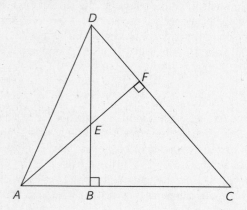

The area of a triangle $= \frac{1}{2}$ (base × height), so the area of

△*ADC* is equal to $\frac{1}{2}(DB \times AC)$ and also equal to

$\frac{1}{2}(AF \times DC)$. Therefore, $DB \times AC = AF \times DC$. Now plug in

the given measurements to find the length of *AF* :

$$(15)(12) = (AF)(18)$$
$$180 = 18AF$$
$$10 = AF$$

You could have also solved this problem using similar tri-

angles. Since △*AFC* and △*DBC* are both right triangles and

share ∠*C*, they are similar, and therefore, the lengths of

their sides are in proportion. So $\frac{AF}{AC} = \frac{DB}{DC}$, or $\frac{AF}{12} = \frac{15}{18}$.

Multiply both sides of the equation by 12 to solve for

AF : *AF* = 10.

9. B

Both figs and clanks are defined in terms of bops, so use
bops as an intermediate step to figure out how many
clanks equal 28 figs. Since 1 fig = 2 bops, 28 figs = 56
bops. Now figure out how many clanks equal 56 bops.
Since 1 clank = 7 bops, 8 clanks = 56 bops. So 8 clanks
= 28 figs.

10. A

Let *x* = the amount of the chemical two days ago. Since
it decays at a rate of 20 percent each day, the amount of
the chemical remaining yesterday is equal to 80 percent of
x, or .8*x*. So the amount of the chemical remaining today
equals 80% of .8*x*, or .64*x*. Therefore, .64*x* is equal to 48
pounds of the chemical. So, .64*x* = 48, and *x* = 75.

11. E

First figure out the number of small 2-by-2-by-4 rectangular solids there are by dividing each dimension of the cube
by one of the dimensions of the small solids.

The cube has dimensions 12-by-12-by-12. So along the

length, we have $\frac{12}{2}$, or 6 solids. Along the width, we have

$\frac{12}{2}$ or 6 solids. Along the height, we have $\frac{12}{4}$ or 3 solids.

That gives us a total of 6 × 6 × 3, or 108 small solids.

The surface area of each small solid is the sum of the
areas of the 6 faces. There are 4 faces that are 2 by 4.
They each have an area of 8. The 2 faces that are 2 by
2 each have an area of 4. So the surface area of each
small solid is 4(8) + 2(4) = 32 + 8 = 40. The combined
surface areas of all the smaller rectangular solids is equal
to the number of solids times the surface area of each, or
108 × 40 = 4,320.

The surface area of the cube is 6 times the area of one
face, or 6 times 12^2, which equals 864.

Since $\frac{4,320}{864} = 5$, the combined surface area of all the

smaller solids is 5 times greater than the surface area of

the original cube.

12. D

The $8x$ in the quadratic equation represents the sum of the products of the outer and inner terms of the equation in factored form, $(x + \_)(x + \_)$. The k represents the product of the last terms. So to factor the equation, think of pairs of numbers that sum to 8 and whose product is a positive integer less than 17. List the pairs:

$(x + 1)(x + 7) = 0$

2 solutions.

$(x + 2)(x + 6) = 0$

2 solutions.

$(x + 3)(x + 5) = 0$

2 solutions.

$(x + 4)(x + 4) = 0$

1 solution.

Since there are 7 different solutions to this equation, answer choice (D) is correct.

13. B

Use $x = 9$ when $y = 3$ to solve for k: $3^3 = k(9)$, so $27 = 9k$ and $k = 3$. Use $k = 3$ and $x = 72$ to solve for y: $y^3 = 3(72) = 216$, so $y = 6$.

14. E

Don't be intimidated by functions—they are often the easiest problems to solve if they center on straight substitution. Plug in −3 wherever you see x:

$f(x) = |\, 6x^2 + 3x \,|$

$f(-3) = |\, 6(-3^2) + 3(-3) \,|$

$f(-3) = |\, 6(9) - 9 \,|$

$f(-3) = |\, 54 - 9 \,|$

$f(-3) = 45$

15. D

Use $a_n = a_1 r^{n-1}$ to solve for r: $36x = 9xr^2$, so $4 = r^2$ and $r = 2$ or -2, but you can eliminate −2 on the grounds provided in the question stem that r is positive. Using $r = 2$, solve for a_7: $a_7 = 9x(2)^6$, so $a_7 = 576x$.

16. E

N is the square of a positive integer t, or $N = t^2$. Then, the integer $t = \sqrt{N}$. The next greater integer is one more, or $t + 1$, which equals $\sqrt{N} + 1$. To find the square, we use the distributive law (FOIL):

$$(\sqrt{N} + 1)^2 = (\sqrt{N} + 1)(\sqrt{N} + 1)$$

$$= (\sqrt{N})^2 + \sqrt{N} \times 1 + 1 \times \sqrt{N} + 1^2$$

$$= N + 2\sqrt{N} + 1$$

Or you can easily solve this problem by picking numbers. We know N is the square of a positive integer. So let's say N is 4, the square of 2. The next greater integer after 2 is 3, and the square of 3 is 9. Therefore, we can eliminate any answer choice that does not result in a value of 9 when N is 4.

Choice (A): $\sqrt{4 + 1} = \sqrt{5}$. Discard.

Choice (B): $4 + 1 = 5$. Discard.

Choice (C): $4^2 + 1 = 16 + 1 = 17$. Discard.

Choice (D): $4^2 + (2 \times 4) + 1 = 16 + 8 + 1 = 25$. Discard.

Choice (E): $4 + 2\sqrt{4} + 1 = 4 + 4 + 1 = 9$. This is what we're looking for, so choice (E) is correct.

Practice Test B
Answer Sheet

Remove (or photocopy) this answer sheet and use it to complete the practice test. See the answer key following the test when finished. The "Compute Your Score" section at the back of the book will show you how to find your score.

Start with number 1 for each section.

SECTION 1

1. Ⓐ Ⓑ Ⓒ Ⓓ Ⓔ
2. Ⓐ Ⓑ Ⓒ Ⓓ Ⓔ
3. Ⓐ Ⓑ Ⓒ Ⓓ Ⓔ
4. Ⓐ Ⓑ Ⓒ Ⓓ Ⓔ
5. Ⓐ Ⓑ Ⓒ Ⓓ Ⓔ
6. Ⓐ Ⓑ Ⓒ Ⓓ Ⓔ

7. Ⓐ Ⓑ Ⓒ Ⓓ Ⓔ
8. Ⓐ Ⓑ Ⓒ Ⓓ Ⓔ
9. Ⓐ Ⓑ Ⓒ Ⓓ Ⓔ
10. Ⓐ Ⓑ Ⓒ Ⓓ Ⓔ
11. Ⓐ Ⓑ Ⓒ Ⓓ Ⓔ
12. Ⓐ Ⓑ Ⓒ Ⓓ Ⓔ

13. Ⓐ Ⓑ Ⓒ Ⓓ Ⓔ
14. Ⓐ Ⓑ Ⓒ Ⓓ Ⓔ
15. Ⓐ Ⓑ Ⓒ Ⓓ Ⓔ
16. Ⓐ Ⓑ Ⓒ Ⓓ Ⓔ
17. Ⓐ Ⓑ Ⓒ Ⓓ Ⓔ
18. Ⓐ Ⓑ Ⓒ Ⓓ Ⓔ

19. Ⓐ Ⓑ Ⓒ Ⓓ Ⓔ
20. Ⓐ Ⓑ Ⓒ Ⓓ Ⓔ

□ # right in section 1

□ # wrong in section 1

SECTION 2

1. Ⓐ Ⓑ Ⓒ Ⓓ Ⓔ
2. Ⓐ Ⓑ Ⓒ Ⓓ Ⓔ

3. Ⓐ Ⓑ Ⓒ Ⓓ Ⓔ
4. Ⓐ Ⓑ Ⓒ Ⓓ Ⓔ

5. Ⓐ Ⓑ Ⓒ Ⓓ Ⓔ
6. Ⓐ Ⓑ Ⓒ Ⓓ Ⓔ

7. Ⓐ Ⓑ Ⓒ Ⓓ Ⓔ
8. Ⓐ Ⓑ Ⓒ Ⓓ Ⓔ

□ # right in section 2

□ # wrong in section 2

9. 10. 11. 12. 13.

14. 15. 16. 17. 18.

Remove (or photocopy) this answer sheet and use it to complete the practice test.

Start with number 1 for each section.

SECTION

3

1.	Ⓐ Ⓑ Ⓒ Ⓓ Ⓔ	5.	Ⓐ Ⓑ Ⓒ Ⓓ Ⓔ	9.	Ⓐ Ⓑ Ⓒ Ⓓ Ⓔ	13.	Ⓐ Ⓑ Ⓒ Ⓓ Ⓔ
2.	Ⓐ Ⓑ Ⓒ Ⓓ Ⓔ	6.	Ⓐ Ⓑ Ⓒ Ⓓ Ⓔ	10.	Ⓐ Ⓑ Ⓒ Ⓓ Ⓔ	14.	Ⓐ Ⓑ Ⓒ Ⓓ Ⓔ
3.	Ⓐ Ⓑ Ⓒ Ⓓ Ⓔ	7.	Ⓐ Ⓑ Ⓒ Ⓓ Ⓔ	11.	Ⓐ Ⓑ Ⓒ Ⓓ Ⓔ	15.	Ⓐ Ⓑ Ⓒ Ⓓ Ⓔ
4.	Ⓐ Ⓑ Ⓒ Ⓓ Ⓔ	8.	Ⓐ Ⓑ Ⓒ Ⓓ Ⓔ	12.	Ⓐ Ⓑ Ⓒ Ⓓ Ⓔ	16.	Ⓐ Ⓑ Ⓒ Ⓓ Ⓔ

right in
section 3

wrong in
section 3

Practice Test B

SECTION ONE

Time—25 Minutes
20 Questions

Solve each of the following problems, decide which is the best answer choice, and darken the corresponding oval on the answer sheet. Use available space in the test booklet for scratchwork.*

Notes:

(1) Calculator use is permitted.

(2) All numbers used are real numbers.

(3) Figures are provided for some problems. All figures are drawn to scale and lie in a plane UNLESS otherwise indicated.

(4) Unless otherwise specified, the domain of any function f is assumed to be the set of all real numbers x for which $f(x)$ is a real number.

Reference Information

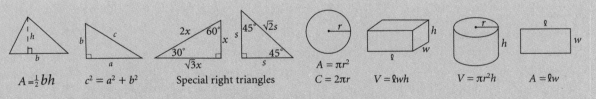

$A = \frac{1}{2}bh$ $c^2 = a^2 + b^2$ Special right triangles $A = \pi r^2$ $V = \ell wh$ $V = \pi r^2 h$ $A = \ell w$
$C = 2\pi r$

The sum of the degree measures of the angles in a triangle is 180.
The number of degrees of arc in a circle is 360.
A straight angle has a degree measure of 180.

1. $(2 \times 10^4) + (5 \times 10^3) + (6 \times 10^2) + (4 \times 10^1) =$

(A) 2,564

(B) 20,564

(C) 25,064

(D) 25,604

(E) 25,640

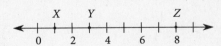

Note: Figure not drawn to scale.

2. On the number line shown above, the length of YZ is how much greater than the length of XY?

(A) 3

(B) 4

(C) 5

(D) 6

(E) 7

KAPLAN

3. If $2^{x+1} = 16$, what is the value of x?

(A) 2

(B) 3

(C) 4

(D) 5

(E) 6

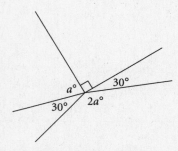

Note: Figure not drawn to scale.

4. In the figure above, what is the value of a?

(A) 50

(B) 55

(C) 60

(D) 65

(E) 70

5. A machine labels 150 bottles in 20 minutes. At this rate, how many minutes does it take to label 60 bottles?

(A) 2

(B) 4

(C) 6

(D) 8

(E) 10

6. If $k(a) = \sqrt{a-2}$ and $k(b) = 4$, what is the value of b?

(A) 18

(B) 16

(C) 6

(D) 4

(E) 0

7. When x is divided by 5, the remainder is 4. When x is divided by 9, the remainder is 0. Which of the following is a possible value for x?

(A) 24

(B) 45

(C) 59

(D) 109

(E) 144

8. In triangle ABC, $AB = 6$, $BC = 12$, and $AC = x$. Which of the following cannot be a value of x?

(A) 6

(B) 7

(C) 8

(D) 9

(E) 10

9. The average of 20, 70, and x is 40. If the average of 20, 70, x, and y is 50, then $y =$

(A) 100

(B) 80

(C) 70

(D) 60

(E) 30

GO ON TO THE NEXT PAGE

NUMBER OF BOOKS BORROWED
FROM MIDVILLE PUBLIC LIBRARY

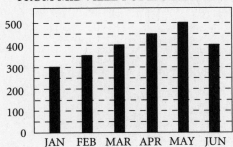

10. According to the graph above, the number of books borrowed during the month of January was what fraction of the total number of books borrowed during the first six months of the year?

(A) $\frac{1}{8}$

(B) $\frac{1}{7}$

(C) $\frac{1}{6}$

(D) $\frac{3}{16}$

(E) $\frac{5}{12}$

11. If 40 percent of r is equal to s, then which of the following is equal to 10 percent of r?

(A) $4s$

(B) $2s$

(C) $\frac{s}{2}$

(D) $\frac{s}{4}$

(E) $\frac{s}{8}$

12. At which of the following points do the graphs of the functions $a(x) = x^2 - 4$ and $b(x) = 6x - 12$ intersect?

(A) $(2, 0)$

(B) $(2, 4)$

(C) $(4, 2)$

(D) $(4, 8)$

(E) $(12, 4)$

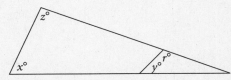

Note: Figure not drawn to scale.

13. In the figure above, which of the following must be true?

(A) $x + r = z + y$

(B) $x + r = z - y$

(C) $x - y = z + r$

(D) $x - r = y - z$

(E) $x + y = z + r$

14. If a "prifact number" is a nonprime integer such that each factor of the integer other than 1 and the integer itself is a prime number, which of the following is a "prifact number"?

(A) 12

(B) 18

(C) 21

(D) 24

(E) 28

GO ON TO THE NEXT PAGE

KAPLAN

15. If $3x + y = 14$, and x and y are positive integers, each of the following could be the value of $x + y$ EXCEPT

(A) 12

(B) 10

(C) 8

(D) 6

(E) 4

18. Dave is arranging five books on a shelf. If all five books must be arranged in one straight line, how many different orders can he put the books in?

(A) 24

(B) 120

(C) 240

(D) 625

(E) 3125

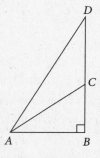

16. In the figure above, the area of triangle *ABC* is 6. If $BC = CD$, what is the area of triangle *ACD* ?

(A) 6

(B) 8

(C) 9

(D) 10

(E) 12

17. What is the minimum number of rectangular tiles, each 12 centimeters by 18 centimeters, needed to completely cover 5 flat rectangular surfaces, each 60 centimeters by 180 centimeters?

(A) 50

(B) 100

(C) 150

(D) 200

(E) 250

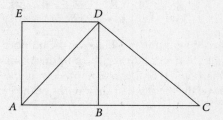

19. In the figure above, side *AB* of square *ABDE* is extended to point *C*. If $BC = 8$ and $CD = 10$, what is the perimeter of triangle *ACD*?

(A) $18 + 6\sqrt{2}$

(B) $24 + 6\sqrt{2}$

(C) $26 + 6\sqrt{2}$

(D) 30

(E) 36

20. Five liters of water were poured from tank *A* into tank *B*, and ten liters of water were then poured from tank *A* into tank *C*. If tank *A* originally had ten more liters of water than tank *C*, how many more liters of water does tank *C* now have than tank *A* ?

(A) 0

(B) 5

(C) 10

(D) 15

(E) 20

IF YOU FINISH BEFORE TIME IS CALLED, YOU MAY CHECK YOUR WORK ON THIS SECTION ONLY. DO NOT TURN TO ANY OTHER SECTION IN THE TEST.

KAPLAN

SECTION TWO

Time—25 Minutes
18 Questions

Solve each of the following problems, decide which is the best answer choice, and darken the corresponding oval on the answer sheet. Use available space in the test booklet for scratchwork.*

Notes:

(1) Calculator use is permitted.

(2) All numbers used are real numbers.

(3) Figures are provided for some problems. All figures are drawn to scale and lie in a plane UNLESS otherwise indicated.

(4) Unless otherwise specified, the domain of any function f is assumed to be the set of all real numbers x for which $f(x)$ is a real number.

Reference Information

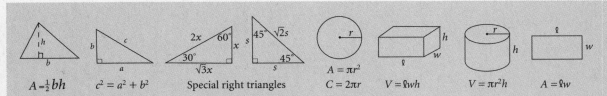

$A = \frac{1}{2}bh$ $c^2 = a^2 + b^2$ Special right triangles $A = \pi r^2$ $C = 2\pi r$ $V = \ell wh$ $V = \pi r^2 h$ $A = \ell w$

The sum of the degree measures of the angles in a triangle is 180.
The number of degrees of arc in a circle is 360.
A straight angle has a degree measure of 180.

1. At a certain school, the ratio of teachers to students is 1:8. Which of the following could be the total number of teachers and students at the school?

(A) 9

(B) 16

(C) 24

(D) 37

(E) 42

2. If $f(x) = 7$, what is the range of $f(x)$?

(A) all real numbers

(B) 7

(C) all real numbers other than zero

(D) all integers

(E) all positive numbers

3. What are all values of x for which $(x + 3)(x - 4)x = 0$?

(A) −3 and −4

(B) 0 and −3

(C) 3 and 4

(D) −3, 0, and −4

(E) −3, 0, and 4

GO ON TO THE NEXT PAGE

*The directions on the actual SAT will vary slightly.

KAPLAN

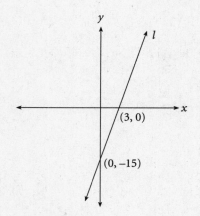

Note: Figure not drawn to scale.

4. Which of the following is parallel to line l in the graph above?

    (A) $y = 3x - 15$

    (B) $y = \dfrac{1}{5}x + 10$

    (C) $y = 5x - 4$

    (D) $y = 15x + 3$

    (E) $y = -15x - 3$

NUMBER OF TVs SOLD AT
STORE X IN 2003

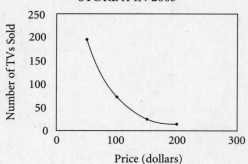

5. The graph above represents the number of televisions sold by Store X in the year 2003. Approximately how many televisions priced at $100 were sold by Store X?

    (A) 0
    (B) 50
    (C) 75
    (D) 100
    (E) 200

6. How many solid wood cubes, each with a surface area of 150 square centimeters, can be cut from a solid wood cube with a total surface area of 5,400 square centimeters if no wood is lost in the cutting?

    (A) 6
    (B) 36
    (C) 30
    (D) 60
    (E) 216

GO ON TO THE NEXT PAGE

KAPLAN

7. The ratio of x to y to z is 3 to 6 to 8. If $y = 24$, what is the value of $x + z$?

   (A) 11
   (B) 33
   (C) 44
   (D) 66
   (E) 88

8. If $r < 0$ and $(4r - 4)^2 = 36$, what is the value of r ?

   (A) -2

   (B) -1

   (C) $-\dfrac{1}{2}$

   (D) $-\dfrac{1}{4}$

   (E) $-\dfrac{1}{8}$

GO ON TO THE NEXT PAGE

KAPLAN

DIRECTIONS FOR STUDENT-PRODUCED RESPONSE QUESTIONS

For each of the questions below (9–18), solve the problem and indicate your answer by darkening the ovals in the special grid. For example:

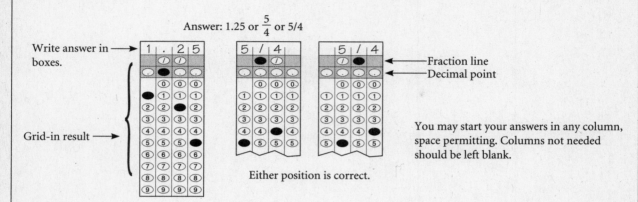

Answer: 1.25 or $\frac{5}{4}$ or 5/4

Write answer in boxes.

Grid-in result

Fraction line
Decimal point

Either position is correct.

You may start your answers in any column, space permitting. Columns not needed should be left blank.

- It is recommended, though not required, that you write your answer in the boxes at the top of the columns. However, you will receive credit only for darkening the ovals correctly.

- Grid only one answer to a question, even though some problems have more than one correct answer.

- Darken no more than one oval in a column.

- No answers are negative.

- Mixed numbers cannot be gridded. For example: the number $1\frac{1}{4}$ must be gridded as 1.25 or 5/4.

  (If $\boxed{1 \mid 1 \mid / \mid 4}$ is gridded, it will be interpreted as $\frac{11}{4}$ not $1\frac{1}{4}$.)

- Decimal Accuracy: Decimal answers must be entered as accurately as possible. For example, if you obtain an answer such as 0.1666..., you should record the result as .166 or .167. **Less accurate values such as .16 or .17 are not acceptable.**

Acceptable ways to grid $\frac{1}{6}$ = .1666. . .

9. If $A = 2.54$ and $20B = A$, what is the value of B?

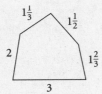

10. What is the perimeter of the figure above?

11. The amount of money a caterer charges for an event is directly proportional to the number of people attending the event. If the caterer charges $780 to cater an event which 60 people attend, how much would she charge for an event which 100 people attend? (Disregard the dollar sign when gridding your answer.)

12. A retailer buys 16 shirts at $4.50 each and she sells all 16 shirts for $6.75 each. If the retailer purchases more of these shirts at $4.50 each, what is the greatest number of these shirts that she can buy with the profit she made on the 16 shirts?

13. Lines ℓ and m intersect at a point to form 4 angles. If one of the angles formed is 15 times as large as an adjacent angle, what is the measure, in degrees, of the smaller angle?

14. If $x = -4$ when $x^2 + 2xr + r^2 = 0$, what is the value of r?

15. Let $n\ast = n^2 - n$ for all positive numbers n. What is the value of $\frac{1}{4}\ast - \frac{1}{2}\ast$?

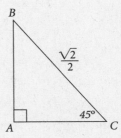

16. What is the area of $\triangle ABC$ shown above?

17. If x is a factor of 8,100 and if x is an odd integer, what is the greatest possible value of x?

18. In a certain class, $\frac{1}{2}$ of the male students and $\frac{2}{3}$ of the female students speak French. If there are $\frac{3}{4}$ as many females as males in the class, what fraction of the entire class speaks French?

IF YOU FINISH BEFORE TIME IS CALLED, YOU MAY CHECK YOUR WORK ON THIS SECTION ONLY. DO NOT TURN TO ANY OTHER SECTION IN THE TEST. | STOP

KAPLAN

SECTION THREE

Time—20 Minutes
16 Questions

Solve each of the following problems, decide which is the best answer choice, and darken the corresponding oval on the answer sheet. Use available space in the test booklet for scratchwork.*

Notes:

(1) Calculator use is permitted.

(2) All numbers used are real numbers.

(3) Figures are provided for some problems. All figures are drawn to scale and lie in a plane UNLESS otherwise indicated.

(4) Unless otherwise specified, the domain of any function f is assumed to be the set of all real numbers x for which $f(x)$ is a real number.

Reference Information

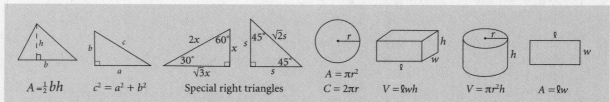

$A = \frac{1}{2}bh$ $c^2 = a^2 + b^2$ Special right triangles $A = \pi r^2$ $C = 2\pi r$ $V = \ell w h$ $V = \pi r^2 h$ $A = \ell w$

The sum of the degree measures of the angles in a triangle is 180.
The number of degrees of arc in a circle is 360.
A straight angle has a degree measure of 180.

1. If 3% of x is 7.5, what is 15% of x?

(A) 17.5
(B) 23.5
(C) 27.5
(D) 36.5
(E) 37.5

2. If $p = -2$ and $q = 3$, then $p^3q^2 + p^2q =$

(A) −84
(B) −60
(C) 36
(D) 60
(E) 84

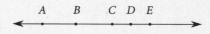

Note: Figure not drawn to scale.

3. In the figure above, B is the midpoint of AC and D is the midpoint of CE. If $AB = 5$ and $BD = 8$, what is the length of DE?

(A) 8
(B) 6
(C) 5
(D) 4
(E) 3

GO ON TO THE NEXT PAGE

KAPLAN

N	P
2	7
4	13
6	19
8	25

4. Which of the following equations describes the relationship of each pair of numbers (*N, P*) in the table above?

(A) $P = N + 5$

(B) $P = 2N + 3$

(C) $P = 2N + 5$

(D) $P = 3N + 1$

(E) $P = 3N - 1$

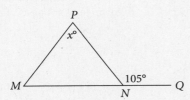

Note: Figure not drawn to scale.

5. In the figure above, *MQ* is a straight line. If *PM = PN*, what is the value of *x* ?

(A) 30

(B) 45

(C) 60

(D) 75

(E) 90

6. Marty has exactly 5 blue pens, 6 black pens, and 4 red pens in his knapsack. If he pulls out one pen at random from his knapsack, what is the probability that the pen is either red or black?

(A) $\dfrac{11}{15}$

(B) $\dfrac{2}{3}$

(C) $\dfrac{1}{2}$

(D) $\dfrac{1}{3}$

(E) $\dfrac{1}{5}$

7. Two hot dogs and a soda cost \$3.25. If 3 hot dogs and a soda cost \$4.50, what is the cost of 2 sodas?

(A) \$0.75

(B) \$1.25

(C) \$1.50

(D) \$2.50

(E) \$3.00

8. If $r + 3 > 6$ and $2r - 4 < 5$, which of the following must also be true?

    I. $r > 2$

    II. $r < 4$

    III. $r < 5$

(A) I only

(B) III only

(C) I and II only

(D) I and III only

(E) I, II, and III

GO ON TO THE NEXT PAGE

KAPLAN

9. Which of the following numbers disproves the statement "A number that is divisible by 2 and by 4 is also divisible by 8"?

    (A) 8
    (B) 20
    (C) 24
    (D) 32
    (E) 80

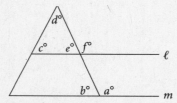

10. In the figure above, if $\ell \parallel m$, which of the following must be equal to a?

    (A) $b + c$
    (B) $b + e$
    (C) $c + d$
    (D) $d + e$
    (E) $d + f$

11. A certain phone call cost 75 cents for the first 3 minutes plus 15 cents for each additional minute. If the call lasted x minutes and x is an integer greater than 3, which of the following expresses the cost of the call, in dollars?

    (A) $0.75(3) + 0.15x$
    (B) $0.75(3) + 0.15(x + 3)$
    (C) $0.75 + 0.15(3 - x)$
    (D) $0.75 + 0.15(x - 3)$
    (E) $0.75 + 0.15x$

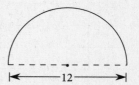

12. The figure above shows a piece of wire in the shape of a semicircle. If the piece of wire is bent to form a circle without any of the wire overlapping, what is the area of the circle?

    (A) 6π
    (B) 9π
    (C) 12π
    (D) 18π
    (E) 36π

13. If $a^2 - a = 72$, and b and n are integers such that $b^n = a$, which of the following cannot be a value for b?

    (A) -8
    (B) -2
    (C) 2
    (D) 3
    (E) 9

GO ON TO THE NEXT PAGE

KAPLAN

	Number of Class Rings Ordered	Number of Class Rings Ordered	Number of Class Rings Ordered
	Size 5	Size 6	Size 7
School X	15	30	35
School Y	12	40	10

	Cost of Class Rings
Size 5	$75
Size 6	$100
Size 7	$125

14. Based on the charts above, how much more does School X spend on class rings than School Y?

    (A) $1,735
    (B) $2,350
    (C) $3,105
    (D) $4,200
    (E) $6,150

15. If $xy = p$ and p is a constant, what happens to the value of x if the value of y is doubled?

    (A) It halves.
    (B) It doubles.
    (C) It remains the same.
    (D) It squares.
    (E) It quadruples.

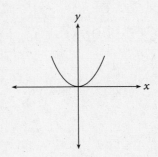

Note: Figure not drawn to scale.

16. If the graph above shows $f(x) = 2x^2$, which of the following is the graph of $f(x) = 2x^2 - 3$?

(A)

(B)

(C)

(D)

(E)

IF YOU FINISH BEFORE TIME IS CALLED, YOU MAY CHECK YOUR WORK ON THIS SECTION ONLY. DO NOT TURN TO ANY OTHER SECTION IN THE TEST. STOP

Practice Test B: **Answer Key**

SECTION ONE

1. E
2. A
3. B
4. E
5. D
6. A
7. E
8. A
9. B
10. A
11. D
12. A
13. D
14. C
15. E
16. A
17. E
18. B
19. B
20. D

SECTION TWO

1. A
2. B
3. E
4. C
5. C
6. E
7. C
8. C
9. .127
10. 9.5 or $\frac{19}{2}$
11. 1300
12. 8
13. $\frac{45}{4}$ or 11.2 or 11.3
14. 4
15. $\frac{5}{4}$ or .062 or .063
16. $\frac{1}{8}$ or .125
17. 2025
18. $\frac{4}{7}$ or .571

SECTION THREE

1. E
2. B
3. E
4. D
5. A
6. B
7. C
8. D
9. B
10. C
11. D
12. B
13. C
14. B
15. A
16. B

Answers and Explanations

SECTION ONE

1. E

$2 \times 10^4 = 20{,}000$. $5 \times 10^3 = 5{,}000$. $6 \times 10^2 = 600$. $4 \times 10^1 = 40$. So the sum is 25,640.

2. A

Find the length of each segment, and then subtract the length of XY from the length of YZ. Y is at 3 on the number line and Z is at 8, so the length of YZ is $8 - 3 = 5$. X is at 1 on the number line and Y is at 3, so the length of XY is $3 - 1 = 2$. So the length of YZ is $5 - 2 = 3$ greater than the length of XY.

3. B

To find the value of x, you need to change 16 into a power of 2: $16 = 2^4$. Therefore, $2^{x+1} = 2^4$. So $x + 1 = 4$, or $x = 3$.

4. E

The number of degrees around a point is 360. Therefore:

$$90 + 30 + 2a + 30 + a = 360$$
$$150 + 3a = 360$$
$$3a = 210$$
$$a = 70$$

5. D

If a machine labels 150 bottles in 20 minutes, it labels 15 bottles every 2 minutes. To label 60, or 4×15, bottles would take 4×2, or 8 minutes.

6. A

We have the function $k(a) = \sqrt{a - 2}$. So $k(b) = \sqrt{b - 2}$. Set $k(b)$ equal to 4 and solve for b:

$$k(b) = \sqrt{b - 2} = 4$$
$$(\sqrt{b - 2})^2 = 4^2$$
$$b - 2 = 16$$
$$b = 18$$

Backsolving would also work well here.

7. E

Since x leaves a remainder of 4 when divided by 5, it must end in either a 4 or a 9, so choice (B) can be eliminated. Since x leaves no remainder when divided by 9, it is evenly divisible by 9. Of the remaining choices only 144 is divisible by 9.

8. A

The sum of the lengths of any two sides of a triangle must be greater than the length of the third side. So $AB + AC$ must be greater than BC; $6 + x > 12$. If $x = 6$, $6 + 6 = 12$ is not greater than 12, so x cannot equal 6.

9. B

Number of terms × average = sum of the terms. For the first group, $3 \times 40 = 120$, so the sum of 20, 70, and x is 120. For the second group, $4 \times 50 = 200$, so $20 + 70 + x + y = 200$. Since the sum of the first 3 terms is 120, $120 + y = 200$, $y = 80$.

10. A

Looking at the graph, you can see that the number of books borrowed in January was 300. To find the total number of books borrowed during the first 6 months of the year, add the values of each bar:

$300 + 350 + 400 + 450 + 500 + 400 = 2{,}400$ books.

So the number of books borrowed in January is $\frac{300}{2400}$ or $\frac{1}{8}$ of the total number of books borrowed during the first 6 months of the year.

KAPLAN

11. D

We're told that 40 percent of $r = s$. The value of 40 percent of r is 4 times the value of 10 percent of r, so 10 percent of $r = \dfrac{1}{4} \times s = \dfrac{s}{4}$.

An alternative method is to Pick Numbers. Since you're dealing with percents, let $r = 100$. Forty percent of $r = s$, so 40 percent of $100 = 40 = s$. You're asked which answer choice is equal to 10 percent of r; 10 percent of $100 = 10$. Now plug the value for s into the answer choices to see which ones give you 10:

(A) $4s = 4 \times 40 = 160$. Eliminate.

(B) $2s = 2 \times 40 = 80$. Eliminate.

(C) $\dfrac{s}{2} = \dfrac{40}{2} = 20$. Eliminate.

(D) $\dfrac{s}{4} = \dfrac{40}{2} = 10$. Works!

(E) $\dfrac{s}{8} = \dfrac{40}{8} = 5$. Eliminate.

Since (D) is the only choice that produces the desired result, it is the correct answer. But remember, when Picking Numbers you need to check all the answer choices; if more than one works, pick new numbers and plug them in until only one answer choice works.

12. A

To figure out where two curves intersect, solve for y in terms of x, then set the two curves equal to each other and solve for x. In this case, the functions represent the y-value of the curves, so you just need to set them equal to each other and solve for x.

$x^2 - 4 = 6x - 12$

$x^2 - 6x + 8 = 0$

$(x - 2)(x - 4) = 0$

$x = 2$ or $x = 4$

Now you need to find the corresponding y-values for each of these values of x. Just plug the value of x into either function to find the appropriate y-value. $a(2) = 2^2 - 4 = 4 - 4 = 0$, and $a(4) = 4^2 - 4 = 16 - 4 = 12$, so these

two curves intersect at the points $(2, 0)$ and $(4, 12)$. Only $(2, 0)$ is an answer choice, so (A) is correct.

13. D

The two overlapping triangles share a common angle, which we can label $p°$. Since the interior angles of any triangle add up to 180 degrees, we have two equations: $x + z + p = 180$ and $y + r + p = 180$. Subtracting p from both sides of each equation, we have $x + z = 180 - p$ and $y + r = 180 - p$. Since $x + z$ and $y + r$ both equal the same quantity, $x + z$ and $y + r$ must be equal to each other. Rearranging $x + z = y + r$, we get $x - r = y - z$, which matches choice (D).

14. C

Check the answer choices. If a number has even 1 factor (not including 1 and itself) that is not a prime number, eliminate that choice:

(A)   12: 4 is not prime. Eliminate.

(B)   18: 6 is not prime. Eliminate.

(C)   21: 3 and 7 are its only other factors, and both are prime. Correct!

(D)   24: 6 is not prime. Eliminate.

(E)   28: 4 is not prime. Eliminate.

15. E

Try different possible values for x and y, eliminating the incorrect answer choices. Since x is multiplied by 3, let's begin with the smallest positive integer value for x: 1. If $3(1) + y = 14$, then $y = 11$, and $x + y = 12$. So choice (A) is out.

If $3(2) + y = 14$, then $y = 8$, and $x + y = 10$. So choice (B) is out. If $3(3) + y = 14$, then $y = 5$, and $x + y = 8$. So choice (C) is also out. If you're really clever, you'll see at this point that answer choice (E) is impossible (which makes it the right choice). After all, the next smallest possible value of x is 4, and since x and y must both be positive integers, neither one can equal 0. (Zero is *not* positive—or negative.) So the sum of x and y must be greater than 4. (Sure enough, if $x = 4$, then $y = 2$, and $x + y = 6$, eliminating choice (D) as well.)

16. A

The area of a triangle $= \frac{1}{2}$(base $\times$ height). Since the area of $\triangle ABC$ is 6, $\frac{1}{2}(AB \times BC) = 6$. If you consider CD as the base of $\triangle ACD$, you will notice that its height is represented by altitude AB. So the area of $\triangle ACD = \frac{1}{2}(CD \times AB)$.

Since $CD = BC$, the area of $\triangle ACD$ can be expressed as $\frac{1}{2}(BC \times AB)$, which you know equals 6.

17. E

Each of the 5 surfaces is 60 by 180 centimeters, so tiles measuring 12 by 18 centimeters can be laid down in 5 rows of 10 to exactly cover 1 surface. There are 5 surfaces, so $5 \times 5 \times 10 = 250$ tiles are needed.

18. B

Any of the five books could be placed in the first spot. Any of the remaining four could be placed in the second spot. Any of the remaining three could go in the third spot, either of the remaining two could go in the fourth spot, and the last book must be placed at the end of the line. Therefore, there are $5 \times 4 \times 3 \times 2 \times 1 = 120$ possible arrangements of the five books.

19. B

The perimeter of triangle $ACD = AD + AB + BC + CD$. You are given the lengths of BC and CD, so you need to find the lengths of AD and AB. Angle DBC is a right angle because it is supplementary to $\angle DBA$, one of the 4 right angles of square $ABDE$. Since right triangle DBC has sides of length 8 and 10, you should recognize it as a 6-8-10 right triangle (a multiple of the 3-4-5 right triangle) and realize that $BD = 6$. (If you didn't recognize this you could have used the Pythagorean theorem to find the length of BD.) BD is also a side of the square and since all sides of a square are equal, $AB = 6$.

So triangle DBA is an isosceles right triangle with sides in the ratio of $1:1:\sqrt{2}$. That means hypotenuse AD is equal to the length of a side times $\sqrt{2}$, so $AD = 6\sqrt{2}$. Now you can find the perimeter of triangle ACD: $6\sqrt{2} + 6 + 8 + 10 = 24 + 6\sqrt{2}$.

20. D

Tank A originally contained 10 more liters of water than tank C, so represent the initial number of liters in each tank in terms of tank A :

tank $A = a$

tank $C = a - 10$

Five liters of water are poured from A to B, and an additional 10 liters are poured from A to C. A total of 15 liters are removed from tank A so it now contains $a - 15$ liters of water. 10 liters are added to tank C so it now contains $a - 10 + 10 = a$ liters. So tank C contains 15 more liters of water than tank A.

KAPLAN

SECTION TWO

1.   A

If the ratio of teachers to students is 1:8, then the people in the school can be divided into groups of 9—1 teacher and 8 students. The total number of teachers and students must therefore be divisible by 9. The only answer choice that is divisible by 9 is 9 itself, (A).

2.   B

Distinguish domain from range. The domain of a function is the set of values for which the function is defined. The range of a function is the set of numbers that constitute the values of the function. For all values of this function, $f(x)$ will always equal 7. So the range is 7.

3.   E

Any number times 0 equals 0. Therefore, at least one of the terms on the left side of the equation $(x + 3)(x − 4)x = 0$ must equal 0. If $x + 3 = 0$, $x = −3$. If $x − 4 = 0$, $x = 4$. The third possibility is that $x = 0$. You could also solve this problem by backsolving, plugging in −4, −3, 0, 3, and 4 to see which numbers make the equation true. Be sure to check all the numbers so you won't be fooled by an answer choice like (B), which has 2 numbers that work in the equation but not all of them.

4.   C

Remember that parallel lines have the same slope and never touch, whereas perpendicular lines have negative reciprocal slopes. Use the points (3,0) and (0,−15) on the graph to figure out the slope of line l: Slope of line

$l = \dfrac{(y_2 - y_1)}{(x_2 - x_1)} = \dfrac{(0 - (-15))}{(3 - 0)} = \dfrac{15}{3} = 5$. So you need a

line with the same slope; only (C) has a slope of 5.

5.   C

Graphs on the SAT can be confusing. Begin by investing a moment to orient yourself to what is being measured on the horizontal and vertical axes, and how the graph itself relates the two. Then focus on the question. First locate $100.00 on the x-axis, draw a line straight up until it hits the line on the graph, and then draw a line from that point straight to the y-axis. It will hit at around 75.

6.   E

Call the length of a side of a small cube s. If the surface area of a small cube is 150, then $6s^2 = 150$, $s^2 = 25$, and $s = 5$. Similarly, each side l of the larger cube can be found by solving the equation $6l^2 = 5,400$. This simplifies to $l^2 = 900$ and $l = 30$. Therefore, six small cubes can be lined up along each edge of the larger cube, as shown in this diagram:

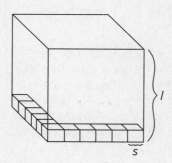

The large cube as a whole, then, contains a total of $6 \times 6 \times 6 = 216$ smaller cubes.

7.   C

Since the ratio of x to y to z is 3:6:8, if $y = 24$ or 4×6, x and z must also be multiplied by 4 for the ratio to hold. So $x = 4 \times 3 = 12$ and $z = 4 \times 8 = 32$, and $x + z = 44$.

8. C

$(4r - 4)^2 = 36$, so $4r - 4$ could equal 6 or −6, since the result is 36 when each of these integers is squared.

But the problem states that $r < 0$, so try −6. $4r - 4 = -6$, $4r = -2$, and $r = -\frac{2}{4} = -\frac{1}{2}$, answer choice (C). (If you try $4r - 4 = 6$ you'll find $r = 2\frac{1}{2}$, which cannot be correct for this question since $r < 0$.)

9. .127

If $A = 2.54$ and $20B = A$, then $20B = 2.54$. So $B = \frac{2.54}{20}$, or .127.

10. 9.5 or $\frac{19}{2}$

The perimeter of the figure is equal to the sum of the lengths of its sides: $2 + 1\frac{1}{2} + 1\frac{1}{3} + 1\frac{2}{3} + 3 = 9\frac{1}{2}$, which is $\frac{19}{2}$ expressed as an improper fraction, or 9.5 expressed as a decimal.

11. 1300

If the amount the caterer charges is directly proportional to the number of people attending, you can set up the problem as a proportion or else use the direct variation equation, $y = kx$, to find the cost per person, then calculate the cost for 100 people.

Proportions:

$\frac{\$780}{60 \text{ people}} = \frac{x}{100 \text{ people}}$

$\$78000 = 60x$

$\$1300 = x$

Variation Equation:

$\$780 = 60k$

$\$13 = k$

$\$13(100) = \$1300$

12. 8

The profit made by the retailer on the shirts is equal to the difference between the selling price and the cost for each shirt, multiplied by the number of shirts: ($6.75 − $4.50) × 16 = $2.25 × 16 = $36.00 profit. To find the number of $4.50 shirts that can be bought for $36.00, you need to divide $36.00 by $4.50, and $\frac{36}{4.5} = 8$.

13. $\frac{45}{4}$ or 11.2 or 11.3

Draw a diagram and label it according to the given information:

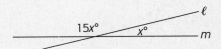

Let the smaller angle measure $x°$. Since the other angle formed is 15 times as large, label it $(15x)°$. Notice that these 2 angles are supplementary, that is, they add up to 180 degrees. Therefore:

$x + 15x = 180$

$16x = 180$

$x = \frac{45}{4}$

So the smaller angle is $\frac{45}{4}$ degrees, which can also be gridded in decimal form as 11.2 or 11.3.

KAPLAN

14. 4

Before you plug in −4 for x, you should factor the given equation:

$$x^2 + 2xr + r^2 = 0$$

$$(x + r)(x + r) = 0$$

$$(x + r)^2 = 0$$

Now plug in −4 for x to solve for r: $(-4 + r)^2 = 0$, $-4 + r = 0$, and $r = 4$.

15. $\frac{1}{16}$ **or .062 or .063**

Plug the values into the given definition:

$$\frac{1}{4}\text{❋} = \left(\frac{1}{4}\right)^2 - \frac{1}{4}$$

$$= \frac{1}{16} - \frac{1}{4}$$

$$= \frac{1}{16} - \frac{4}{16}$$

$$= \frac{-3}{16}$$

$$\frac{1}{2}\text{❋} = \left(\frac{1}{2}\right)^2 - \frac{1}{2}$$

$$= \frac{1}{4} - \frac{1}{2}$$

$$= \frac{-1}{4}$$

So:

$$\frac{1}{4}\text{❋} - \frac{1}{2}\text{❋} = \frac{-3}{16} - \left(\frac{-1}{4}\right)$$

$$= \frac{-3}{16} - \left(\frac{-4}{16}\right)$$

$$= \frac{1}{16}$$

This can also be gridded as .062 or .063.

16. $\frac{1}{8}$ **or .125**

You should recognize that right $\triangle ABC$ is a 45-45-90 triangle, with side lengths in a ratio of $1:1:\sqrt{2}$. Therefore, the length of the 2 equal legs AB and AC is $\frac{1}{2}$.

To find the area of the triangle, plug the values of the base and height (the lengths of the two equal legs) into the area formula:

Area of a triangle $= \frac{1}{2}$(base × height)

$$= \frac{1}{2}\left(\frac{1}{2}\right)^2$$

$$= \frac{1}{2}\left(\frac{1}{4}\right)$$

$$= \frac{1}{8}, \text{ or } .125$$

17. 2025

You're given that x is a factor of 8,100 and it's an odd integer. To find the greatest possible value of x, begin factoring 8,100 by using its smallest prime factor, 2, as one of the factors. Continue factoring out a 2 from the remaining factors until you find an odd one as shown below:

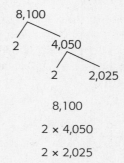

8,100

2 × 4,050

2 × 2,025

Since 2,025 is odd, you can stop factoring; it is the greatest odd factor of 8,100.

18. $\frac{4}{7}$ or .571

Translate the problem into math: Let b = number of boys; let g = number of girls. So $b + g$ = total number of students in the class.

$\frac{1}{2}$ of the boys speak French, so $\frac{1}{2}b$ = the number of boys who speak French.

$\frac{2}{3}$ of the girls speak French, so $\frac{2}{3}g$ = the number of girls who speak French.

Therefore, $\frac{1}{2}b + \frac{2}{3}g$ = total French speakers.

So the fraction of the class that speaks French

$$= \frac{\frac{1}{2}b + \frac{2}{3}g}{b + g}$$

Since there are $\frac{3}{4}$ as many girls as boys in the class,

$g = \frac{3}{4}b$. Plug in $\frac{3}{4}b$ for g into the fraction above:

Fraction of the class that speaks French:

$$= \frac{\frac{1}{2}b + \frac{2}{3}\left(\frac{3}{4}b\right)}{b + \frac{3}{4}b}$$

$$= \frac{\frac{1}{2}b + \frac{1}{2}b}{\frac{7}{4}b}$$

$$= \frac{b}{\frac{7}{4}b}$$

$$= \frac{4}{7}, \text{ or } .571$$

SECTION THREE

1. E

One way to solve this problem is to find the value of x. If 3 percent of x is 7.5, then $.03x = 7.5$. Divide both sides by .03 to get $x = 250$. 15 percent of 250 is $.15(250) = 37.5$. Another way is to notice that 15 percent of x is the same as 5 times 3 percent of x. Since you know 3 percent of x is 7.5, you can easily multiply 7.5 by 5 to get 37.5.

2. B

Plug in −2 for p and 3 for q: $p^3q^2 + p^2q =$
$(-2)^3 3^2 + (-2)^2 3 = (-8)(9) + 4(3)$, or $(-72) + 12 = -60$.

(Note that a negative number raised to an *even* power becomes positive, but a negative number raised to an *odd* power stays negative.)

3. E

Keep track of the lengths you know on the diagram. B is the midpoint of AC so $AB = BC$. Since $AB = 5$, $BC = 5$. $BD = 8$, so $BC + CD = 8$. $BC = 5$, so $5 + CD = 8$, $CD = 3$. D is the midpoint of CE, so $CD = DE = 3$.

4. D

Try each answer choice until you find one that works for all of the pairs of numbers.

Choice (A), $P = N + 5$ works for 2 and 7, but not for 4 and 13.

Choice (B), $P = 2N + 3$ also works for 2 and 7, but not for 4 and 13.

Choice (C), $P = 2N + 5$, doesn't work for 2 and 7.

Choice (D), $P = 3N + 1$, works for all four pairs of numbers, so that's the answer.

KAPLAN

5. A

$\angle PNM$ is supplementary to $\angle PNQ$, so $\angle PNM + 105° = 180°$, and $\angle PNM = 75°$. Since $PM = PN$, triangle MPN is an isosceles and $\angle PMN = \angle PNM = 75°$. The interior angles of a triangle sum to 180 degrees, so $75 + 75 + x = 180$, and $x = 30$.

6. B

Probability is defined as the number of desired events divided by the total number of possible events. There are $5 + 6 + 4$, or 15 pens in the knapsack. If he pulls out 1 pen, there are 15 different pens he might pick, or 15 possible outcomes. The desired outcome is that the pen be either red or black.

The group of acceptable pens consists of $4 + 6$, or 10 pens. So the probability that one of these pens will be picked is 10 out of 15, or $\frac{10}{15}$, which we can reduce to $\frac{2}{3}$.

7. C

Pick variables for the 2 items and translate the given information into algebraic equations. Let $h =$ the price of a hot dog and $s =$ the price of a soda. The first statement is translated as $2h + s = \$3.25$, and the second as $3h + s = \$4.50$. If you subtract the first equation from the second, the s is eliminated so you can solve for h:

$$3h + s = \$4.50$$
$$- (2h + s = \$3.25)$$
$$\overline{\quad h \quad = \$1.25}$$

Plug this value for h into the first equation to solve for s:

$$2(\$1.25) + s = \$3.25$$
$$\$2.50 + s = \$3.25$$
$$s = \$0.75$$

So 2 sodas would cost $2 \times \$0.75 = \$1.50$.

8. D

Inequalities can be solved just like equations (remember to reverse the sign of the inequality if you multiply by a negative number). So if $r + 3 > 6$, you can subtract 3 from both sides of the inequality to find that $r > 3$. Add 4 to both sides of the inequality $2r - 4 < 5$ to get $2r < 9$, then divide both sides by 2 to get $r < 4.5$. We now know that $3 < r < 4.5$. Since r is greater than 3, it is also greater than 2, and I is true. Similarly, since r is less than 4.5, it must also be less than 5, and III is true. II, however, is not necessarily true—r could be less than 4, or it could be greater than 4.

9. B

Since numerical solutions are offered in the answer choices, Backsolving is a good strategy for solving this problem. 8 is divisible by 2, 4, and 8, so it does not disprove the statement. 20 is divisible by 2 and 4, but is not divisible by 8, so it disproves the statement.

10. C

$a = f$, since all the obtuse angles formed when two parallel lines are cut by a transversal are equal. f is an exterior angle of the small triangle containing angles c, d, and e, so it is equal to the sum of the two nonadjacent interior angles, c and d. Since $a = f$ and $f = c + d$, $a = c + d$, answer choice (C).

11. D

The first 3 minutes of the phone call cost 75 cents or $0.75. If the entire call lasted x minutes, the rest of the call lasted $x - 3$ minutes. Each minute after the first 3 cost 15 cents or $0.15, so the rest of the call cost $0.15(x - 3)$. So the cost of the entire call is $0.75 + $0.15(x - 3)$.

If this isn't clear, Pick Numbers. Let $x = 5$. The first 3 minutes cost $0.75 and the additional $5 - 3 = 2$ minutes are $0.15 each. So the entire call costs $0.75 + 2($0.15) = $1.05. Plug 5 for x into all the answer choices to see which ones give you $1.05:

(A) $0.75(3) + 0.15x = 2.25 + 0.15(5) = 2.25 + 0.75 = 3.00$. Eliminate.

(B) $0.75(3) + 0.15(x + 3) = 2.25 + 0.15(5 + 3) = 2.25 + 1.20 = 3.45$. Eliminate.

(C) $0.75 + 0.15(3 - x) = 0.75 + 0.15(3 - 5) = 0.75 - 0.30 = 0.45$. Eliminate.

(D) $0.75 + 0.15(x - 3) = 0.75 + 0.15(5 - 3) = 0.75 + 0.30 = 1.05$. Works!

(E) $0.75 + 0.15(5) = 0.75 + 0.75 = 1.50$. Eliminate.

The only choice that yields the desired result is (D), so it must be correct.

12. B

Before you can find the area of the circle, you need to find the length of the wire. The wire is in the shape of a semi-circle with diameter 12. Since circumference $= \pi d$, the length of a semicircle is half of that, $\frac{\pi d}{2}$. So the length of the wire is $\frac{\pi(12)}{2}$, or 6π. When this wire is bent to form a circle, the circumference of this circle will equal 6π. So the length of the circle's diameter must equal 6, and the radius must be 3. Now you can find the area of the circle:

$$\text{Area} = \pi r^2 = \pi(3)^2 = 9\pi$$

13. C

If $a^2 - a = 72$, then $a^2 - a - 72 = 0$. Factoring this quadratic equation: $(a - 9)(a + 8) = 0$. So $a - 9 = 0$ or $a + 8 = 0$, and $a = 9$ or $a = -8$. b to the nth power equals a, so b must be a root of either 9 or -8. Look through the answer choices to find the choice that is not a root of either 9 or -8:

(A) -8: $(-8)^1 = -8$, so this can be a value for b.

(B) -2: $(-2)^3 = -8$, so this can be a value for b.

(C) 2: $2^3 = 8$, *not* -8, so this answer *cannot* be a value for b.

(D) 3: $3^2 = 9$, so this can be a value for b.

(E) 9: $9^1 = 9$, so this can be a value for b.

So (C) is the only answer choice that cannot be a value for b.

14. B

Ask yourself, "Am I answering the question?" when you are done with your calculations. Often problems require multiple steps, and there are trick answers that are close to what you want but not quite right. Cross-reference the charts to calculate what each school spends:

School $X = 15(\$75) + 30(\$100) + 35(\$125) = \$8,500$

School $Y = 12(\$75) + 40(\$100) + 10(\$125) = \$6,150$

School X – School $Y = \$8,500 - \$6,150 = \$2,350$.

15. A

If $xy = p$ and p is a constant, pick numbers for x and y and use them to solve for p. Say $x = 2$ and $y = 3$, so $(2)(3) = p$ and $p = 6$. Now double y and use $p = 6$ to solve for x: $x(6) = 6$, so $x = 1$. The value of x halves when the value of y is doubled.

16. B

Plug in 0 for x:

$$f(x) = 2x^2 - 3$$
$$f(x) = 2(0)^2 - 3$$
$$f(x) = -3$$

The only options are (B) and (E). Even though no numbers are shown on the graphs, plug in 2 for x.

$$f(x) = 2x^2 - 3$$
$$f(x) = 2(2)^2 - 3$$
$$f(x) = 5$$

All values for $f(x)$ for choice (E) are negative, so the only correct choice is (B).

Compute Your Score

Step 1: Figure out your Math raw score. Refer to your answer sheet for the total number right and the total number wrong for all three sections in the practice test you're scoring. (If you haven't scored your results, do that now, using the answer key that follows the test.) You can use the chart below to figure out your Math raw score section by section. Multiply the number wrong by .25 and subtract the result from the number right in that section. Add the number of Grid-Ins you got right without subtracting anything. Add the scores together and round the result to the nearest whole number.

PRACTICE TEST A

	Number Right	Number Wrong	Raw Score
Section One:	☐	− (.25 × ☐) =	☐
Section Two:	☐	− (.25 × ☐) =	☐
Section Two: (GRID-INS)	☐	− (NO WRONG ANSWER PENALTY) =	☐
Section Three:	☐	− (.25 × ☐) =	☐
		Math Raw Score =	☐
			(rounded up)

PRACTICE TEST B

	Number Right	Number Wrong	Raw Score
Section One:	☐	− (.25 × ☐) =	☐
Section Two:	☐	− (.25 × ☐) =	☐
Section Two: (GRID-INS)	☐	− (NO WRONG ANSWER PENALTY) =	☐
Section Three:	☐	− (.25 × ☐) =	☐
		Math Raw Score =	☐
			(rounded up)

KAPLAN

Step 2: Find your practice test score. Use the table below to find your practice test score based on your Math raw score.

FIND YOUR PRACTICE TEST SCORE*

Raw	Scaled	Raw	Scaled	Raw	Scaled
54	800	30	540	6	340
53	790	29	530	5	330
52	760	28	520	4	320
51	740	27	520	3	310
50	720	26	510	2	290
49	710	25	500	1	280
48	700	24	490	0	260
47	680	23	480	−1	240
46	670	22	480	−2	220
45	660	21	470	−3	200
44	650	20	460	−4	200
43	640	19	450	−5	200
42	630	18	450	−6	200
41	630	17	440	−7	200
40	620	16	430	−8	200
39	610	15	420	−9	200
38	600	14	410	−10	200
37	590	13	410		or below
36	580	12	400		
35	580	11	390		
34	570	10	380		
33	560	9	370		
32	550	8	360		
31	550	7	350		

* Since the College Board has not yet released precise scoring information for the NEW SAT, these numbers are approximates.

Don't take your scores too literally. They are intended to give you an approximate idea of your performance There is no way to determine precisely how well you have scored for the following reasons:

- Practice test conditions do not precisely mirror real test conditions.
- Various statistical factors ad formulas are taken into account on the real test.
- For each grade, the scaled score range changes from year to year.

Note for International Students

If you are an international student considering attending an American University, you are not alone. Nearly 600,000 international students pursued academic degrees at the undergraduate, graduate, or professional school level at U.S. universities during the 2004–2005 academic year, according to the Institute of International Education's Open Doors report. Almost 50 percent of these students were studying for a bachelor's or first university degree. This number of international students pursuing higher education in the United States is expected to continue to grow. Business, management, engineering, and the physical and life sciences are particularly popular majors for students coming to the United States from other countries.

If you are not a U.S. citizen and you are interested in attending college or university in the United States, here is what you'll need to get started.

- If English is not your first language, you'll probably need to take the TOEFL (Test of English as a Foreign Language) or provide some other evidence that you are proficient in English. Colleges and universities in the United States will differ on what they consider to be an acceptable TOEFL score. A minimum TOEFL score of 213 (550 on the paper-based TOEFL) or better is often required by more prestigious and competitive institutions. Because American undergraduate programs require all students to take a certain number of general education courses, all students—even math and computer science students—need to be able to communicate well in spoken and written English.

- You may also need to take the SAT or the ACT. Many undergraduate institutions in the United States require both the SAT and TOEFL for international students.

- There are over 3,400 accredited colleges and universities in the United States, so selecting the correct undergraduate school can be a confusing task for anyone. You will need to get help from a good advisor or at least a good college guide that gives you detailed information on the different schools available. Since admission to many undergraduate programs is quite competitive, you may want to select three or four colleges and complete applications for each school.

- You should begin the application process at least a year in advance. An increasing number of schools accept applications year round. In any case, find out the application deadlines and plan accordingly. Although September (the fall semester) is the traditional time to begin university study in the United States, you can begin your studies at many schools in January (the spring semester).

- In addition, you will need to obtain an I-20 Certificate of Eligibility from the school you plan to attend if you intend to apply for an F-1 Student Visa to study in the United States.

*All test names used in this section are registered trademarks of their respective owners.

KAPLAN ENGLISH PROGRAMS*

If you need more help with the complex process of university admissions, assistance preparing for the SAT, ACT, or TOEFL, or help building your English language skills in general, you may be interested in Kaplan's programs for international students.

Kaplan English Programs were designed to help students and professionals from outside the United States meet their educational and career goals. At locations throughout the United States, international students take advantage of Kaplan's programs to help them improve their academic and conversational English skills, raise their scores on the TOEFL, SAT, ACT, and other standardized exams, and gain admission to the schools of their choice. Our staff and instructors give international students the individualized attention they need to succeed. Here is a brief description of some of Kaplan's programs for international students:

General Intensive English

Kaplan's General Intensive English course is the fastest and most effective way for students to improve their English. This full-time program integrates the four key elements of language learning—listening, speaking, reading and writing. The challenging curriculum and intensive schedule are designed for both the general language learner and the academically bound student.

TOEFL and Academic English

Our world-famous TOEFL course prepares you for the TOEFL and also teaches you the academic language and skills needed to succeed in a university. Designed for high-intermediate to advanced-level English speakers, our course includes TOEFL-focused reading, writing, listening, speaking, vocabulary, and grammar instruction.

General English

Our General English course is a semi-intensive program designed for students who want to improve their listening and speaking skills without the time commitment of an intensive program. With morning class time and flexible computer lab hours throughout the week, our General English course is perfect for every schedule.

OTHER KAPLAN PROGRAMS

Since 1938, more than 3 million students have come to Kaplan to advance their studies, prepare for entry to American universities, and further their careers. In addition to the above programs, Kaplan offers courses to prepare for the ACT, GMAT, GRE, MCAT, DAT, USMLE, NCLEX, and other standardized exams at locations throughout the United States.

Applying to Kaplan English Programs

To get more information, or to apply for admission to any of Kaplan's programs for international students and professionals, contact us at:

Kaplan English Programs
700 South Flower, Suite 2900
Los Angeles, CA 90017, USA
Phone (if calling from within the United States): 800-818-9128
Phone (if calling from outside the United States): 213-452-5800
Fax: 213-892-1364
Website: www.kaplanenglish.com
Email: world@kaplan.com

*Kaplan is authorized under federal law to enroll nonimmigrant alien students. Kaplan is accredited by ACCET (Accrediting Council for Continuing Education and Training).

FREE Services for International Students

Kaplan now offers international students many services online—*free of charge*!
Students may assess their TOEFL skills and gain valuable feedback on their English
language proficiency in just a few hours with Kaplan's TOEFL Skills Assessment.
Log onto www.kaplanenglish.com today.
